Faces of Ireland

1875~1925

Faces of Ireland

Brian M. Walker ~ Art Ó Broin & Seán McMahon

The Amaryllis Press

To our families

First American edition published in 1984 by
The Amaryllis Press, Inc. Publishers,
212 West 79th St., New York
NY 10024

First published in Northern Ireland by
The Appletree Press Ltd
7 James Street South
Belfast BT2 8DL

Designed by Spring Graphics Co.

Library of Congress Catalog Card Number
84-070584

ISBN 0-943276-03-9

Contents

BOOK FOUR: LEINSTER

Foreword

The first book in the *Faces* series appeared in 1974. Through the work of contemporary photographers and writers it illustrated life in Ulster between 1880 and 1914, a period of great social and economic, as well as political change in Ireland. Following the book's success it was decided to prepare three further volumes, each dealing with one of the remaining three provinces of the country during approximately the same period. The four books have now been brought together in this omnibus edition, which we hope will provide a coherent and very special picture of the many different faces of life in Ireland during the late nineteenth and early twentieth centuries.

The book contains over 350 photographs, the largest single collection of Irish photographs covering this period. Besides the work of the famous Robert French and R. J. Welch, the photographs of a host of others are included, most of which have never been published before. A considerable number are the work of photographers unknown to the wider public before their discovery and appearance in the *Faces* volumes. We are pleased that the series may thus have helped to create a more widespread awareness of the great value of our photographic heritage.

Besides the work of photographers, the book contains extracts from the writings of contemporary authors, some famous but others who are virtually unknown today, and whose work is largely

unavailable. All were of their age, and their writings provide
indispensable, personal records, which the compilers feel provide a
deeper insight into the period than other more official historical
documents. The selection of literary writings also provides a broader
panorama of Irish literary endeavour in the period than has been
attempted before.

    This volume, however, is not merely a collection of photographs,
plus a collection of literary extracts. Rather it is an attempt to
juxtapose the two sources and to capture the spirit of the age in a way

A Love Letter.

Dear Sarah Jane, you've often said
That, whun a went tae see Belfast
A ocht tae get my picter taen,
So, dear, a've got it tuk at last.

The card it's on is terble nice,
Altho' my face is rether plain ;
A niver wud a got it din,
But jist to please my Sarah Jane.

The man a seen was very kin',
He made me kame an' brush my hair ;
Then tuk me to a darlin' room,
An' set me in a cushined cher.

The wa's wur a wi' picters hung--
A niver seen as nice a place--
And luking glesses here an' there,
A spose tae let me see my face.

He then brocht oot a nice wee box—
My ! thon maun be a cliver man—
Sez he : " Sit studdy, if ye pleese,
An' luk as pleesint as ye can."

A thocht o' *you*--that made me lauch :
The man stud waitin' for a minit,
An' when he cuvered up the box,
He said he had my picter in it.

He sent it till me thro' the post,
Young Jemmy Saunners brocht the letter;
A hope ye'll be as pleesed as me,
Acanse nae picter cud be better.

Noo ye maun get yer likeness taen,
Be shair an' no mistak the hoose
A'll gie ye the address at fut,
Because nae ither's only use.

ADDRESS :

WILLIAM · ABERNETHY,

PHOTOGRAPHER,

29 High Street (opposite Bridge Street),

Belfast.

no single medium could. Usually there is a straightforward connection between the two; at other times the relation is less obvious, but it always exists.

The books are arranged in the order in which they were first published. Each section contains an introduction with brief historical information and comment on the particular selection. Taken as a single volume, this omnibus edition will give the reader the opportunity to experience the fascinating and varied pattern of life throughout the four provinces of Ireland during this important and eventful period.

Ulster

Brian M. Walker

Preface

I am very grateful to the many people who have helped me write this book. In particular I am much indebted to those friends who gave me continual encouragement during the time I was writing it especially Mary Punch, Patrick and Elizabeth Roche, William Vaughan, John and Yvonne Healy, Douglas Perrin and David and Felicity Haire. I also wish to thank for their generous help, Terence McCaughey, Olive Baskin, Christopher Woods, Jack Johnston, Jim Gracey, Sam Hanna Bell and Mrs W. G. Kirkpatrick.

My work was greatly assisted by information and good advice from Bill Crawford, Brian Hutton and the staff of the Public Record Office of Northern Ireland, Brian Turner, Noel Nesbit and the staff of the Ulster Museum, Brendan Adams, Aiken McClelland and the staff of the Ulster Folk Museum, and James Vitty, Paula Howard and the staff of the Linenhall Library. Gratitude for their assistance must also be expressed to the staffs of the National Library of Ireland, the Royal Irish Academy, the British Museum, Queen's University Library, the Belfast Central Library and Armagh Museum.

My thanks are especially due to Merv and Pen Jones for their excellent work in designing the book and to the publisher for his invariable patience and efficiency. For their help in the production of the book I am grateful to J. P. McAlinden, S. Campbell, E. Kydd, P. McAvoy, P. Boyd and D. J. P. Webster.

To those people and institutions who gave permission for their photographs and extracts to be used I am much indebted.

Finally thanks must be extended to the governors of the Linenhall Library and the trustees of the Esme Mitchell Trust, without whose generous support the book might not have been published.

Introduction

This book, for several reasons, is not a conventional type of history. In the first place, it adopts the unusual approach of looking at life in Ulster at the turn of the century through the work and lives of two different types of contemporary artist—the photographer and the writer. In the second place the selection of artists includes not only well known photographers like R. J. Welch and famous poets such as William Allingham but also local photographers, poets, novelists and playwrights. Presented in an original manner, the material in the book seeks to illustrate life in the province at this time in a way which is both appealing and interesting as well as novel.

The period illustrated in these pages runs from the early 1880s to around 1915—a time which witnessed important changes and events in Ulster. On the political front it saw the advent of the Unionist and Nationalist parties, the riots of 1886 and 1907, the Belfast strike of 1907, the 1912-14 home-rule crises and the outbreak of the First World War. But important as these political occurrences were they were probably overshadowed in most people's everyday lives by the social and economic changes taking place in the province.

By 1901 Belfast was a city of 349,180 people, compared with 87,062 in 1851, and still rapidly expanding. Her shipyards and ropeworks were among the largest of their kind in the world. Linen factories were to be found not only in Belfast but in large numbers throughout the north of Ireland. Communications were improving with the introduction of the motor car and electric tram. In the countryside great changes were taking place with the tenant farmers gradually coming into ownership of their land; also new mechanised methods of farming were being adopted. Thanks to the education acts of the early part of the nineteenth century illiteracy was now largely a thing of the past.

This scene of progress and improvement was of course only part of the whole picture. In many areas traditional patterns of working and living remained. With the tremendous economic growth went other more disturbing features. Conditions were frequently harsh in the factories, sanitation was very inadequate in much of the new housing and life for many with no social security must often have been desperate. In the countryside farm labourers gained little from the changes. Social inequality was a glaring feature of the period. Such was the world in which our artists lived.

For the photographer equipped with his recently acquired craft, some facets of this much contrasting scene could be recorded in a new and exciting way. This he did, not in a matter of fact way but often vividly in a manner that captured something of the feeling of life in these years. We can see this clearly for example in the stark scene of the two women labouring in the field at Glenshesk, in the superbly impressive picture

of the S.S.s *Titanic* and *Olympic* in the shipyards, or in the simple, silent portrait of the Newcastle fishwives that tells so much of suffering and toil. These photographs effectively illustrate not only life at this time but also the very remarkable skill of the photographers.

By the 1880s photography was well established in the province. The Ulster Amateur Photographic Society was founded in 1885. According to the census reports there were 74 professional photographers in Ulster in 1881 and by 1911 the number had risen to 223. For the professional photographer his job could have a number of aspects. Primarily he would have been concerned with private portraits. Increasingly, however, as the century went on he supplied photographs for postcards and book illustrations. Then when in the early part of the twentieth century photographs could be reproduced in newspapers his work took on an added dimension.

Of the photographers included in the book the first who should be mentioned is Robert John Welch (1859-1936). Born in Strabane, Co. Tyrone, he came to Belfast in 1875 to train. Besides being official photographer to a number of firms like Harland and Wolff he spent much of his career travelling around the country recording its scenery, antiquities and the life of its people; many of these photographs were used as illustrations in books. The principal collection of his plate glass negatives is in the Ulster Museum, Belfast.

Our next two photographers were also connected with Strabane. J. A. Burrows, about whom little is known, ran a photographic business in the town from about 1901 to 1913 when it was bought by Herbert Frederick Thomas Cooper. Born in 1874 at Hammersmith, London, Cooper settled in Strabane and ran the business until his death in 1960. The Cooper Collection, which includes some of Burrow's work, has now been deposited in the Public Record Office of Northern Ireland by his son, Mr H. D. H. Cooper. It is the largest single collection of photographs in Ireland, numbering over 200,000 plate glass negatives, few of which have been published in book form before. The collection is chiefly concerned with routine family, wedding and passport photographs but around 20,000 cover a wide range of events in Counties Tyrone and Donegal.

Another important photographer included is William Alfred Green (1870-1958). Of Co. Down stock, he was educated in Lisburn, County Antrim. He became an apprentice assistant to R. J. Welch and then went into business on his own. Green had a special interest in folk customs and agricultural practices and devoted much of his time recording these, especially in the Toome Bridge area of Co. Antrim. Most of his work was done between 1910 and 1930. His photographs are in the Ulster Folk Museum, Cultra, Co. Down. Also in the Ulster Folk Museum are the photographs of Rose Shaw, an amateur photographer, who photographed rural life in the Clogher Valley, Co. Tyrone, where she lived in the early part of this century.

After these photographers, all of whom had close connections with Ulster, mention must be made of Robert French (1841-1917). A Dubliner, he was chiefly responsible for taking the photographs in the Lawrence Collection in the National Library of Ireland. William Mervyn Lawrence, the original owner of this collection, ran a photographic business in Dublin and he employed French to travel to every part of Ireland taking photographs for his picture postcard work. As well as being used for postcards these photographs were used for advertisements and book illustrations.

In addition to the work of these six photographers, material has come from other collections of photographs. The Sprott Collection in Portadown College, Portadown, Co. Armagh, is a collection of lantern slides by various photographers depicting life in Portadown from about 1880 to 1940. Miscellaneous collections in the Linenhall Library, the Royal Irish Academy, the Public Record Office of Northern Ireland and the Ulster Museum provided suitable photographs as did a number of private albums. Where possible, in these latter cases, the photographer has been identified and his name given along with the location of the photograph. Some of the dates of the photographs are uncertain, but nearly all lie between 1880 and 1915.

Just as the photographer with his precise, factual illustrations can tell us much about life at this time so also can the writer with his subjective, imaginative accounts. For example, the poetry of Patrick MacGill, a one time navvy, gives an insight into the harsh depersonalised life of the navvy in a way that a mass of statistics about canals and railways could not. In Louis Walsh's play, *The pope at Killybuck*, we can see something of the humour and prejudice of the Northern countryside. Again in Sir Samuel Ferguson's poem, 'In Carey's footsteps' we have the intensely felt reaction of an individual to political violence, a subject unfortunately not unfamiliar to us today. The attitudes and prejudices sometimes shown in these writers' works are often revealing.

A number of general points can be made about the selection of authors. All are imaginative writers who were either born and brought up in Ulster or who spent an important part of their lives there. The political, social and religious backgrounds of these people differed considerably as did the subjects they wrote about. All were influenced to some degree by their connection with Ulster and so these extracts from their work along with the notes on the authors give us an interesting insight into life in the province at this time with all its differing personal experiences.

Next it can be noted that the authors represent both a narrower and a wider selection of literary talent than is customary in most anthologies. Each author is connected with Ulster and nearly all these examples of their work were written between 1880 and 1915. But at the same time they include not only playwrights who wrote for the Abbey Theatre and the Ulster Literary Theatre but also several who wrote for amateur drama groups. Again there are famous poets like William Allingham and unknown poets such as Thomas Given, a farmer from Cullybackey, Co. Antrim. Some wrote in Ulster Scots vernacular, some in Irish and some in Queen's English. Over thirty writers are included. Also there are examples of religious verse, folk song and political doggerel as well as extracts from literary and satirical magazines. All together the selection provides a valuable cross section of cultural activity during this period.

Standards differed considerably between these authors as the extracts clearly show. Some like Sir Samuel Ferguson and William Allingham wrote material of the highest quality which can have a strong impact even today. Others like Margaret Dobbs were effective in their local context. In the case of certain of the writers, however, it may seem to the present day reader that their work is of little literary value. But if should be remembered that this is what people at the time wrote and what they read. A novelist such as Rosa Mulholland attracts no attention today from the reader or critic but in her time her books were serialized in newspapers all over the country and she was undoubtedly influential in creating and reinforcing social and political attitudes. These extracts do give us some idea of the general literary taste of the period.

Finally comment must be passed on the arrangement of material in the book. It is neither simply a collection of photographs nor an anthology of Ulster writers, but an experiment to bring the two together. The association between image and text may at times seem tenuous. But it exists and it is left to the reader to discover it. In some cases the photographs are linked with the writers themselves, not the extracts. Although every county in Ulster is represented by writers and photographs some, because of the availability of material, are better represented than others.

Such then are the aims and methods of *Faces of the Past*. It portrays people and conditions and contemporaries' personal expressions about them. It reflects something of the diverse social, political and cultural personality of Ulster at this time. Besides all this, it shows the very considerable artistic talent emanating from the province in these years, not only at a sophisticated level of thinking and creating but also at the local level in the countryside. The choice of photographs and extracts is of course the author's personal one but it is hoped that the material selected will give the reader an interesting and evocative record of life in Ulster at the turn of the century.

AT WORK

Haymaking, 1915 style (Cooper Collection, Public Record Office of Northern Ireland)

Workers leaving the Belfast shipyards, 1911.
The Titanic can be seen in the background.
(Welch Collection, Ulster Museum).

Right: *Linen bleach greens such as this one somewhere in Co. Antrim, were a common sight in Ulster. The linen was laid out in the fields and carefully turned to allow slow and even atmospheric bleaching to take place. (Lawrence Collection, National Library of Ireland).*

Thomas Given, a farmer from Cullybackey, Co. Antrim, was one of three brother poets. As was the custom of many rural poets, he wrote for local newspapers. Also like many others he used the dialect of his own district. He does not seem to have been a weaver himself at any stage, but his use of various weaving terms in this poem suggests that he had a good knowledge of the trade. Given died in 1917 at the age of 67.

Below: *A handloom damask weaver at Waringstown, Co. Down, around 1890. By this time independent weavers were few in number, the factories having usurped their position. (Sprott Collection, Portadown College)*

THE WEAVER QUESTION

We read o' meetings to support
   The risin' nerra-gauge,
Which is to be the strength and fort
   O' every comin' age.
We read o' controversies lang,
   O' puirhoose jaw and vapour,
But seldom does the weavers' wrang
   Bedeck the public paper
          On ony day.

Oor wabs are lang an' ill to weave—
   Sometimes the yarn is bad—
Till scanty claes, wi' ragget sleeve,
   Is seen on lass an' lad.
But noo guid fortune we'll attain,
   For orators sae thrifty
Will gar the dreeper clip his chain
   Wa' doon tae twa-an'-fifty
          On ilka day.

Queels maun be wun when claith is wroucht,
   An' pickers, shears an' treadles,
Tallow an' temples maun be boucht,
   An' floor tae dress the heddles.
Then meat tae gar the wee yins leeve,
   Maun come as weel's the tackle,
But shure the wages we receive
   Wud hardly buy them treacle
          Tae meal this day.

How aisy 'tis for men tae preach
   Whun riches they hae got,
An' wae self-interest's purse-hurt screech,
   Ca' us a sinfu' lot.
But, haud a wee! ye men o' wealth!
   Though noo for breath yer pantin',
We ax nae favours gained by stealth—
   It's justice that we're wantin'—
          Nae mair this day.

I ne'er was blessed wae gift o' gab,
   Like some great learned men,
Instead o' school, I wove my wab,
   Before that I was ten.
Though noo I'm auld an' gray's my hair,
   I've studied weel the sense o't
For work let us get wages fair,
   Nae matter 'boot the length o't
          On ony day.

Thomas Given from G. R. Buick's *Poetical works of the brothers Given* (Belfast, 1900), pp 190-1.

HERE, approximately, are a few instances of the wages paid to women in the spinning and weaving mills of Belfast. Preparers, spreaders, drawers and rovers get from 8s. 6d. to 11s. per week; spinners earn from 11s. 6d. to 13s.; reelers from 15s. to 17s.; weavers and winders from 8s. to 14s.; though those who are engaged in fine weaving or damask work earn up to 18s. to 19s. As for male workers in these industries, skilled labourers like flax-dressers are paid from 24s. to 28s. per week, and roughers from 20s. to 24s.

These figures, however, give a rather flattering idea of the wages paid in the textile industries, for it must be remembered that it is always possible that either the cut-throat competition which continually goes on between the spinning and the weaving industries, or some other cause of trade depression, may result in the mills working only short time. Towards the end of 1907, for instance, all the spinning mills were working for half-time for nearly twelve months, and a friend of mine tells me of a reeler he knew, a married woman, who was trying during all that time to support a family on 6s. 3d. a week. Skilled male labourers, like flax-roughers, were for a time making as low a wage as 10s. 6d. weekly. The workers, indeed, suffer when trade is bad, but they do not gain in proportion when trade is good . . . . .

Warehouse girls' wages, however, are no better than those of factory-workers. In a fairly decent house, a woman stitcher earns from 10s. and 11s. to 18s. a week on the piece-work system, and printers—girls who stencil on to the linen the perforated design—are paid as low as 7s. 6d. Ornamenters make about 12s. weekly.

The deadliest sin in the labour conditions of Ireland is neither the low wage paid to unskilled labourers nor that paid to women. It is the system under which boys and girls hardly out of their infancy are employed in the mills at a wage of 3s. 6d. a week. The child half-timer in Lancashire is often an object of sympathy. The plight of the Ulster half-timer, however, is infinitely more pitiable. In Lancashire the child really works half-time every day of the week and goes to school during the other part of the day. In Ulster the child works full time during three days in the week, and attends school on the remaining days. The results which follow, when children of twelve years old or thereabouts are kept working for ten hours a day during three days in the week in a humid atmosphere of from 70 to 80 degrees Fahrenheit, might have been foreseen. Vitality is slowly squeezed out of them, and it is hardly an exaggeration to say that from the age of 15 upwards they die like flies.

The death rate in Belfast among young people between the ages of 15 and 20 is double what it is in Manchester. That this is due neither to inherited lack of vitality not to the condition of Belfast houses is proved by the fact that in the first five years of their life children die less rapidly in Belfast than in Manchester. Miss Martindale,* who is as enviably free from the vice of dogmatism as she is from that of melodrama, believes that the over-crowded, ill-ventilated and insufficiently-warmed state of some of the schools may be a partial cause of the high deathrate among these boys and girls, but there can be little doubt that the half-time system is a ruling cause of such an unnatural rate of mortality.

Robert Lynd, *Home Life in Ireland* (London, 1904), pp 229-30.

a government inspector of factories.

Right: *Reeling linen yarn in a Belfast spinning mill (Lawrence Collection, National Library of Ireland)*

Below: *Ornamenting finished linen (Welch Collection, Ulster Museum)*

Robert Lynd was born in Belfast in 1879 and educated at the Royal Belfast Academical Institution and Queen's College (now Queen's University). He wrote a number of novels and travel books about Ireland. These include *The mantle of the emperor* (London, 1906) and *Rambles in Ireland* (London, 1912). A republican and Gaelic Leaguer from his youth, he also edited some of the works of James Connolly - *Labour in Ireland: Labour in Irish history, The reconquest of Ireland* (Dublin and London, 1917). However, his considerable renown as a writer rests not so much upon these works as on his essays, many of which were written during the time he was literary editor of the *News Chronicle*. He wrote under the pseudonym of Y.Y., and among his books of essays are *The art of letters* (London, 1920), and *Books and authors* (London, 1929). A number of his best essays were published in London in 1933 in the volume *Y.Y. An anthology of essays*, selected, with an introduction, by Eileen Squire. Robert Lynd died in 1949.

Delft merchant, High Street, Portadown, 1892 (Sprott Collection, Portadown College)

LINES ON PORTADOWN

Hail, Portadown! thou bonny gem,
   The rising star of Erin's Isle,
The seat of enterprising men,
   Who have caus'd thy trade to smile;

Who, by their increasing labour,
   Have made you a princely home,
Where the townsman and the stranger
   Are alike sweet friendship shown.

Through thee flow the lovely waters
   Of the far-famed river Bann,
Where thy social sons and daughters
   Spend convivial evenings on.

Proudly stand thy lofty buildings
   Once where nought but ruin stood,
Beautifi'd with costly gildings,
   Though yet in their infant bud.

Magic-like thy domes are rising,
   Tow'ring upwards to the sky;
And what makes the scene more prizing
   Is, no lordling's hand was nigh.

Thy factory-bells are heard each morn
   Chiming with the songster's lay,
Calling thousands to perform
   The various duties of the day.

Here the hand of trade is making
   Business marts triumphant rise;
While art with her a part has taken
   In the noble enterprise.

So let us unite together,
   And let discord die away;
Let us strive to help each other
   As we journey on life's way

Robert Donnolly, *Poetical works of Robert Donnolly*
(Portadown, 1882), pp 180-1.

A Portadown shopkeeper, 1892 (Sprott Collection, Portadown College)

Robert Donnolly was the author of hundreds of poems on people and places in Portadown and the surrounding area. These were often printed on broadsheets, sometimes illustrated by Donnolly himself. A native of Portadown, Co. Armagh, he was apparently a weaver by trade. He published two books of poetry; the first, *Poems on various subjects,* was published at Armagh in 1867 and the second in 1882 (see above). Some of his poems were written in praise of specific tradesmen and merchants. In his writing he speaks highly of the industrial growth taking place around him.

FOR a country where political agitations follow each other as rapidly as plagues in an Eastern City it is curious how little constructive thought we can show on the ideals of a rural civilization. But economic peace ought surely to have its victories to show as well as political war. I would a thousand times rather dwell on what men and women working together may do than on what may result from majorities at Westminster. The beauty of great civilization has been built up far more by people working together than by any corporate action of the State.

In these socialistic days we grow pessimistic about our own efforts and optimistic about the working of the legislature. I think we do right to expect great things from the State, but we ought to expect still greater things from ourselves. We ought to know full well that if the State did twice as much as it does we would never rise out of mediocrity among the nations unless we have unlimited faith in the power of our personal efforts, to raise and transform Ireland and unless we translate the faith into works.

The State can give a man an economic holding, but only the man himself can make it into an Earthly Paradise, and it is a dull business, un-worthy of a being made in the image of God, to grind away at work without some noble end to be served, some glowing ideal to be attained...............

"What dream shall we dream, or what labour shall we undertake?" you may ask, and it is right that those who exhort should be asked in what manner and how precisely they would have the listener act or think. I answer : the first thing to do is to create and realize the feeling for the community and break up the evil and petty isolation of man from man. This can be done by every kind of co-operative effort where combined action is better than individual action. The parish cannot take care of the child as well as the parents, but you will find in most of the labours of life combined action is more fruitful than individual action.

Some of you have found this out in many branches of agriculture, of which your dairying, agricultural, credit, poultry, and flax societies are witness. Some of you have combined to manufacture; some to buy in common; some to sell in common. Some of you have the common ownership of thousands of pounds' worth of expensive machinery. Some of you have carried the idea of co-operation for economic ends further, and have used the power which combination gives you to erect village halls and to have libraries of books, the windows through which the life and wonder and power of humanity can be seen. Some of you have light-heartedly, in the growing sympathy of unity, revived the dances and songs and sports which are the right relaxation of labour.

Some Irishwomen here and there have heard beyond the four walls in which so much of their lives are spent the music of a new day, and have started out to help and inspire the men and be good comrades to them; and, calling themselves United Irishwomen, they have joined, as the men have joined, to help their sisters who are in economic servitude, or who suffer from the ignorance and indifference to their special needs in life which pervade the administration of local government. We cannot build up a rural civilization in Ireland without the aid of Irish women. It will help life little if we have methods of the twentieth century in the fields and those of the fifth century in the home..........
Working so, we create the conditions in which the spirit of the community grows strong.

George Russell, *Co-operation and nationality* (Dublin, 1912), pp82-3, 88-91.

At first sight, this extract may seem a strange one to include for the poet George William Russell, or, as he was better known, AE. But in fact Russell had a considerable interest in economic affairs, especially in relation to the land. In 1897 he became an official of the Irish Agricultural Organization Society and from 1906 to 1923 he was editor of its magazine, *The Irish Homestead*. It is of course for his very considerable literary ability that Russell is best remembered. Born at Lurgan, Co. Armagh, in 1867, he moved at an early age to Dublin. He became one of the most influential members of the Irish literary revival at the turn of the century and wrote a large number of books of verse, stories and plays, nearly all of a mystical nature. Russell's play, *Deidre*, was staged in Dublin in 1902 by the Irish National Dramatic Company. His volume, *Collected poems*, was published in London in 1913 (2nd ed. London, 1926). Other writings include *The Candle of Vision* (London, 1918) and *Interpreters* (London, 1922). In addition to being a writer Russell was a painter, the subjects often being mystical ones like his poetry. He died in 1935.

Above: *The committee of the Irish Co-operative Women's Guild, York Street Branch, Belfast—part of Russell's co-operative movement but hardly rural (Mr. Fred Heatley's private collection)*

Above left: *This photograph of the creamery at Donemana, Co. Tyrone was taken around 1910. By this time the co-operative movement had become an important feature of the agricultural scene throughout Ireland. At the end of 1910 there were 381 local co-operative societies belonging to the Irish Agricultural Organization Society with a total membership of just under 95,000. (Cooper Collection, Public Record Office of Northern Ireland)*

OLD AND NEW

I see the older men
Of Ireland bent and bowed,
By marsh and rushy fen
Dig out from fibrous shroud
The peats, and shape the turf-stacks red
With centuries' slow rest beneath the bog,
Where rotted rivers hold in dead
Embrace both elk, and steed, and leafen log.
Up higher on the fold
Of living earth that lies
With healthy hill-fed mould
Thrown open to the skies,
I see the young men toil the full
Long day to tear the fragrant earth apart,
And fling the seed so beautiful
About their mother's unforgetting heart.

Shane Leslie, *Songs of Oriel* (Dublin, 1908), p. 37.

*Turf cutting at Gortconny bog, Co. Antrim
(Welch Collection, Ulster Museum)*

Sir John Randolph (Shane) Leslie, (1885-1971), from Glaslough, Co. Monaghan, was educated at Eton and Cambridge. He was a cousin of Sir Winston Churchill. He wrote a large number of biographies, histories, novels and poems. His volumes of poetry include *Verses in peace and war* (London, 1922), and *Poems and ballads* (London, 1933). He was keenly interested in ghosts and wrote several books about them - *Fifteen odd stories* (London, 1935), and *Shane Leslie's ghost book* (London, 1955). His other works include *The Oxford Movement* (London, 1933), and *George the Fourth* (London, 1926).

O ut beyond the swaths the mowers toiled on, smitten pitilessly by the sun. Both were stripped to the shirt and trousers, neck-bands open, sleeves rolled high, hats pushed back upon nape and crown. Hughy's shirt was wet below the armpits, soaked about the neck and waist, clinging tight to his back as a cotton skin; but Peter's flapped dry as a bone. When Hughy, turning for a new swath, wiped his brow his arm glistened from wrist to elbow; but Peter's scraped over the parched wrinkles with a withered sound of dryness. The sun sucked at Peter unavailingly, warmed him as it might warm a stone, wrought nothing but freckles on the brown leanness of his arms; but Hughy it smote, working in him riot and ferment, boiling his blood, baking his bones, making him smoke along the stubble.

They worked hard, stopping only to whet scythes, or trudge to the drinking can, or turn down between the mounded rows, their feet crushing the eyes of fallen daisies, pressing the life from tumbled thistle and meadow-sweet, driving corncrakes in panic through the grass or crushing wounded frogs into the stubble.

The burden of work and of the day was heavy, but they bore it unmurmuringly; accepting it as they accepted most things—hunger and cold, pain and trouble, life and death—with an air of sullen indifference, of philosophic resignation to the inevitable—the inevitable before which your sapient ran cheerfully nor lingered to be kicked. They looked out upon the glories of earth and sky, the wonders of sunshine and shade, with indifferent eyes, seeing only what a thousand times they had seen, and knew by heart, and hoped by God's mercy to see often again. It was just the trees with them, the crops, the grass, the hills and the cattle, the valleys and the meadows, the sun that shone and the men that worked.

S. F. Bullock, *Irish pastorals* (London, 1901), pp84-5.

Mowing corn at Toome, Co. Antrim (Green Collection, Ulster Folk Museum)

This extract comes from 'The mowers', a short story included in Shan F. Bullock's *Irish pastorals;* it is set in the Cavan-Fermanagh border countryside, as were many of his novels. Born in 1865 at Crom, Co. Fermanagh as John William Bullock, he was brought up around Crom Castle where his father was steward. He eventually went to London where he spent most of his life as a civil servant. For his work on the secretariat of the Irish Convention of 1917 he was awarded the M.B.E. His best known novels are *The loughsiders* (London, 1924), *Dan the dollar* (Dublin, 1907), and *The squireen* (London, 1903). He wrote an autobiographical volume entitled *After sixty years,* published in London in 1931. He also wrote poetry and a play, *Snow drop Jane,* which was produced in Belfast in 1915. He died in 1935.

Harvesters and a steam threshing machine around 1915 (Cooper Collection, Public Record Office of Northern Ireland)

These two girls at Glenshesk, Co. Antrim, are putting the finishing touches to 'lazy beds' of seed potatoes. The 'lazy beds' were made by digging ditches and putting the soil to one side on top of the seeds. This photograph probably dates from the late nineteenth century. (Welch Collection, Ulster Museum)

Joseph Campbell, or Seosamh MacCathmaoil as he was sometimes called, was born in Belfast in 1879. He was an early contributor to the Ulster Literary Theatre, his play, *The little cowherd of Slainge*, being performed by the Theatre in 1905. But it is undoubtedly for his poetry and songs that Campbell is best remembered. He drew much of his inspiration from the northern countryside, particularly the counties of Antrim and Donegal. Along with the musician Herbert Hughes he collected traditional Ulster songs; 'My Lagan love' is probably the best known of these. Many of his poems were religious in nature. In *The gilly of Christ* (Dublin, 1907), he set the life of Christ among the people and fields of Ulster's countryside. After spending some time in Dublin and London, Campbell settled in Co. Wicklow. His play, *Judgement*, was performed at the Abbey Theatre in 1911. Campbell was a staunch republican and was imprisoned during the Irish civil war. On being released in 1924 he went to the United States. In 1935 he returned to Co. Wicklow where he died in 1944. A collected edition of his poetry, *Poems of Joseph Campbell*, introduced by Austin Clarke, was published in Dublin in 1963.

HARVEST SONG

O reapers and gleaners,
Come dance in the sun:
The last sheaves are stooked
And the harvest is done.

The thistle-finch sings,
And the corn-plover cries,
And the bee and the moth
Flit about in the skies.

For Jesus has quickened
The seed in the mould,
And turned the green ears
Of the summer to gold.

The hill-folk all winter
Have clamoured for bread,
And here is enough
For a host to be fed!

Last year was a lean year,
And this is a fat,
And poor folk have cause
To be thankful for that.

So, reapers and gleaners,
Come dance in the sun,
And praise Mary's Child
That the harvest is done.

Joseph Campbell, *The rushlight*
(Dublin, 1906), p.54.

*This farmer in the Mourne mountains above Kilkeel,
Co. Down, is winnowing corn. Winnowing is the process of shaking or hand threshing corn to remove the
chaff from the head of corn. This scene was photographed around 1915. (Green Collection, Ulster Folk
Museum)*

Above: *A school classroom, location unknown. From the tidy appearance of all the children it is clear they knew a photographer was coming to the school! (Public Record Office of Northern Ireland)*

Right: *The master and pupils of Black's school, Strabane, Co. Tyrone (Cooper Collection, Public Record Office of Northern Ireland)*

THE school-house faced the Market Square. It was a dingy, dilapidated-looking building, both inside and out.

A few rude desks and forms, well worn, and diminishing in size, owing to well applied and constant whittling with jack-knives; the master's desk in the corner, together with the usual wall covering of maps and alphabetical charts, completed the furnishing of the apartment.

There was a distinct air of disorder and untidiness about the place—the same might be said regarding not a few of its inhabitants.

The master, David Grahame, commonly called "Fractions," owing to his recognised ability for land measuring, and the puzzling calculations connected therewith, was a tall, well-built, fresh-complexioned man, with a somewhat marked cast of features, keen grey eyes, prominent nose, and a firmly set mouth. His age may have been fifty-five.

Many were the stories told of his talents and versatility—all going to prove to what heights he might have risen, had good luck appointed him to a wider field.

Not only had he laid the groundwork of some eminent scholars, and accomplished not a few wonderful geometrical and algebraical feats, but he also possessed a smattering of legal knowledge, which enabled him to be of much service in the drawing up of wills and agreements. Added to all this "the Master" displayed a distinct aptitude for theological argument and debate, having had more than one wordy tussle with the minister himself: the minister, it is said, coming off a good second.

Archibald McIlroy, *When lint was in the bell* (Belfast, 1897), pp15-16.

This description of a school and a teacher comes from reminiscences of his younger days by the author, Archibald McIlroy. Born at Ballyclare, Co. Antrim, he worked in the bank and in business. He was also a local councillor. He contributed to many magazines and was the author of several works and sketches describing Ulster life. His books include *The auld meeting house green* (Belfast, 1898), *A banker's love story* (London, 1901) and *The humour of Devil's Island* (Dublin, 1902). He was drowned in 1915 at the age of fifty-five on the *Lusitania*.

RUN DOWN

IN the grim dead end he lies, with passionless filmy
    eyes,
English Ned, with a hole in his head,
Staring up at the skies.

The engine driver swore as often he swore before —
    "I whistled him back from the flamin' track,
An' I could n't do no more."

The gaffer spoke through the 'phone "Platelayer
    Seventy-one
    Got killed to-day on the six-foot way,
By a goods on the city run.

    "English Ned was his name,
    No one knows whence he came,
  He didn't take mind of the road behind
    And none of us is to blame."

    They turned the slag in the bed
    To cover the clotted red,
Washed the joints and the crimsoned points,
   And buried poor English Ned.

    In the drear dead end he lies,
    With the earth across his eyes,
    And a stone to say,
    How he passed away
    To a shift beyond the skies.

This photograph of railway workers was taken at Lifford in Co. Donegal around 1911 (Cooper Collection, Public Record Office of Northern Ireland)

Patrick MacGill, *Songs of the dead end* (London, 1913), p.132.

Born at Glenties, Co. Donegal, in 1891, Patrick MacGill left school at the age of 10. Four years later he emigrated to Scotland where he worked as a navvy, a platelayer and a labourer. His first volume of poems about the life of a navvy, *Gleanings from a navvy's scrapbook* (Greenock, 1911), was immediately popular and was followed by *Songs of a navvy* (Windsor, 1912), and *Songs of the dead end* (London, 1913). In the next year he wrote *Children of the dead end*, published in London, a semi-autobiographical novel set in the farmlands of the Lagan countryside (north-east Donegal) and in Scotland. During the 1914-18 war, he served in the London Irish Rifles, an experience which prompted him to write a number of books depicting the horror of war - *The great push - an episode of the Great War* (London, 1916), *Soldier songs* (London, 1917) and *The amateur army* (London, 1915). His play about war, *Suspense*, was published in London in 1930. Other works of importance include *Maureen* (London, 1921), *The glen of Carra* (London, 1934) and *The rat pit* (London, 1915). MacGill went to the United States in 1930. He died in 1963.

32 *An office of the Belfast Ropework Company on the Newtownards Road, Belfast, January 1899 (Linenhall Library)*

BY THE WATER

The last of the coal schooners about 1893 at the Queen's Quay, Belfast. (Welch Collection, Ulster Museum)

SEA WRACK

THE wrack was dark an' shiny where it floated in
    the sea,
There was no one in the brown boat but only him
    an' me;
Him to cut the sea wrack, me to mind the boat,
An' not a word between us the hours we were afloat.
    The wet wrack,
    The sea wrack,
    The wrack was strong to cut.

We laid it on the grey rocks to wither in the sun,
An' what should call my lad then, to sail from
    Cushendun?
With a low moon, a full tide, a swell upon the deep,
Him to sail the old boat, me to fall asleep.
    The dry wrack,
    The sea wrack,
    The wrack was dead so soon.

There' a fire low upon the rocks to burn the wrack
    to kelp
There' a boat gone down upon the Moyle, an' sorra
    one to help!
Him beneath the salt sea, me upon the shore,
By sunlight or moonlight we'll lift the wrack no
    more
    The dark wrack,
    The sea wrack,
    The wrack may drift ashore.

Moira O'Neill, *Songs of the Glens of Antrim* (London, 1900), pp10-11.

Moira O'Neill was the pen-name of Nesta Higginson, later Mrs. Nesta Skrine. Born at Cushendun in the Glens of Antrim, she is best known for her songs and poems of the Glens. The first edition of *Songs of the Glens of Antrim* was published in London in 1900, and ran into many editions and impressions. In 1921, also in London, *More songs of the Glens of Antrim* was brought out. Earlier writings include *An Easter vacation* (London, 1893), and *The elf errant* (London, 1895). A collected volume of her poems was published in 1933 - *Collected poems of Moira O'Neill* (London). She eventually went to Canada but returned to Ireland to live in Co. Wicklow, where she died in 1955 at the age of 90.

Left: *Seaweed gatherers at work near Fair Head, Co. Antrim. Notice the jetty for the Ballycastle coal field. (Welch Collection, Ulster Museum)*

Below: *Burning seaweed for kelp in an Antrim coast glen. Materials extracted from the kelp, as the burnt seaweed was known, were used in the production of bleaching materials and glass. (Green Collection, Ulster Folk Museum)*

NANCY [Energetically]: I'll have the kettle on the boil in two twos. [During the foregoing the minister has gone over to Bell, and shakes her hand, which he holds long and tenderly, looking steadily into her face. Bell is downcast.]

MINISTER [With a half-guilty start moving over to side of table]: No, thank you, I'll not mind.

JOHNNY [Interrogatively, glancing at clock]: You must be cold, out at such a late hour in this weather. [He looks searchingly across at Bell.]

NANCY [Taking down tea-caddy]: Aye, a good cup o' tay will warm you up.

MINISTER: Thank you all the same, but I'll not stay now. [Nancy puts the caddy back with an air of disappointment.] I came round by the quay and heard some of the men talking of going off and trying a night at the fishing.

NANCY: The weather's not settled yet; maybe it's only a calm between storms.

MINISTER: One of them urged that they should take the big sail they used when the "Annie" won the race last autumn at the regatta.

JOHNNY [Angrily to Nancy] It'll be that young scape-grace Rob [Bell starts] He's up to every divilment [To minister], sav'n your presence.

He nearly swamped himself in the yawl the other day tryin' how much wind she would stand without sinkin' the lee gunnel.

MINISTER: I couldn't make them out in the darkness, as the beached boats were between them and me, but I heard the same voice say, as if to itself: "It's win or lose tonight."

[Bell agitated, but pleased.]

JOHNNY: The racin's never out of his head.

NANCY [Coming from fire after taking kettle off and hanging bellows]: It's dangerous work at this time o' year.

MINISTER [Moving towards Nancy]: So I thought I'd just look in and give you a word of warning. [Bell is listening at the door, and her face lights up as she appears to recognise a footstep. Minister shakes hands with Nancy.]

NANCY: We're obleged to you. Johnny'll put sense into Rob or any o' the boat's crew that comes to take him from his fireside, and his wife and chile at such a time and in such weather.

J. H. Cousins, *The racing lug* from Robert Hogan and James Kilroy (ed.), *Lost plays of the Irish renaissance* (Dixon, California, 1970), pp 42-3.

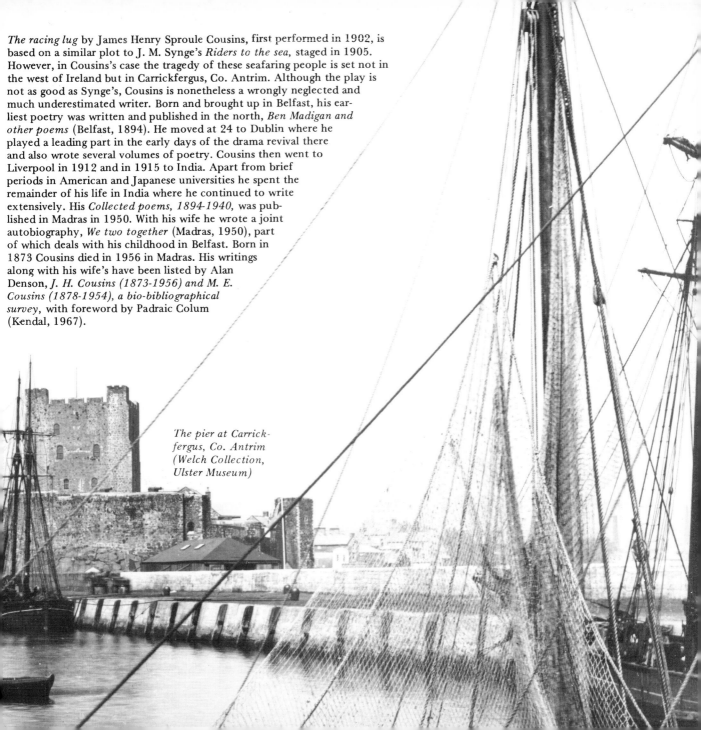

The racing lug by James Henry Sproule Cousins, first performed in 1902, is based on a similar plot to J. M. Synge's *Riders to the sea*, staged in 1905. However, in Cousins's case the tragedy of these seafaring people is set not in the west of Ireland but in Carrickfergus, Co. Antrim. Although the play is not as good as Synge's, Cousins is nonetheless a wrongly neglected and much underestimated writer. Born and brought up in Belfast, his earliest poetry was written and published in the north, *Ben Madigan and other poems* (Belfast, 1894). He moved at 24 to Dublin where he played a leading part in the early days of the drama revival there and also wrote several volumes of poetry. Cousins then went to Liverpool in 1912 and in 1915 to India. Apart from brief periods in American and Japanese universities he spent the remainder of his life in India where he continued to write extensively. His *Collected poems, 1894-1940,* was published in Madras in 1950. With his wife he wrote a joint autobiography, *We two together* (Madras, 1950), part of which deals with his childhood in Belfast. Born in 1873 Cousins died in 1956 in Madras. His writings along with his wife's have been listed by Alan Denson, *J. H. Cousins (1873-1956) and M. E. Cousins (1878-1954), a bio-bibliographical survey,* with foreword by Padraic Colum (Kendal, 1967).

The pier at Carrick-fergus, Co. Antrim (Welch Collection, Ulster Museum)

Ardglass fishing boats returning to harbour (Lawrence Collection, National Library of Ireland)

Samuel Kennedy Cowan was one of six northern poets who had a selection of their works published together in 1896. Born at Lisburn, Co. Antrim, in 1850, Cowan graduated from Dublin University. He was probably most renowned in his day as a writer of Christmas-card verse. Legend has it that he regularly wrote up to 400 rhymes and verses for a single Christmas. Many of his lyrics were set to music by composers including Sir Arthur Sullivan. Among his volumes of poetry are *Poems* (London, 1873), *Victoria the good* (Newry, 1897), and *From Ulster's hills* (Belfast, 1913). Besides all this Cowan was a major in the militia. He died in 1918.

*Three fishwives from
Newcastle, Co. Down
(Green Collection,
Ulster Folk Museum)*

DUNDRUM BAR

THEY sailed away with never a care,
   Under the light of moon and star,
For the tide was full and the wind was fair
   At Dundrum Bar.
Five good fishermen, steady and brave,
Ready to battle with wind and wave,
   Each for his own,
With their nets aboard, all trim and strong,
They sailed away with cheer and song,
Sou'-sou'-east, toward Annalong,
   Where deep seas moan.

Lamps on the land through the live-long night,
   Steadily gleaming, broad and far,
Streamed, like a golden lane of light,
   Thro' Dundrum Bar.
Beacon-lamps of home were they,
Trimmed by true hands lovingly,
   Each for her own;
Lamps, alas! that, thro' the dark,
Never again shall light their bark,
Lying alone and low and stark,
   Where deep seas moan!

All night long and the livelong day,
   Watching, waiting, each for her own,
Gazed they fondly, and far away,
   Where deep seas moan.
Gazed till, lo! before the gale,
Was it sail, or seaweed pale,
   Or shattered spar
Saw they, drifting, still and white,
All in the golden lane of light
Shed by the shore-lamps, shining bright,
Thro' Dundrum Bar?

It was neither seaweed pale,
   Neither sail nor shattered spar,
Drifting ashore before the gale,
   Thro' Dundrum Bar.
Nay; but the corse of one was it
Whose ghost the lamps of love had lit
   Back to his own;
For love from love no death can keep,
For love is mighty, and love is deep
And vast as the graves of them that sleep
   Where deep seas moan.

S. K. Cowan, *Sung by six. Collected poems of six poets* (Belfast, 1896), pp 51-3.

Regatta day at Bangor, Co. Down (Lawrence Collection, National Library of Ireland)

NORTH SEA BUBBLES

In the South there dwelt an Earl
Who possessed a fine 'Black Pearl'
Of goodly lines and build was she,
Her size in tons 'three forty three'.

The Earl had once expressed desire
His jewel rare to let on hire,
So, to a Celt on pleasure bent,
His well beloved pearl he lent.

Then Captain Bond so staunch and true
His mates, his boatswain and the crew-
Twenty-five hands on board, all hearty-
Were joined from Redburn by our party.

The Irishman, his wife and son,
John Harrison and Arthur Dunn,
Miss Fowler, too, of Rahinstown,
In hunting field of great renown.

From Aberdeen the good ship sails,
Not fearing North Sea storm or gales,
And soon we reach the shore beyond
Secure, and safely 'under Bond'.

(cont.)

R. G. Dunville, *North Sea bubbles* (Belfast, not dated), pp13-15.

Members of the Annesley family from Castlewellan, Co. Down, aboard their yacht on the way to Cowes, 1893 (Annesley Collection, Public Record Office of Northern Ireland)

Robert Grimshaw Dunville (1838-1910) was a member of the famous Dunville whiskey family whose advertisements in Ulster newspapers at the end of the nineteenth century assured readers that their stocks of whiskey in Belfast were the largest in the world! Besides being a whiskey distiller, he was an aspiring poet. These aspirations, however, received little acknowledgment. In his *Dictionary of Irish poets*, D. J. O'Donoghue mentions a volume of poetry called *The voyage*, published by him in 1891, which, O'Donoghue remarks, he 'sensibly suppressed' after its publication. Smarting, no doubt, from the criticism of this first book, Dunville had his second book, *North Sea bubbles*, published privately for friends. As can be seen from the above passage, it was hardly a serious work. But had he produced this book for children, there can have been little doubt of its success. *North Sea bubbles* deals with a trip he made with his family and some friends from their home at Redburn, near Holywood, Co. Down, in a boat called the *Black Pearl*. The book is pleasantly illustrated by the author and would have fascinated young readers.

CASSIE: May I bring in the bicycle out o' the rain? Dear sakes, what's the matter, Ellen! Have ye bad news?

ELLEN: Ach, no! But she's getting old, and it doesn't take much to vex her. She's fretting, like, because I'm going to America, and she'd like me to stay here. But it's no use thinking o't.

CASSIE (*Propping bicycle against dresser and coming up to Mary*):- Ach, now, Mrs. Macauley, don't you be taking on like that; don't now. What's going to America that it should fret ye? What else does anybody be doing in the glens? Isn't it three out of four, and five out of six, and six out of seven in every house that goes? There's nothing else for them to do. This is a poor country, and out there there's plenty o' work and lashings o' money, and why wouldn't they go! I'm real thankful I'm out there myself, so I am, and it's thankful ye should be that Ellen's going for she'll do fine.

MARY: I'm not thankful, then; I'm sore displeased at her, Cassie, leaving me me lone and going off to sport herself in America, or the dear knows where. It's not you that knows what it is to have your childer glad to leave ye, and ye may be thankful this day that ye're not married. Ye'll never have the heart-break that I have, and it's well for ye.

CASSIE: 'Deed that's just what I'm thinking meself, when I'm back here and see the empty houses and the old men and women that's filling the country. I wouldn't live here not for all the gold in America. But come now, Mrs. Macauley, rise off that trunk and come and sit by the fire. You'll be better so. (*She leads Mrs. Macauley to chair by fire and sits down beside her*). Listen now, and I'll tell ye. Ellen's got the wish to go to America, and don't you be stopping her. What would she do here at all at all! Shure this is no country for them as is young and stirring. She'll send you back more money in a year than ever she'd make in all her life in Ireland. Don't ye know that?

MARY: It's me daughter's company, not the money I'd want. Why wouldn't she stay here and marry a decent man, and wouldn't that be better nor pounds and pounds? Ye know it would.

M. E. Dobbs, *She's going to America*, included in *Village plays* (Dundalk, 1920), pp37-8.

Right: *Belfast Quays around 1910. Notice both the sail and steam boats. (Lawrence Collection, National Library of Ireland)*

Below: *American liner at Moville, Co. Donegal, probably around 1890. This boat stopped to take on passengers from Derry brought by tender from Moville. (Lawrence Collection, National Library of Ireland) In 1883 over 15,000 people left through Derry for Canada and the U.S.A.*

This play, *She's going to America*, set in the Glens of Antrim, was first performed at Cushendall in September 1912. It deals with the problem of emigration and its effects on the local community. In the introduction to the volume containing this and three other plays, the authoress, Margaret Emmeline Dobbs, explains that they were written specially for a company of village actors and were designed to meet the difficulties of production in a country district. Three of the plays were staged at Cushendall in a hay loft turned into a long narrow hall, with stage, scenery and lighting of local construction. Margaret Dobbs was born in Co. Antrim and spent much of her life in the Glens of Antrim. She was an Irish scholar of some note. She died in 1961 aged 88.

QUAYS. BELFAST. 4745. W.L.

Members of the Belfast Naturalist Field Club on a boat trip on Lough Erne, Co. Fermanagh, July 1892. The B.N.F.C. was founded in 1863. Along with the Belfast Natural History and Philosophical Society, founded in 1821, it has done much to promote the study of the geology, botany, archaeology and history of the province. (R. W. Welch, **Praeger Album,** *Royal Irish Academy)*

44

A SONG OF FREEDOM

In Cavan of little lakes,
As I was walking with the wind,
And no one seen beside me there,
There came a song into my mind :
It came as if the whispered voice
Of one, but none of humankind,
Who walked with me in Cavan then,
And he invisible as wind.

On Urris, of Inish-Owen,
As I went up the mountainside,
The brook that came leaping down
Cried to me, for joy it cried;
And when from off the summit far
I looked o'er land and water wide,
I was more joyous than the brook
That met me on the mountainside.

To Ara, of Connacht's isles,
As I went sailing o'er the sea,
The wind's word, the brook's word,
The wave's word, was plain to me—
"As we are, though she is not.
As we are shall Banba be—
There is no King can rule the wind
There is no fetter for the sea."

Alice Milligan

Henry Morgan (ed.), *Poems by Alice Milligan* (Dublin, 1954), P. 1.

Born at Omagh, Co. Tyrone, about 1866, Alice Milligan was educated in Belfast and London. She founded and edited with Ethna Carbery, the Belfast published magazine, the *Shan Van Vocht*, which, for the three years that it ran, had an important influence on Irish republicanism. She also wrote several novels and plays as well as books of poetry. The poem given here was first published in 1904. She died in 1953.

Mermen discovered in Lough Oughter, Co. Cavan, by the B.N.F.C. What eventually happened to these mermen is unfortunately not revealed in the Club's records! (Welch Collection, Ulster Museum)

IN THE CITY

Castle Place, Belfast, about 1908 (Lawrence Collection, National Library of Ireland)

Belfast shipyards 1910. S.S. Olympic and S.S. Titanic are both nearly completed. (Hogg Collection, Ulster Museum)

Donegall Place, Belfast, around 1908. The new City Hall was opened in 1906. (Lawrence Collection, National Library of Ireland)

Belfast—when you reach it—is not calculated to charm the eye. It has the features of any English manufacturing town so far as its buildings are concerned, and the finest structures it can show (without disparaging its handsome Town Hall) are the vast fabrics which rise in the dockyards, such ships as have never been built in the world before—marvels of symmetry and strength. To see them in the building up is to watch, perhaps, the most impressive exhibition of human skill and energy.

Stephen Gwynn, *Ulster* (London, 1911), p.15.

Stephen Lucius Gwynn (1864-1950) was born in Dublin but spent many of his early and most formative years in Co. Donegal. From 1906 until 1918 he was a Nationalist M.P. He was the author of a large number of novels, Irish travel books, biographies and volumes of poetry. In 1899 he wrote a popular Ulster travelogue, *Highways and byways in Donegal and Antrim* (London). His *Collected poems* were published in 1923 in London. Among Gwynn's novels and short story collections are *John Maxwell's marriage* (London, 1903), and *The glade in the forest* (Dublin, 1907). He also wrote an interesting autobiography called *Experiences of a literary man* (London, 1926).

These photographs are from an album about a Belfast temperance missionary around 1910. Above is a young man who has learnt the better of his ways and is signing the pledge under the watchful eyes of the missionary and a policeman! Top right is the missionary (on the right) in a public house on the Shankill Road and below right is a court scene. (D. H. Hogg, Linenhall Library.)

Bernard Magennis (1833-1911) was born at Ballybay, Co. Monaghan. He was a national school teacher for a time, and wrote verse in newspapers such as the *Dundalk Democrat* and the *Northern Whig*. He lived for a number of years in New York and Lancashire. A prominent temperance advocate, he edited a Dublin paper, *The Social Mirror and Temperance Advocate*. His books include *Anti-humbug, or Mansion House banquets midst Ireland's poverty* , (Manchester, 1890) and *The catapult, a satire* (Dublin, 1897). Other members of the Magennis family, especially Peter Magennis,. were well-known poets in south-west Ulster.

THE BOYS OF OUR DAY

We live in an age of great progress 'tis clear,
Though some think our progress doth crab-like appear,
And assert that each step in advance that we take
Another still backward we slip—by *mistake;*
And so be where we started it's plain to my mind,
Neither moving an inch, nor yet stopping behind;
Having prefaced thus far, I'll proceed to portray,
As I find them before me, the boys of our day.

See that urchin who out from his pocket doth draw
An old dhudeen pipe which he sticks in his jaw!
He wants with *men's* age, not his own to keep pace,
As you'll see by his wizen'd and smoke begrimed face.
Mark his impudent phiz and his comical leers,
Though he's little yet over a half score of years!
He's so fast from his nature he's run clean away,
This specimen bright of the boys of our day!

. . . .

There are others who sit in a corner obscure,
And call for their glasses of Jameson's pure;
With a smack on their lips and delight in each soul,
They drain to the dregs the accursed damning bowl,
'Till the roses of youth on their cheek soon have fled,
And the spring-time of life scarcely blooms 'till 'tis dead,
While all that is pure is corroding away,
And in crime they grow hoary, these boys of our day.

They prefer such amusements as *manly* are thought,
But the pleasures *they* bring oft too dearly are bought;
Those pleasures are false, vicious pastimes impart,
And leave still behind them a sting in the heart;
Behold the poor waifs and the strays that now roam
The streets of the cities abroad and at home.
What brought them to that? If they speak truth, they'll say
Parental neglect of the boys of our day!

Bernard Magennis, *Lamh Dearg or the Red Hand*
(Dublin, 1887), pp 147-9.

Uladh means Ulster. It is still often necessary to state as much : we intend to insist. Draw an imaginary line across Ireland from that great bight, Donegal Bay, in the west, to Carlingford Lough, on the east, and draw it not too rigidly : north of that you have Ulster. This Ulster has its own way of things, which may be taken as the great contrast to the Munster way of things, still keeping on Irish lands.

Cities like Londonderry and Belfast have drawn all its best energies towards them. And though of late years the city has been more a stumbling block to the right intellectual and artistic progress of the country yet, in spite of influences and disabilities operating against it, a certain characteristic temperamental and mental trend has been lent to the town by the country, and a certain local intellectual activity has persisted there. We wish to locate this, and to afford it an outlet in literary expression.

Exactly what that local temperament and artistic aptitude are *Uladh* wants to discuss. *Uladh* would also influence them, direct and inform them. And as the Theatre is the most essential of all art activities, and the surest test of a people's emotional and intellectual vitality, *Uladh* starts out as the organ of the Theatre, the Ulster Literary Theatre, but proposes to be as irrelevant to that movement and its topics as is deemed necessary.

We recognise at the outset that our art of the drama will be different from that other Irish art of drama which speaks from the stage of the Irish National Theatre in Dublin, where two men, W. B. Yeats and Douglas Hyde, have set a model in Anglo-Irish and Gaelic plays with a success that is surprising and exhilarating. Dreamer, mystic, symbolist, Gaelic poet and propagandist have all spoken on the Dublin stage, and a fairly defined local school has been inaugurated. We in Belfast and Ulster also wish to set up a school; but there will be a difference.

At present we can only say that our talent is more satiric than poetic. That will probably remain the broad difference between the Ulster and the Leinster schools. But when our genius arrives, as he must

sooner or later, there is no accounting for what extraordinary tendency he may display. Our business is, however, to plod along gathering matter for his use, practising methods, perfecting technique, and training actors.

We have most to fear for the young men in that, if they do not find an outlet in Ulster, they will either go away, or gravitate upon the sloblands of American or English magazine work, which is purely commercial and has no pretention to literature whatever. It expresses nothing, means nothing; it aims at being sixpence-worth. We do not aim at being sixpence-worth; we aim at being priceless, for honesty and and good purpose are priceless. If we do not attain to all this, we shall at least attain to something unique in Ulster, smacking of the soil, the winds on the uplands, the north coast, the sun and the rain, and the long winter evenings.

Uladh will be non-sectarian and non-political; each article will be signed by the writer as an expression of his own individual views; other views may be put forward in another number. In any case, our pages will be kept free from the party-cries of mob and clique and market-place. Honesty in all matters of taste and opinion will, we hope, characterise our matter. Our contributors are mostly young men, of all sects and all grades of political opinion.

The journal will be run on broad propagandist lines. Propagandism on broad lines, we think, is desirable at this juncture. There is a strong undercurrent of culture in the North, and this we will endeavour to tap, and, if possible, turn into native channels. As a good Ulsterman, and a friend of this venture, has truly said: "We have it to effect a great deal—the voice of the Press is far-reaching. We may roll the stone that has been only pushed at by others. Then will the heroes of the North ride forth again: at present they only sleep within the cavern of dark prejudice and ignorance and distrust."

If we succeed in accomplishing this much, if we roll the stone, if it is in our power to awaken the heroes to activity and the people to sympathy and life, surely our existence will be justified.

Above left: *Forrest Reid - novelist (Mr. Stephen Gilbert's private collection)*

Above right: *Francis Joseph Bigger - antiquarian (R.W. Welch, Praeger Album, Royal Irish Academy)*

Below: *Scene from an Ulster Literary Theatre production of Rutherford Mayne's The turn of the road. The actors from left to right are John Campbell, Lily Hughes, J. Storey, Lewis Purcell and W. R. Gordon. (Mr. S. H. Bell's private collection)*

Uladh i, no. 1 (Nov. 1904), pp 1-3.

The extract on the left is from the opening editorial of the Belfast literary magazine, *Uladh*. Although it ran for only 4 numbers its contributors included notable writers such as Robert Lynd, Forrest Reid, Carl Hardebeck, Bulmer Hobson, Francis Joseph Bigger, AE, Alice Milligan and George and Norman Morrow. One of its purposes was to promote the Ulster Literary Theatre which was founded in 1904 and ran until 1934. Various factors contributed to the Theatre's failure to equal the Abbey Theatre in Dublin. Prominent no doubt amongst these factors were lack of really outstanding writers like Yeats and Synge, failure to find permanent premises, absence of wealthy patrons, inadequate publishing and bookselling facilities, and a certain puritanical attitude in the north towards the theatre. Nonetheless the Ulster Literary Theatre did have considerable success and was responsible for bringing to the fore important playwrights like Rutherford Mayne.

Above: *Bishop Street, Derry, in the 1880s. At the end of the street can be seen the old Corporation Hall. (Robert French, Linenhall Library)*

Below: *Waterloo Place. Derry, around 1905 (Lawrence Collection, National Library of Ireland)*

Although born in Co. Wicklow in 1818, Mrs. Cecil Frances Alexander was closely associated with Derry city; she lived in Bishop Street from 1867 to 1895 when her husband was Bishop of Derry and Raphoe. She was a prolific and very able writer of hymns, many of which are still popular today, such as 'There is a green hill far away' and 'Once in royal David's City'; the first of these is supposed to have been written as she sat in her study looking out over the Derry hills. At this time there were a number of prominent hymn writers in Ulster. In 1896, the year after her death, a collected volume of Mrs. Alexander's poetry and hymns was published in London. Both her husband, William Alexander, and their daughter, Eleanor, were also well known writers.

ST. PATRICK'S BREASTPLATE.

I BIND unto myself to-day
    The strong Name of the Trinity,
By invocation of the same,
    The Three in One and One in Three.

I bind this day to me for ever,
    By pow'r of faith, Christ's Incarnation;
His baptism in Jordan river;
    His death on Cross for my salvation;
His bursting from the spicèd tomb;
    His riding up the heav'nly way;
His coming at the day of doom;
    I bind unto myself to-day.

I bind unto myself to-day
    The virtues of the star-lit heaven,
The glorious sun's life-giving ray,
    The whiteness of the moon at even,
The flashing of the lightning free,
    The whirling wind's tempestuous shocks,
The stable earth, the deep salt sea,
    Around the old eternal rocks.

. . . .

Christ be with me, Christ within me,
    Christ behind me, Christ before me,
Christ beside me, Christ to win me,
    Christ to comfort and restore me,
Christ beneath me, Christ above me,
    Christ in quiet, Christ in danger,
Christ in hearts of all that love me,
    Christ in mouth of friend and stranger.

I bind unto myself the Name,
    The strong Name of the Trinity;
By invocation of the same,
    The Three in One, and One in Three.
Of Whom all nature hath creation:
    Eternal Father, Spirit, Word:
Praise to the Lord of my salvation,
    Salvation is of Christ the Lord.

Versified from the Irish by **C. F. Alexander**, *Poems* (London, 1896), pp 59-62.

Part of the crowd at the city hall for the unveiling of Queen Victoria's statue in 1903 by King Edward VII (Welch Collection, Ulster Museum)

THE ROYAL VISIT TO IRELAND
Letter from " Robin" to H.R.H. Prince Albert Victor
(Afterwards Duke of Clarence).

Ballycuddy, County Down,
May the tenth, 18 and 89.

"Dear Prince Albert Victor,

A'm prood tae heer that ye ir railly cumin' tae see Bilfast agen. Mony an' mony a time Peggy an' me haes been crackin' aboot ye since the last time that ye cummed wi' yer da an' ma. There wuz yin thing aboot ye, dear Prince, that struck Peggy mair nor ocht else, an' that was this : Ye'll hae min' o' that terble wat day that cummed on; weel, whun the fowk wuz cheerin' ower ocht ye sut in the kerridge wi' yer hat aff, an' the rain teemin' on ye like oot o' dishes. Peggy said ye wur a guid waen, an' wud make a gran' King sum day, jist if ye wudnae forget yersel' and grow prood. "Peggy, dear " sez I, "rale nobility is niver prood; it's only empty, ignerant upstarts that forgets themsels."

Hooaniver, pittin' that tae yin side, A'm prood, as A said afore, that yer cummin' back tae Bilfast. It shews that ye likit it whun ye wur there afore,' an' it shews at the same time that yer a wise, studdy young man whun yer royal Da an' Ma ir no afeerd tae trust ye awa' oot o' their sicht sae far.

A hope, dear Prince, ye'll no' feel affendit wi' me acause A tak' the liberty o' writin' ye this letter. A hae kent a' yer femily weel since A wuz a boy at Skule, an' A hae iver taen a great interest in the conserns o' the Royal Femily. A'm gaun up tae see ye, ov coorse, an' what fur noo? In echteen hunner an' foarty nine, whun yer Granda an' Granma cummed till Bilfast, A wuz there tae cheer wi' the tither fowk. Yer dear Granma didne ken me then, but she's a grate freen o' mine noo. They tell me ye redd the story A writ aboot me bein' interduced till the Queen in Glescoe last yeer; an' then ye ken that yer Da an' me ir auld akwantenances an' brither Freemasons. Shew him this letter, an' he'll tell ye a' aboot me an' whaur A leev.

. . . .

There'll harly be a chance o' my gettin' a aurd wi' ye while yer ower, there'll be sich a wheen o' the gran' fowk roon ye iverywhaur ye gang. Weel, weel, A maun pit up wi' the dissappointment, but ig A had ten minnits wi' ye

A wud gie ye a wheen hints that micht be usefu' till ye.

Dear Prince, A'm feered ye'll be tired readin' by this time, so A maun stap. The dear man, if ye wud cum doon to Bangor fur a day but the fowk wud like it. Ye cud hae a birl on the Switchback Railway, an' then ye cud see the Masonic Hall, an' the waterworks, an' a wheen ither places.

Wi' sincere and kind respekts frae me an' mine tae you an' yours,

A remain, Yer humble, loyal, an' law-abidin' servant,

Rabin Gordon."

W. G. Lyttle, *Robin's readings; part 1 - 3* (Belfast), pp 53-5.

Born at Newtownards, Co. Down, in 1844, Wesley Guard Lyttle was known as 'Robin', the author of a large number of poems and sketches in the dialect of a Co. Down farmer. In this character he used to give public readings which were extremely popular. In published form, *Robin's readings* ran through many editions. He also wrote several novels using a Co. Down dialect - *Sons of the sod* (Bangor, 1886) and *Betsy Gray, a tale of ninety-eight,* which was republished recently (Newcastle, Co. Down, 1968). As well as writing, Lyttle had a varied career which included running a Bangor newspaper, the *North Down and Bangor Gazette,* and he was one of the first to teach shorthand in Belfast. He died in 1896.

Some of the decorations in Donegall Square for the royal visit to Belfast in 1885. The White Linenhall has been specially decorated. Note the interesting writings on the arch. (R. W. Welch, Linenhall Library)

NEW TRAMWAYS COMMITTEE

AN IMAGINARY MEETING

WHO'LL BE CHAIRMAN?

The newly appointed members of the Tramways Committee met at the Town Hall the other day to appoint their chairman and make preliminary arrangements, when there was a full attendance. The proceedings were animated, if not interesting, and are fully reported below.

SIR SAMUEL BLACK—"Your first business is to appoint a chairman, and following my usual custom, I would suggest that you elect my old friend, Sir Dan——" (Loud cries of "No dictation," "You've played that game too long," &c., &c.

(Collapse of Sir Samuel temporarily.)

Alderman John M'Cormick is, as chairman of the Law Committee, moved to the chair in order to conduct the election.

Alderman JOHN M'CORMICK— "My Lord Mayor, Sir Daniel, and both Sir Roberts, and also gentlemen, this is the proudest moment of my life. Still, I shall not unnecessarily detain you by any simple words of mine, and will therefore be brief—ed. (hear, hear!) Before asking for nominations for the chairmanship, you will permit me to say in the very fewest of polysyllabic dithyrambics that such an unparalleled concatenation of the most brilliant intellectual attainments as are personified in the prominent personages composing the corruscation to be known henceforward as the Municipal Tramways Committee could not be equalled outside that noble city whose proud motto is *'Pro tanto quid retribuamus'.*"

Councillor M'INNES. — "Rats."

Ald. JOHN M'CORMICK—"I beg your pardon. Permit me to finish. To proceed then, we are not limited in our field of choice. The transincorporation of the street tramways system will effect a perfect metampsychosis in our conditions of vehicular traffic which no inconceivable predetermination can relieve from uncertainty. It is, therefore, your duty to select a member whose character shall be ascendant, predominant, commanding, controlling, regnant, sovereign, superior, and supreme to all such paltry considerations as laying lines economically, or such twopenny halfpenny trivialities as *halfpenny fares.* I know of no one, I say I know of no one in your number who fulfils all those conditions. Yet perhaps I exaggerate. There is ONE, but modesty and my position forbids me mentioning him.

Councillor W. MACARTNEY.—What about the deputations?

At this stage enter Councillors J. N. M'Cammond, James M'Entee, and Alderman W. Harper, the former singing—

"We'd a high old spree,
Me and M'Entee,

and the Alderman—

"We had, by gum-um-um."

Alderman Sir JAMES HENDERSON —"I quite concur in every word which Alderman John M'Cormick has excellently mentioned in his most excellent speech. Indeed, I think he put the matter in a most excellent way, but I do not see why his modesty or position should have prevented him mentioning my name, since it was evidently me whom he referred to."

Councillor WM. MACARTNEY — "What about the deputations?"

Alderman HARPER—"I'm sorry I came in a little late, but surely the Committee will not pass over one for the chairmanship who has the very highest qualifications." (Chorus of "Who? Who?") The Alderman, continuing — "Names, my Lord Mayor, names are unnecessary. I refer to the senior Alderman, the senior member of the Corporation present—one who, in the words of the poet, has

'With contemplative view surveyed mankind and womankind from China to Peru,'

and—may I say—picked up and dropped again a good few half-guineas during the process."

Councillor WM. MACARTNEY — "What about the deputations?"

Sir DANIEL—"Oh! d—— the deputations!"

Alderman WM. M'CORMICK (Falls) —"Are we never going to get down to business? We cannot all be chairman, so I wonder how it would do to co-opt an outsider. What price the Bishop? He has a great name for managing things,"

Sir JEAMES—"All betting news is strictly prohibited except in the most excellent columns of my most excellent newspaper."

Major Councillor CUNNINGHAM— "Aw! it-er is a gweat pity my Awldehman —I wefer to Awldehman Wobinson—is not heah. He has a vewy high opinion of me, and in my mititawy capacity-er I am accustomed to command-er."

Councillor W. MACARTNEY — "What about the depu——"

He is immediately and ignominiously removed by "James," Sergeant-at-Mace.

Councillor M'INNES—"Now, if you're nearly all done praising yourselves, I would like to make a nomination which I am sure will meet with unanimous approval. (Question.) Our chairman, whoever he may be, must be the embodiment of tact —(hear, hear!)—moderation—(hear, hear!) — suavity, courtesy, and consideration for the feelings of others. (Applause). I therefore have much pleasure in moving that Councillor William Walker——"

(Exeunt M'Innes gallantly defending himself against a storm of ink-pots; and break-up of the meeting in confusion.)

(It is long odds that they will be compelled to adopt old Sir Samuel's suggestion ultimately.)

Nomad's Weekly, no. 256, 18 June 1904.

Tram at the Whitehouse terminus, Dec. 1905 (A. R. Hogg, Linenhall Library). Horse drawn trams were introduced to Belfast in 1872 and replaced by electric trams in 1905.

Nomad's Weekly was a weekly Belfast satirical magazine first brought out in 1899 and which ran until 1914. During this time, under the editorship of Alfred S. Moore it mercilessly satirized politicians, churchmen, trade union officials, corporation councillors and businessmen. No person or institution was safe from its searching columns. It led the field in many areas of social reform such as shorter hours for shop assistants. At one stage it claimed a readership of 40,000 people.

RAINEY: So ye're here at last, are ye? Kapin' the tay waitin'!

TOM: Och, sure, A cudden help it. A wus wi' Hughie!

RAINEY: Aye, ye're sure t'be late if ye're wi' him. Where's he?

TOM: A left him in Royal Avenue talkin' to Michael O'Hara.

RAINEY: What, thon Papish fella?

TOM: Aye, they went intil the Sinn Feiners' Hall thegither. *[He sits down and takes off his boots.]* He'll not be long. *[He takes off his coat and loosens his waistcoat.]*

RAINEY: A don't like Hughie goin' after Papishes. He knows a quare lock o' them.

MRS. RAINEY: Och, now, what harm is there in that. A'm sure Micky O'Hara's as nice a wee fella as ye cud wish t' meet.

RAINEY: Aw, A've nathin' agenst him, but A don't like Cathliks an' Prodesans mixin' thegither. No good ivir comes o' the like o' that.

[Tom goes into the scullery where the splashing noise is renewed.]

MRS. RAINEY: They'll have to mix in heaven, John.

RAINEY: This isn't heaven.

MRS. RAINEY: Indeed, that's true. What wi' stracks an' one thing an' another, it might be hell.

RAINEY: There's no peace where Catholiks an' Prodesans gits mixed up thegither. Luk at the way the Cathliks carry on on the Twelfth o' July. Ye have t' have the peelers houlin' them back for fear they'd make a riot. D'ye call that respectable or dacent?

MRS. RAINEY: Well, God knows, they git plenty of provokin'. What wi' them men that prache at the Custom House Steps an' yer or'nge arches an' the way the *Tellygraph* is always goin' on at them, A wonder they don't do more nor they do.

RAINEY: Aw, ye wur always one fur Cathliks!

MRS. RAINEY: A belave in lavin' people alone. Come on, an' have yer tay fur dear sake. Sure ye'd go on talkin' fur a lifetime if A wus to let ye.

St J. G. Ervine, *Mixed marriage* included in *Four Irish plays* (London, 1914), p.3.

Right: *Mountpottinger crossroads, East Belfast, close to where St J. Ervine lived (Green Collection, Ulster Folk Museum)*

Far right: *The Newtownards Road, East Belfast (Green Collection, Ulster Folk Museum)*

Mixed marriage was first performed at the Abbey Theatre in 1910. Set in contemporary industrial Belfast, the play centres upon a strike and a mixed marriage. The author, St John Greer Ervine, was born in Belfast in 1883; he lived at Ballymacarrett in East Belfast, until he was 18, when he went to London and started to write. During 1915-16 he spent a brief period as manager of the Abbey Theatre before going to the war-front in Europe where he was injured and had a leg amputated. He settled in the south-west of England and continued writing. Although the greater part of his life was spent away from Ulster, many of his finest novels and plays are about the province and its people. His plays include *John Ferguson* (Dublin, 1915), *Boyd's shop* (London, 1936), and *Friends and relations* (London, 1947). Among the novels he wrote were *Mrs. Martin's man* (London, 1914), and *The first Mrs. Fraser* (London, 1929). He also wrote a life of Lord Craigavon, which was published in London in 1949 - *Craigavon, Ulsterman.* To a certain extent these works reflect Ervine's changing political views. In his early days he was strongly socialist and rather nationalistic. Later he became a firm unionist. St John Ervine died in 1971.

AROUND THE PROVINCE

A 1913 luxury tour, by charabanc, (Welch Collection, Ulster Museum)

Driving for the Tennis Hole, Ladies Course, Ballycastle, Co. Antrim (Welch Collection, Ulster Museum)

DELINA appeared just now on the platform, deeply moved at the blending masses who rushed at the last moment to catch the boat train.

With a warm hand-shake Lord Gifford bade his railway friend adieu, and conducted Delina to a gorgeous saloon that stood in readiness to convey them to their verdant destination. Its springy seats of all sizes, colour, and form, upholstered in velvet of richest make, imparted to their bodies the ease they craved, and caused Delina, whilst lying buried in sinking silence, to cast her thoughts on the immediate past into the near tide along which she was so closely and swiftly driven. Only forty minutes did they enjoy their room of refinement.

A first class saloon car (Welch Collection, Ulster Museum)

As the train slowly puffed into Larne Harbour station Delina suddenly jumped to her feet, and became pale as milk.

"What's the matter, dear?" spake Lord Gifford, rising hurriedly to his feet. "Is there anything wrong?"

"Oh, everything," she gasped, in despair, "for I've forgotten my little bundle. I left it in the waiting-room above."

"Bosh, child; what about it! Far nicer things, I presume, will await you once we are safely landed on the other side."

"But—but—I'd love to have it. My brooch is in it, and two embroidered handkerchiefs my mother gave me years ago, besides other wee things I've learned to love."

As there was little time to be lost, and to satisfy her wish, meagre as it was, Lord Gifford resolved to le her have it. He beckoned on the station-agent—now that the train had arrived at a standstill—whose genial manner and exemplary courteousness are widely known, and stated the case to him. Lord Gifford then gave him his card, making the necessary alterations in his address and asked that it be forwarded immediate

Stroking his long, soft beard, that once claimed to be more gingered in colour, the station-agent answered him gently, yet assuredly, with the words, "Certainly so; it will have every attention."

Shortly afterwards, they were so steadily and quietly guided along from Larne Harbour and its fine, deep lough, above the shimmering and flashy waves o moonlit quash, that before they got completely free from viewing past possibilities, they were standing on Stranraer Harbour.

The quick despatch of business occasioned quicker despatch of trains. Before they found time to decide whether or not to proceed direct to London, the train steamed away, and soon stole from their view

A fine hotel, however, came to their rescue. A peep into the supper-room showed the half-frightened maid tall ferns shedding a fanciful shade upon the neatly arranged flowers that decked the long table's snowy cover; hospitality, be it said, peeped from its very mirrors; the fruits of the earth, the fish of the sea the fowls of the air, and the flesh of beasts, were nimbly sitting in their glass, china, and silver dishes, crushing, apparently, the table's face with their tempting delicacies. Around this well-lighted room sat many a jolly rover, inhaling the heated perfume of rosy Bacchus, and sniffing contentedly at the delightful combined odour of the huge supper-table. Further along oozed the fragrant scent of a Chinese plant, that mixed refreshingly with the fainter, more ethereal odour of the exquisite flowers, whose faces stood ele-

elegantly daubed, some deep, others deeper, with natural paints of every conceivable natural shade, and whose delightful differences of tint grew more faint as the night advanced; while the cheery click of china pleasantly greeted the ear, as the hungry fingers of a travelling throng craved to touch it.

Partaking heartily of a well-cooked supper, sleep soon found purchasers in Lord Gifford and Delina Delaney.

A. McK. Ros, *Delina Delaney*, (Belfast, 1898; 2nd ed., London, 1935), pp 72-5.

Amanda McKittrick Ros was without doubt the most eccentric Ulster writer of her day. Born near Drumaness, Co. Down, in 1860, she trained as a teacher and went to Larne where she married Andrew Ross, the local stationmaster (he is mentioned in this extract). As a writer she has been variously described. On the one hand she has been called the world's worst novelist and on the other a sort of literary 'Grandma Moses'. The latter description is clearly the fairer one. Completely lacking in literary sophistication, she wrote the most extraordinary and delightful prose. She was the authoress of *Delina Delaney* and of two other novels, *Irene Iddlesleigh* (Belfast, 1897), and *Helen Huddleson* (London, 1969); this last book was completed by Jack Loudan after her death. She also wrote poetry, including *Poems of puncture* (London, 1912) and *Fumes of formation* (Belfast, 1933). These works contain many references to her pet hates - lawyers and literary critics - one unfortunate lawyer who crossed her path was lampooned with the name Mickey Monkeyface McBlear. Her admirers formed clubs which met to exchange quotations from her writings; members of these clubs included Lord Beveridge, E. V. Lucas and Lord Oxford. She died in 1939. A good biography of her has been written by Jack Loudan-*O rare Amanda* (London, 1954; 2nd ed., 1969).

Dining room in the Slieve Donard Hotel, Newcastle, Co. Down (Lawrence Collection, National Library of Ireland)

Right: *Ballyshannon, Co. Donegal (Welch Collection, Ulster Museum)*

Below: *Excursion steamer on the Erne at Enniskillen, Co. Fermanagh (Lawrence Collection, National Library of Ireland)*

UNDER THE GRASS

Where those green mounds o'erlook the mingling Erne
  And salt Atlantic, clay that walked as Man
A thousand years ago, some Vik-ing stern,
  May rest, or nameless Chieftain of the Clan;
And when my dusty remnant shall return
  To the great passive World, and nothing can
With eye, or lip, or finger, any more,
  O lay it there too, by the river shore.

The silver salmon shooting up the fall,
  Itself at once the arrow and the bow;
The shadow of the old quay's weedy wall
  Cast on the shining turbulence below;
The water-voice which ever seems to call
  Far off out of my childhood's long-ago;
The gentle washing of the harbour wave;
  Be these the sights and sounds around my grave.

Soothed also with thy friendly beck, my town,
  And near the square gray tower within whose shade
Was many of my kin's last lying down;
  Whilst, by the broad heavens changefully arrayed,
Empurpling mountains its horizon crown;
  And westward 'tween low hummocks is displayed,
In lightsome hours, the level pale blue sea,
  With sails upon it creeping silently:

Or, other time, beyond that tawny sand,
  An ocean glooming underneath the shroud
Drawn thick athwart it by tempestuous hand;
  When like a mighty fire the bar roars loud,
As though the whole sea came to whelm the land—
  The gull flies white against the stormy cloud,
And in the weather-gleam the breakers mark
  A ghastly line upon the waters dark.

A green unfading quilt above be spread,
  And freely round let all the breezes blow:
May children play beside the breathless bed,
  Holiday lasses by the cliff-edge go;
And manly games upon the sward be sped,
  And cheerful boats beneath the headland row;
And be the thought, if any rise, of me,
  What happy soul might wish that thought to be

William Allingham, *Irish songs and poems* (London, 1887), pp 123-4.

This rather sombre poem was written by William Allingham in his last years as he contemplated death. After Ferguson, Allingham is undoubtedly the greatest poet in this anthology. The town referred to in the poem is of course Ballyshannon, Co. Donegal, where he was born in 1824. Educated at Ballyshannon he spent much of his early life in the north of Ireland while serving in the bank and the customs service. He became a close friend of Tennyson and was associated with members of the pre-Raphaelite group. After 1863 he lived permanently in England, returning only for brief periods to Ireland. From 1874-9 he was editor of *Fraser's Magazine.* Throughout his writing his upbringing remained a constant influence. Perhaps his best work was *Laurence Bloomfield,* published in book form in 1864. Consisting of twelve chapters of verse it was a powerful commentary on social conditions in the Irish countryside. Allingham wrote several other books of poetry containing famous poems of his such as 'The winding banks of Erne' and that well known poem 'The fairies'. He also wrote a play *Ashby Manor* (London, 1883). He died in 1889. For a good selection of his work see *William Allingham, an introduction* (Dublin, 1971) by Professor Alan Warner, and John Hewitt's, *The poems of William Allingham* (Dublin, 1967).

An open air auction scene in Portadown, Co. Armagh, about 1885. (Sprott Collection, Portadown College)

The pope at Killybuck is a comedy, the main theme of which is Orange-Green rivalry over land. This extract is from an auction scene. It was first performed at Ballycastle, Co. Antrim, in 1915 by the Dalriada Players who were one of a number of flourishing amateur dramatic societies to be found around the countryside at the time. When put on commercially in Belfast in 1917 its title was changed to *The auction at Killybuck* for fear that the original title would cause a riot. But in fact from its first production the play has greatly amused audiences throughout Ulster. Its author was Louis Joseph Walsh, a solicitor, born at Maghera, Co. Londonderry. After practising for a time in Co. Londonderry he served as a district justice in Co. Donegal. As well he was the author of a number of humorous plays and stories, mainly set in Ulster. Among these plays are *The guileless Saxon: an Ulster comedy in three acts* (Dublin, 1917), and *Equity follow the law* (Belfast, 1935). His collections of short stories include *Yarns of a country attorney: stories and sketches of life in rural Ulster* (Dublin, 1918). He was also the author of *On my keeping and theirs: a record of experiences 'on the run' in Derry gaol and Ballykinlar internment camp* (Dublin, 1921). Walsh died in 1942.

[Job Wilson and William John consult for a moment with much head-shaking, whilst the auctioneer keeps repeating "Going at the biddin' of £460. Any advance?"]

WILLIAM JOHN: £465.

ALEX: What do you say now, Mr. Convery? Will I put you down for £475?

[Dominick appears to hesitate.]

ALEX: Come on, man, a ten poun' note never raired ye, and before I wud let wan o' these black-nebbed, sour-faced Prisbyterians into a place I wanted, I wud either have it myself or I wud make the man that bought it over my head pay dear for it.

DOM: All right, I'll give ye £475.

ALEX: Come on, William John. Is it £485? Nivir let it be sayed that a Papish put the cowe on ye. We bate them at Derry, Aughrim, and the Boyne; and we'ill bate them the day too. I wud allow no man that wus n't the right soort to own a fut o' lan' in oul' Killybuck.

[William John and Job again consult]

WILLIAM JOHN [feebly] : £480.

ALEX: £480 now offered. Any advance? Speak out, Dominick. The Swaterban blood was always plucky, and I hope you won't let a Prisbyterian get the better o' you for the sake of a wheen o' poun's.

DOM: Well, I suppose I may offer you £485; but I'm thinkin' it's me last bid.

ALEX: Now, Mr. Wilson, send forward the hosts of Israel. Where's the use o' talkin' again' the Home Rule Bill, if you let a five or ten poun' note keep ye from savin' Killybuck from all the horrors o' Popery, brass money and wooden shoes. Come, William John. Nivir say: "Die."

WILLIAM JOHN: I'ill give you another ten shillings.

ALEX: I cannot take any smaller bids that £5. Do you say £490?

WILLIAM JOHN [after much nudging from Job, and as if he were expressing his consent to the amputation of his two legs] : £490.

ALEX: £490 now offered. Any advance?

DOM: £495.

ALEX: Make it £500, William John.

WILLIAM JOHN: Naw, naw! It's over dear as it is, an' I went agin' me mind goin' this far.

L. J. Walsh, *The pope at Killybuck* (Dublin, 1915), p. 22

A COUNTRY LAD'S OBSERVATIONS AT THE HIRING FAIR IN BALLYMENA.

Weel, freens, A gat me tae the toon,
Although big clouds were hoverin' roon,
An whiles an odd yin did come doon
    Tae we got drack'd;
Yet mony a sinburnt-luckin' croon
    Seem'd tae be cracked.

The hale toon seemed tae be aware
That Sethurday was Hiring Fair,
And that ferm-servants wud be there
    For a big day,
Who meant tae hae a treat sae rare
    Wae six months' pay.

Here and there wus a wee ban'
The centre-piece a big ould man,
What mak's his leevin' off the lan'
    Without a doot;

Bit see him view the horny han'
    'Ere he spak' oot.

"Tell me, my man, noo can you sow,
And can you milk, and plough, and mow,
And build a load of hay or stro'
    For market day?
If you can do these things, say so
    I'll fix your pay."

The toon assumed its usual gait,
Folk mashing roon at nae wee rate,
Each lucking' for their ain dear mate
    In blank despair;
And so may I if I keep blate
    To the next Fair.
November, 1899.

Adam Lynn, *Random rhymes from Cullybackey* (Belfast, 1911), pp 13-14.

Adam Lynn was born at Cullybackey, Co. Antrim, and worked in the linen industry. He wrote poetry for local papers such as the *Ballymena Observer*. During this period many newspapers had regular poetry columns and also published extracts from novels by popular authors. Writing in his local dialect, Lynn dealt with subjects like the Cullybackey cycling club, 'the twelfth', and the river Maine. No other works of his appear to have been published in book form.

Left: *Carrickmacross fair, Co. Monaghan (Lawrence Collection, National Library of Ireland)*

Right: *Customers at a fair in Portadown, Co. Armagh, about 1892 (Sprott Collection, Portadown College)*

Below: *Lending a hand in Castlewellan, Co. Down (Green Collection, Ulster Folk Museum)*

HE was gone without waiting for an answer, and in a few minutes was driving along the road in a small, light tax-cart.

Having driven about a mile up and down hill, he descried in the still lurid semi-darkness a little, broken-down vehicle standing outside a cabin-door, through which shone the glow of burning turf.

"Hum! I thought there was a break-down," he said. "I guessed how it would be when I heard Batt had sold her the broken-kneed pony." And, calling an urchin to hold his horse, he walked up the stone causeway to the cabin-door.

There he paused a moment, raised his hat and passed his hand over his forehead, frowned, and stepped over the threshold.

Bawn did not hear what was said; she was talking to the child, and the master of Tor had advanced and was standing beside her before she looked up. The gentleman stood observing her with a strange look on his face, noting her fair, smooth brow, her fresh, symmetrical cheeks, her laughing lips and eyes. In her black serge dress and shawl of shepherd's plaid she was exactly the same Bawn who had wrestled for her liberty with Somerled on board the steamer.

Bawn was sitting on a "creepy" stool before the blazing turf, her hat had been taken off, and her golden head was shining in the ruddy light. A barefooted child was standing before her, finger in mouth, staring with fascinated eyes at the beautiful stranger, greatly to the delight of an aged man who sat shaking his head in the chimney-corner. Two sturdy men in sou'wester hats were directing Andy where to go for the loan of a little car to carry his mistress further, and a decent-looking woman was taking oat-cakes from a "griddle."

"But, sure, here's Misther Rory himself. Never fear but the masther'll pull ye out of the hobble."

She looked up with an unconscious, unexpecting smile, and saw the identical Somerled standing before her.

The smile died on her lips; the colour went out of

her cheeks; she rose and drew back a step, and looked him in the face. Impulsively trying to speak, her ready tongue was for once at fault. She drew her shawl around her, and met his eye defiantly.

Rosa Mulholland, *A fair emigrant* (London, 1888), pp 207-8.

Rosa Mulholland, born in Belfast in 1841, the daughter of a local doctor, was the authoress of many popular novels and books of poetry. She married John (later Sir John) Gilbert the antiquarian and deputy keeper of the public records in Dublin. Dickens encouraged her early work and published some of her short stories in *Household Words*. Her novels include *Marcella Grace* (London, 1886), and *The wild birds of Killeevy* (London, 1883). She died in 1921. About this time there were a number of Ulster women novelists writing books of a popular and sentimental nature: among others were M. T. Pender and M. de la C. Crommelin. The works of these writers were serialized in newspapers all over the country and undoubtedly influenced public opinion with their views, often telling, directly or indirectly, of Ireland's woes or England's glories.

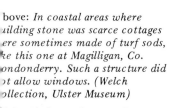

Above: In coastal areas where building stone was scarce cottages were sometimes made of turf sods, like this one at Magilligan, Co. Londonderry. Such a structure did not allow windows. (Welch Collection, Ulster Museum)

Right: A domestic scene (Rose-shaw Collection, Ulster Folk Museum)

Thomas Caulfield Irwin, born in 1823 at Warrenpoint, Co. Down, was educated privately and in his youth travelled to Europe and north Africa. The family fortunes seem to have collapsed around 1848 and from that time on he appears to have been frequently impoverished. In later years he became eccentric, and even mad at times. From 1848 he contributed verse to many magazines, including the *Dublin University Review;* his writing was often of a high standard. His books of poetry include *Poems* (Dublin, 1866), and *Poems, sketches and songs* (Dublin, 1889). He also wrote a series of prose sketches, *Winter and summer stories* (Dublin, 1879). A good selection of Irwin's work can be found in *Irish poets of the nineteenth century,* (London, 1951), edited by Geoffrey Taylor. He died in Dublin in 1892.

SONNET

A roadside inn this summer Saturday:-
The doors are open to the wide warm air,
The parlour, whose old window views the bay,
Garnished with cracked delph full of flowers fair
From the fields round, and whence you see the glare
Fall heavy on the hot slate roofs and o'er
The wall's tree shadows drooping in the sun.
Now rambles slowly down the dusty street
The lazy drover's clattering cart; and crows
Fainter through afternoon the cock; with hoes
Tan faced harvest folk trudge in the heat:
The neighbours at their shady doors swept clean,
Gossip, and with cool eve fresh scents of wheat,
Grasses and leaves, come from the meadows green.

T. C. Irwin, *Versicles* (Dublin, 1883), p.45.

Far left: *Weary harvester enjoying her meal of potatoes and buttermilk (Green Collection, Ulster Folk Museum)*
Below: *Crosskey Inn, a former stage coach inn at Toome, Co. Antrim. (Green Collection, Ulster Folk Museum)*

JOHN [He looks at her, and then begins in a bashful manner]: You weren't at Ballyannis School fete; Sarah?

SARAH: No. But I heard you were there. Why?

JOHN [coming still closer]: I was expecting to see you.

SARAH [contemptuously]: I don't believe in young girls going to them things.

JOHN [gazing at her in astonishment]: But God bless me, they wouldn't call you young! [SARAH turns up her nose disgustedly.] I missed you. Man, I was looking for you all roads.

SARAH: I'm not a fool sort of young girl that you can just pass as idle hour or two with, John Murray, mind that.

JOHN: I never thought that of you, Sarah.

SARAH: Some people think that.

JOHN [astonished]: No.

SARAH: They do. There's Andy just after warning me this morning about making a fool of myself.

JOHN [puzzled]: But you never done that, Sarah.

SARAH: Well, he was just after giving me advice about going round flirting with Tom, Dick and Harry.

JOHN: Ah no, You never done that. Sure I knowed you this years and years, and you never had a boy to my knowing.

SARAH [offended]: Well I had, plenty. Only I just wouldn't take them. I refused more than three offers in my time.

JOHN [incredulously]: Well! Well! And you wouldn't have them!

SARAH: No.

JOHN: Why now?

SARAH (looking at him meaningly): Well—I liked somebody else better.

JOHN [piqued]: Did he—the somebody—did he never ask you?

SARAH: He might yet, maybe.

JOHN [hopelessly to himself]: I wonder would it be any use then me asking her.

SARAH: And I'm beginning to think he is a long time thinking about it. [Knocking at the door.]

JOHN [angrily]: Ach! Who's that?

BROWN [opening yard door and looking in]: Me, sir. Mr. Dan wants to know could you not come out a minute, and show the gentleman what way you can stop the feedboard working.

JOHN: Don't you know yourself, you stupid headed lump you. Away back at once.

Rutherford Mayne, *The drone*, from *The drone and other plays* (Dublin, 1912), pp 27-9.

Above right: *Flower show at Sion Mills, Co. Tyrone, 1910 (Cooper Collection, Public Record Office of Northern Ireland)*

Right: *Take your partners! At the Foresters hall, Strabane, Co. Tyrone (Cooper Collection, Public Record Office of Northern Ireland)*

Rutherford Mayne was the pen-name of Samuel Waddell. Born in Japan in 1878, but brought up in Belfast, he joined the Ulster Literary Theatre in 1904, first as an actor and then as a playwright. His earliest play, *Turn of the road*, was performed by them in 1906. This was followed in 1908 by *The drone*, probably his most famous play, and one which has been performed in many countries since. These plays along with two others done at this time were published in 1912 (see above). Between 1912 and 1923 other works of his were staged by the Ulster Theatre group and the Abbey Theatre, but unfortunately they were not published. Like his earlier plays these were usually set in the Ulster countryside. Two later published works were *Bridge head* (London, 1939) and *Peter* (Dublin, 1944). He died in 1967.

His sister, Helen Waddell, was also a noted writer.

The main literary activity in Irish during this period in Ulster took the form of the collection of orally preserved material. People such as J. H. Lloyd, Rev. Lawrence Murray and Enrí Ó Muirgheasa, stimulated by the renewal of scholarly interest in Irish which occurred in these years (Eoin MacNeill and George Sigerson were two prominent Ulster figures in the new scholarship), set about gathering Irish poems and songs from the Ulster countryside. As well as *Céad de cheoltaibh Uladh*, Enrí Ó Muirgheasa was responsible for another book of collected Ulster Gaelic poetry, *Dhá chéad de cheoltaibh Uladh* (Dublin, 1934). This poem is a love song which came from Mairéad nic Mhuircheartaigh, an inhabitant of Rathlin Island, Co. Antrim. The poem is an interesting example of Rathlin dialect in which the vocabulary and idiom have pronounced Scots Gaelic characteristics. By 1885 a considerable number of people in Ulster still spoke Irish. This was especially so in north-west Donegal which has remained to this day one of the chief Irish speaking areas in Ireland.

Paddy the cliff climber, Rathlin Island, Co. Antrim – a well known local personality (Welch Collection, Ulster Museum).

MO MHÁIRE ÓG *(A Rathlin Song.)*

D'éaluigh m'athair 's d'éag mo mháthair,
   Is chan fheil mo cháirdean le fághail;
Acht cad atá mé gan crodh gan toigh,
   A bheith in dtóir ar Mháire Óig.

       Luinneóg.
Hó-ró-ró 's gur thú mo rún,
Thug me an gaol, 's cha b'aithreach liom,
Do'n nighin úd an chúil dualaigh dhuinn,
Is gur teith liom fhéin mo Mháire Óg.

Chan fheil duine uasal ó nó barún,
   Nó fear óg anns na fearann,
Nach bhfeil dúil aca le bainis,
   Ach chuile fhear, le Máire Óig.

Chan fheil duine 'sa ghleann úd thall—
   Eadar bun 's bárr a' ghleann'—
Nach bhfeil ag bagairt ar mo cheann
   Ar son a bheith in dtóir ar Mháire Óig.

Acht ná cuireadh sin ort-sa brón
   Fad is bhéas mo chuideacht beo
Congbhóchaidh mise duit-se an lón,
   Is má bha scór ann gheobhaidh sin dram.

Anonymous

Enrí Ó Muirgheasa, *Céad de cheoltaibh Uladh*, (Dublin 1915), p. 101.

SHE was a stout, plain, ruddy-faced woman, and she was standing in her kitchen—the kitchen of the gardener's lodge—with a big apron covering the front of her striped cotton dress, and her sleeves rolled back from bare strong arms which, like her rough hands, were flaked with flour, for she was baking. The boy did not resemble her. He was slender, while she was stout; he was fine, while she was coarse; he seemed subtle, while she was simple; and there was an enigmatic expression in his dark, narrow, wide-set eyes—something half-mocking, half-ironic—which now and then made her feel vaguely uneasy. Subtle—and with little of that air of engaging innocence one expects of rustic youth. Brown-skinned, attractive, yet not quite agreeable. Her only child probably, her only son at all events—that could be gathered from the way she looked at him as she bent down to kiss him with a certain superficial roughness.

They lived—she and the boy and the boy's father— in the front lodge of the demesne, within sight and sound of the sea—and she came to the gate to see him off, watching his slender figure on the white, dusty, sunlit road as long as it remained in sight. At the curve of the road he looked back and waved his hand. He never forgot to do that; he knew it pleased her; and for that matter he never forgot anything. She waved too, but she returned to her baking with a sigh. She couldn't have told you

why she sighed, except that she wished she knew a little more about him; and there was nobody—least of all his taciturn unnoticing father—to whom she could express what she felt. She could not clearly express it to herself. She sometimes wondered if he would be a successful man, but more frequently, and with vague misgivings she was ashamed of, she hoped he would be a good one. For he *was* a good boy—always considerate and—and discreet. That was a very queer word to use. She did not like it, and did not know why she had used it. In any case, he would not be a gardener like his father, for he was clever. Mr. Connell had said that he ought to go to college, and that with scholarships it might be managed. He was now nearly fifteen and still at the village school. But in her day-dreams she already saw him, after a brilliant University career, returning home, stiffly garbed in black, assistant and successor to the present minister.

Forrest Reid, *Retrospective adventures* (London, 1941), pp 221-1.

Left: *Three Walker brothers, Belfast, 1892. From right to left: Thomas, who became a Presbyterian minister, James, a Church of Ireland curate, and Carlisle, who, amongst other things became grandfather of the author! (author's collection)*

Far left: *A gate lodge of Belvoir estate, Knockbreda, Co. Down, home of Lord Deramore (author's collection)*

This extract is from a short story 'The accomplice,' written in 1913 and first published in 1917. The author, Forrest Reid (1876-1947), was born in Belfast and spent most of his life there. He was responsible for a number of important novels including *Uncle Stephen* (London, 1931), *Brian Westby* (London, 1934), *The retreat* (London, 1936), *Uncle Tom* (London, 1944) and *Peter Waring* (London, 1937). He also wrote two interesting volumes of autobiography, *Apostate* (London, 1926), and *Private road* (London, 1940); the first of these contains a vivid portrait of life in Victorian Belfast. A contributor to the magazine *Uladh*, Reid wrote articles for many other magazines including the *Westminster Review* and the *Ulster Review*. In addition he reviewed books for the *Manchester Guardian*, an occupation which for some time was his only source of income. He was a close friend of E. M. Forster, and other important contemporary English writers. In 1953 a critical study of his work was written by Russell Burlingham, *Forrest Reid, a portrait and a study* (London, 1953).

THE CIRCUS

THE circus! what a brilliant sight!
  Fine horsemanship was there, sir;
Fine ladies, too, rode round the ring,
  Of clothing somewhat bare, sir.
These boldly dashed through paper hoops,
  Displaying feats of daring;
And posed in many a curious way
  To keep the youngsters staring.

One man could play with glittering knives
  As though they were but toys, sir;
Another one could fling like balls
  Two handsome little boys, sir.
My friends were much amused to see
  The "dwarf" at big men rushing;
But ah, those ladies, semi-clad—
  They kept some females blushing!

Their "afterpiece" was but a sham,
  Unworthy to be seen, sir;
They must have thought their audience here
  Was truly very green, sir.
But when they come to town again,
  They surely must display less
Of female charms. or, much I fear,
  Some female friends will pay less.

J. W. Montgomery, *Fireside lyrics* (Downpatrick, 1887), pp 59-60.

Known as the Bard of Bailieborough, John Wilson Montgomery was a native of Virginia, Co. Cavan. He spent some years as master of the workhouse at Bailieborough but the greater part of his life was spent in Downpatrick, Co. Down, where he was clerk to the poor law board of guardians. He was an enthusiastic antiquarian, frequently writing pieces on local antiquities for newspapers. His best literary work was probably his first volume of poems, *Rhymes Ulidian* (Downpatrick, 1877). In addition to this and *Fireside lyrics*, he wrote a small volume of prose sketches, *Round Mourne* (Bangor, 1908). He died in 1911 at the age of 76.

Above left: *Mr. John Duffy, of the famous Duffy's circus, and friend, Strabane, Co. Tyrone (Cooper Collection, Public Record Office of Northern Ireland)*

Above right: *Perhaps like some of those naughty dancers mentioned above — Buff Bill's Dixie Girls, Strabane, 1910! (Cooper Collection, Public Record Office of Northern Ireland)*

Right: *Young spectators at a Punch'n Judy show, Doagh, Co. Antrim (author's collection)*

Twas just in the middle av Ballygullion sthreet I met Billy av the Hills, the last man in life I thought to meet there on a market-day. In his spare time Billy does be makin' an odd dhrop av potheen; an' the market-day bein' a throng day for the polis in Ballygullion, 'twas ginerally Billy's throng day outside av it, deliverin' a wee keg here an' there.

"You're a sight for sore eyes, Billy," sez I. "What has fetched ye intil the town the day?"

"Ye know ould Dick Taafe, me uncle be marriage," sez Billy. "His brother's dead, away in Donegal, an' he's goin' off to the funeral in the mornin'. I'm sleepin' in the house a night or two to keep the aunt company, an' I come in the day to rise me uncle in good time for the thrain; for he's desperate heavy-headed, and the aunt's little better, though she wouldn't give in till it. Come on down an' have a crack before ye go home,"

So away we goes down to the house, an' whin we got that length, who should be there wi' Mrs. Taafe but wee Jinks, the pedlar,—Peddlin' Tam as they call him,—wi' a whole packful av stuff spread out on the table.

"Good-evenin', gintlemen," sez he. "Ye might come an' give me a hand. I'm just thryin' to sell the misthress here the very thing she wants."

"What's that?" sez Billy. "It'll be somethin' in the way av clothes, I'm thinkin'."

"Not a bit av it," sez the pedlar, "it's just an alarm clock. Sure her heart's broke wi' wakin' the man in the mornin's; an' this is the boy'll do it for her."

"I don't believe in thim conthrivances," sez she; "ye could niver depend on thim."

"Hould on till I show ye how she works," sez Tam, "an' then ye'll change your mind. She's set for five," sez he; "now listen till her ringin', for it's herself can do it."

"Ay, there ye are now," sez the aunt. "Sure it's seven o'clock now, an' she'd be ringin' two hours slow. That'd be a dale av use in the mornin'."

"But ye can set her for any time ye like," sez Tam. "Wait a minit an' I'll set her to seven."

"An' mightn't ye as well get up to raise the house as get up to set the clock to do it," sez she. "It bates me to see the use av it at all."

I wish ye'd seen the pedlar's face. 'Twas little compliment to the ould woman's brains was in the back av his head, I'm thinkin'.

Lynn Doyle, *Ballygullion* (Dublin, 1908), pp 98-100.

Left: Market day in Lisburn, Co. Antrim (Green Collection, Ulster Folk Museum)

Below: *O'Donnell's wine and spirit store, Lifford, Co. Donegal. Mr. Hugh O'Donnell, the proprietor, is standing in the centre (Cooper Collection, Public Record Office of Northern Ireland)*

Lynn Doyle was the pseudonym of Leslie Alexander Montgomery. Born near Downpatrick, Co. Down, in 1873, he was the author of a number of plays staged by the Ulster Literary Theatre. These include *The lilac ribbon, The turncoats* and *Love and land.* However, Lynn Doyle is best remembered for his humorous stories about the imaginary Ulster district of Ballygullion and its people. They tell of fairs, poaching, politics and everyday events, all amusingly portrayed. The above extract is from a chapter called 'The alarm clock'. Later editions of the book were illustrated by William Conor. Other books on Ballygullion followed, including *Ballygullion ballads* (London, 1936). Doyle also wrote an autobiography, *An Ulster childhood* (Dublin, 1921). By profession he was a banker, serving as a branch manager at Cushendall, Co. Antrim, Keady, Co. Armagh, and Skerries, Co. Dublin. He died in 1961.

THE FLOWER OF MAGHERALLY

'Twas at a fair near Banbridge town
   I met this blooming maiden O;
Sure Adam was not more surprised
   When he first saw Eve in Eden O!

Her yellow hair in ringlets fair,
   Her shoes of Spanish leather O!
She is the girl that won my heart,
   And keeps it in the tether O!

And let them all say what they can,
   Or let them scoff or rally O!
She is the darlin' of my heart,
   An' the flower of Magherally O!

Journal of the Irish Folk Song Society,
(London, 1904; reprinted, 1967) vol. 12,
no. 2, pp 57-8.

Right: *Arriving in town (Sprott
Collection, Portadown College)*
Left: *Observers at the pig market in
Woodhouse Street, Portadown, about
1885 (Sprott Collection, Portadown
College)*

This folk song was recorded by a Miss Maud Houston who learnt it from a Mrs. Ryan, who in her turn heard it sung on a Belfast street by a ballad monger! During the period covered by this book, Maud Houston and others like Joseph Campbell, F. J. Bigger and Padric Gregory continued the work begun by Dr. George Petrie and Edward Bunting in collecting folk songs and music. Right up to the present day folk song is a living, active cultural tradition to be found throughout the Ulster countryside. These songs tell of many things — emigration, love, work, politics and important events. Some of the songs being sung at the turn of the century can be read in the journals of the Irish Folk Song Society in this period. More recently a collection of Ulster folk songs has been made by Robin Morton, *Folk songs sung in Ulster* (Cork, 1970)

THERE was no nonsense about the Alexanders. So the head of the family had been asserting so vehemently since he had built his house, calling it Ardreagh, that the shrewd ones among his hearers felt certain that there must have been a good deal of nonsense about the Alexanders, or he would not have been so urgent in his protestations to the contrary. But those who were the shrewdest knew perfectly well that all James Alexander meant by his protestations was that he would not alter his dinner hour from one o'clock to half-past seven, though he could well afford to do so, in imitation of the gentry, and that he would not "set up" a butler or a footman as several ostentatious families whom he could name had done as soon as they had got on a bit in the world, or even sooner.

"We began life as plain people and we intend to remain plain people," he said when his neighbours had rallied him in the unambiguous way they adopt in the North of Ireland when they wish to be satirical, about the building of the house. "Late dinner, swallow-tail coat and white choker? No fears! Many's the time I've eat my dinner in my shirt-sleeves, and felt nothing the worse for it, and many's the time I'll do it again if I've a mind to. And if I don't put on a white choker when I'm at my dinner, you may be sure that I'll have no man at the back of my chair with one round his neck. And them that that's not good enough for can stay away from my house."

This ostentatious unostentation deceived no one. Everyone knew that he was overflowing with pride at being able to build Ardreagh; and for having a dining-room four feet longer than the corresponding apartment in Danesfort, the mansion which Mr. Megarry of the Ballyboye Mills had built for himself, and the Megarrys were one of the old families in Ballyboye,

having held their mill since long before the Civil War in America set all the linen lappers in Belfast looking about to see where they could build a mill. Mr. Alexander had been one of the lads in the Megarrys' mill at Ballyboye.

"What's the length of thon room?" he had asked his architect when the plans of Ardreagh were laid before him, and he laid a finger upon the biggest of the squares outlined before him.

"Twenty-five feet, not including the bay window," replied the architect.

"And what's the size of the biggest room at Danesfort—you built Danesfort, didn't you?"

"Twenty-six feet, I believe."

"Then make mine thirty. I'll show them what I can do, though Megarry give me many's a clout on the ear when he looked into the carding-room, and him and me was one age."

The architect smiled.

"You've given him many a clout since, Mr. Alexander, by all accounts," said he.

"Ay, many's a one—many's a one; and this'll be another—make

it a good four feet longer. It'll be a brave wee clout that he'll feel when it gets abroad that Jimmy Alexander has built a dining-room in his new house more'n four feet longer nor the best Charlie Megarry could do with. I wouldn't keep it a secret if I was you; it may do you good in your business to let people know that you can build such a room."

"You may trust to me, Mr. Alexander, but I doubt if Mr. Megarry will feel it to be as sore a clout as your getting the big order for the Green Star sheets last year—a thousand dozen, wasn't it?" said the architect.

Mr. Alexander's eyes gleamed, his mouth twitched as if he were licking his lips.

"A clout? Yon was no clout, it was a dunch—man, but I hit him a quare dunch that day."

"It will be a long day before that thousand dozen sheets turn into clouts," remarked the architect.

And when he got back to his office in Belfast he gave a good imitation of his client's gloating over the prestige conferred upon him by the possession of a thirty-foot dining-room; and his partner, who was an adept at cubic measure as it related to the increasing of the dimensions of a room beyond the limits contracted for, took good care that Mr. Alexander paid fully for the luxury of "clouting" the man who had been severe to him in his youth forty years before.

And the people before whom Mr. Alexander protested himself to be a plain man and without any

nonsense grinned and asked if it was true that Mr. Megarry was adding another ten feet to his dining-room. There is no great subtlety in the sarcasm of the North of Ireland business man.

F. F. Moore, *The Ulsterman, a story of today* (London, 1914), pp29-31.

Above: *An interior view of Derryvolgie house, South Belfast (Welch Collection, Ulster Museum)*

Born at Limerick in 1855, Frank Frankfort Moore was brought up in Belfast where he was educated at the Royal Belfast Academical Institution. From 1876-92 he was on the reporting staff of the *Belfast News Letter*. He then moved to England where he spent the remainder of his life. His first major novel, *I forbid the banns*, published in 1893 in London, was extremely successful. Other novels include *The jessamy bride* (London, 1897) and *Castle Omeragh* (London, 1903). *The Ulsterman*, from which the above extract is taken, is set in the Ulster of the 1912-14 home-rule crisis period amongst a self-made linen family. As well at this time he was the author of *The truth about Ulster* (London, 1914). His novels were frequently serialized in magazines like *The Graphic* and *The Queen*. Moore also wrote a number of plays which were performed in London and Dublin. He died in 1931.

Wrong turn – car in the canal basin, Strabane, Co. Tyrone, 1910
(Cooper Collection, Public Record Office of Northern Ireland)

POLITICS ETC

A motor cycle unit of the Ulster Volunteer Force, 1913 (Public Record Office of Northern Ireland)

Eviction scene in Co. Fermanagh, probably in the late 1880s (Lawrence Collection, National Library of Ireland)

VICTORY

West Belfast for Ireland!

My countymen, arise, rejoice,
  Democracy has won the day;
For West Belfast, in ringing voice,
  Proclaims against the tyrant sway.
Uplift your souls in joyful song,
  Attune your lyres to hymns of praise,
For Right has triumphed over Wrong,
  And numbered are Oppression's days.

Our Standard Bearer is returned
  To voice our sentiments again;
The people trampled on and spurned
  And shackled with vile slavery's chain,
Have risen boldly at the sound
  Of holy Freedom's clarion blast,
The foes of Progress to confound
  In staunch, unconquered West Belfast.

Upon the ramparts can be seen
  Our banner waving proudly still,
The Orange blending with the Green,
  New emblem of the people's will—
The people's will that reigns supreme
  In what concerns a nation's life—
Democracy's bold choice redeem
  From cruel, vain, religious strife.

Then let me grasp your Orange hand!
  I greet you as a patriot brother,
Let both work for our Fatherland,
  And mutual aid give to each other;
My foes are yours, and yours are mine,
  And we must fall or stand united;
Our native strength we must combine,
  Living no more as slaves benighted.

NO SURRENDER

Within the bounds of British sway
  Old Ireland clamours restlessly,
But come what will or come what may
  The Union rules her destiny.

Out in the cold with birthright sold,
  We dare not let her thus decline;
To Britons bold keep firm your hold
  Lest poverty of fate be thine.

Her rash desire our hearts inspire
  Old Erin's honour to maintain;
Vanish vampire! guard the Empire,
  That rules supreme the rolling main.

With equal laws in freedom's cause
  Proud "Britons never shall be slaves;"
A "Home Rule" clause in Union laws
  Dispelled shall be by loyal braves.

March forward, then, bold Ulster men,
  Resound your harp right manfully;
O'er hill and glen, o'er Shamrock stem
  Uphold the flag of UNITY—

Top right: *Joseph Devlin, Ulster Nationalist leader (Public Record Office of Northern Ireland)*
Top left: *Capt. James Craig, later Lord Craigavon, Ulster Unionist leader (Public Record Office of Northern Ireland)*
Bottom right: *William Walker, Ulster Labour leader*
Bottom left: *J.B. Armour, Ulster Liberal leader (J.K.C. Armour's private collection)*

These two examples of political doggerel date from the 1910 (Dec.) general election. The one on the right was printed in the *Northern Whig* 2 Dec., 1910, while the other on the left, celebrating Joe Devlin's victory in the December election, was printed on a broadsheet. This particular broadsheet came from the collection in the Belfast Central Library. Other interesting collections of ballad broadsheets can be found in Queen's University and the Ulster Folk Museum.

George A. Birmingham was the pseudonym of Canon James Owen Hannay. Born in 1865 at what is now 75 University Road, Belfast, Birmingham was an author of considerable ability and vast productivity. He wrote 44 novels, 3 plays, an opera libretto and 16 other books. The novel from which this extract is taken is set, like a number of his works, in the north. Although it was published in the middle of 1912, it tells of guns being brought secretly into ports and volunteers marching through the streets of Belfast. This was all very soon to happen. Some of his other novels are interesting portraits of the changing social scene in Ireland at the turn of the century, especially *The seething pot* (London, 1904), *Spanish gold* (London, 1908) and *The bad times* (London, 1907); this last book is set in the west of Ireland around the time of the land war in the early 1880s. Birmingham spent 21 years as rector in Westport, Co. Mayo. He left Westport in 1913 - partly because of objections from local people who thought themselves portrayed in one of his books. In 1924 he moved to England where he was rector of several parishes before his death in 1950.

Unionist clubs marching to Belfast City Hall to sign the Ulster covenant, opposing home-rule, 28 Sept. 1912 (Welch Collection, Ulster Museum)

Sir Edward Carson signing the Ulster covenant. To the left are Lord Charles Beresford and Lord Londonderry. To the right are Capt. James Craig and J. H. Campbell. (Public Record Office of Northern Ireland)

THE reading-room of the club is on the first floor, and the window commands an excellent view of Donegall Place, one of the principal thoroughfares of Belfast. The club stands right across the eastern end of the street, and the traffic is diverted to right and left along Royal Avenue and High Street. At the far, the western end, of Donegall Place, stands the new City Hall, with the statue of Queen Victoria in front of it. There again the traffic is split at right angles. Some of the best shops in the town lie on either side of this street. A continuous stream of trams passes up and down it, to and from the junction, which is directly under the club windows, and is the centre of the whole Belfast tramway system. It is always pleasant to stand at the reading-room window and watch the very busy and strenuous traffic of this street. As a view point on that particular morning the window was as good as possible. Donegall Place is the chief and most obvious way from the northern and eastern parts of the city to the place where the meeting was to be held.

Between eleven o'clock and twelve the volunteers began to appear in considerable numbers. I saw at once that I had been wrong in supposing that they meant to spend the day in bed. One company after another came up Royal Avenue or swung round the corner from High Street, and marched before my eyes along Donegall Place towards the scene of the meeting. Small bodies of police appeared here and there, heading in the same direction. Now and then a few mounted police trotted by, making nearly as much jangle as if they had been regular soldiers. The hour fixed for the meeting was one o'clock, but at noon the number of men in the street was so great that ordinary traffic was stopped. A long line of trams, unable to force their way along, blocked the centre of the thoroughfare. The drivers and conductors left them and went away. Crowds of women and children collected on the roofs of these trams and cheered the men as they marched along.

G. A. Birmingham, *The Red Hand of Ulster*, (London, July 1912; reprint Dublin, 1973), pp 242-3.

THOMPSON: I was promoted this year to be one of King William's Generals.

GRANIA: And you lead your fighting kerns into the heat of battle?

THOMPSON: *[confidently]* : Indeed, to tell you the truth, I never got the length of the field.

GRANIA: That is strange.

THOMPSON: I was takin' a short cut through the meadows, and while I was climbing a ditch, my ould gun burst in my hands, an' that is all I mind. I must a lay there all day and then maybe in the night I wandered about, not knowin' where I was, and then I must have fell asleep, and when I wakened up in the mornin' I didn't know where I was, and I'm damned if I know now—excuse me.

GRANIA: And you know not if your army was victorious or not?

THOMPSON: Sure I told you I was on King William's side. Of course we won the day.

GRANIA: Why do you say "of course"? The fortunes of war are so uncertain.

THOMPSON: Sure it wasn't a real fight. It was a sham fight or a pageant fight.

GRANIA: A make-believe. *[Thompson nods his head]*

THOMPSON: Aye, the very thing.

GRANIA: But *have* you been in a *real* fight?

THOMPSON: O aye, I was in a scrap in Portadown last Sunday.

GRANIA: And whom were you fighting in Portadown?

THOMPSON: The Hibernians.

GRANIA [*shocked*]: The Hiberniana! But are not all the people in Erinn Hibernians?

THOMPSON: In sowl they're not.

GRANIA: Are all the people in Portadown Hiberniana?

THOMPSON: Talk sense, woman dear.

GRANIA [*looking towards audience*]: Many changes must have come o'er Erinn since the days of Cuchulain and Oisin. Then we were all Hibernians. [*To Thompson.*] I wish dearest that you were an Hibernian too.

THOMPSON: You'll never see the day. [*Rising from couch.*] And what's more, I'll have nothing more to do with you, for I'm no believer in mixed marriages.

Gerald McNamara, *Thompson in Tir-na-n-Og* (Dublin, n.d.),p 24

Thompson in Tir-na-n-Og was first performed in 1912 at the Grand Opera House in Belfast. The play centres round an Orangeman, Thompson, who, after his gun blows up accidentally on his way to the Scarva field on the 13th of July, wakes up in the land of eternal youth, Tir-na-n-Og, peopled by Celtic gods and heroes. The scene which follows, where Orange and Hibernian views confront each other in a marvellous burlesque, has amused Ulster audiences ever since. Harry Morrow, the real name of the author, Gerald McNamara, was one of six very talented Morrow brothers who contributed much to the Ulster stage in the early part of the century. He was a founder member of the Ulster Literary Theatre, and was an actor as well as a playwright. His other plays, which unfortunately were mostly never published, include *Suzanne and the sovereigns, The throwbacks, No surrender* and *Who fears to speak?* Some of his sketches and short plays were, however, published in the *Dublin Magazine.* Born in 1866, he died in 1938.

Far left: *Twelfth platform, Strabane area, about 1912 (Cooper Collection, Public Record Office of Northern Ireland)*

Below: *Ancient Order of Hibernians, Cloughcorr, no. 463, in 1911 (Cooper Collection, Public Record Office of Northern Ireland)*

This extract is taken from a novel the first part of which is set in the Belfast of the 1880s and 1890s. The attack described here is almost certainly based on the attack on the the Shankill Road R.I.C. barracks in the riots of 1886. James Douglas, author of *The unpardonable sin,* was born and brought up in Belfast. He moved to London where he worked as a journalist, becoming editor of the *Sunday Express* in 1920, a position he held for eleven years. His other writings include *Poems and songs of Robert Burns,* published in London in 1906, and *The man in the pulpit* (London, 1905). He died in 1940 at the age of 73.

Waving his cap in the air, Andy dashed at the railings and seizing the spikes endeavoured to clamber over them. The crowd was suddenly stung to madness, and surged forward, hurling stones over Andy's head. Andy had one foot over the railings, and was about to drop into the garden, when he heard a man behind him cry out - 'Duck, boys, duck; they're going to fire.'

Lifting his eyes, he saw through the window three policemen dropping on their knees and raising their rifles to their shoulders. There was a blinding flash of flame and a noise like thunder, and Andy rolled off the railings into the garden in a tumbled heap.

But it was too late to check the onset of the infuriated mob. The railings collapsed under the weight of the impact of the solid mass. They

Left: *Shankill Road R.I.C. barracks after the attack on it, June 1886, in which eight people were killed. (Welch Collection, Ulster Museum)*

Right: *Funeral of victims of Belfast riots, 1907, at Dunville Park.*

poured through the window, and the barrack-room was filled with a confused press of combatants. The police defended themselves desperately, swinging their rifles by the barrel and dealing savage blows at the heads of their assailants as they appeared at the window. They fought behind a rampart of senseless bodies, but it was evident that the crowd would in the end break down their defence. The inspector realised that the situation was critical, and ordered six of his men to fire upon the crowd from the windows on the first floor.

'Give them buck-shot first' said he, 'and then ball if necessary.'

The six policemen fired simultaneously into the seething mass below. A roar of pain and rage burst forth, and in a mad panic the rioters broke and fled. The police fired a second round of buck-shot into the flying mass. Several of the running men stumbled and fell on the road, then dragged themselves to their feet and staggered into shelter. Some of them found refuge in side streets; others rushed into houses, the doors of which were opened by friendly hands. In a few moments the street was empty and silent; only a dark leaf remained in the garden under the broken railings.

The police were so deeply engrossed with the task of attending to their wounds, and to the wounds of the rioters who had been left behind, that they did not observe an old, grey-haired woman stealing softly towards the boy. She lifted him tenderly in her arms and carried him away.

James Douglas, *The unpardonable sin* (London, 1907), pp 132-4.

THE WATCHWORD

"Take and Hold."

O, hear ye the watchword of Labor.
    The slogan of they who'd be free,
That no more to any enslaver
    Must Labor bend suppliant knee.
That we on whose shoulders are borne
    The pomp and the pride of the great,
Whose toil they repaid with their scorn,
    Should meet it at last with our hate.

Chorus.

Then send it afar on the breeze, boys,
    That watchword, the grandest we've known,
That Labor must rise from its knees, boys,
    And take the broad earth as its own.

Aye, we who oft won by our valor,
    Empire for our rulers and lords,
Yet knelt in abasement and squalor
    To that we had made by our swords.
Now valor with worth will be blending,
    When, answering Labor's command,
We arise from the earth and ascending
    To manhood, for Freedom take stand.

Chorus.

Then out from the field and the city,
    From workshop, from mill and from mine,
Despising their wrath and their pity,
    We workers are moving in line.
To answer the watchword and token
Nor pause till our fetters we've broken,
    And conquered the spoiler and drone.

Chorus.

James Connolly, *Songs of freedom by Irish writers* (New York, 1907), p.3.

SCENES FROM BELFAST STRIKE 1907

Above: *Lorry overturned by strikers in Gt. George's Street.*
Top left: *Motor waggon and police escort in Donegall Street.*
Bottom left: *Maxim gun section of the Middlesex Regiment in Ormeau Park. (Linenhall Library)*

James Connolly was born in Edinburgh in 1868 of Irish parents. In 1895 he moved to Ireland and became a leading member of the Irish trade union and socialist movements. From 1911 to 1914 he was centred in Belfast. Most of his writing took the form of political and historical works but he was also the author of a number of poems including 'Hymn of freedom' and 'Freedom's sun'. As well he was the author of *Under which flag*, a three act play which was staged in 1916 in Liberty Hall, Dublin. The script of this play was lost until recently but in 1970 it was performed again in Dublin. In the 1916 Easter Rising in Dublin he took a leading role; for this action he was executed on May 12th. A new biography of him has recently been written by Samuel Levenson — *James Connolly, a biography* (London, 1973).

A hideous thought. I'll walk a while in the Park
And rid my mind of it. I wish to God
I had not said it: though no man can say
I counselled or advised it: only this;
I did not, as I ought, advise *against*—
Express some detestation—say, at least,
Such crimes are cowardly, and Irishmen,
Having the true faith, should be bold to act
The manlier part.
                Yes, here I'm in the Park.

. . . .

       What's here? A fence of hurdles. Oh I see.
This is the Polo-Ground. But, what, what, what,
I'm here in Carey's footsteps!—Yes, 'twas here,
This very spot, I'm certain that he stood
Waiting,—foul images, I say begone!
Why should ye haunt my mind? What hand had I
In Carey's plot or Brady's butcherings?
I do detest them; and I ask myself
Pardon for words of question, where all's sure.
But, 'tis the mischief of such thoughts as these—
Of fire, assassination, dynamite—
One can't allow them entrance in the mind,
But straight the mind will turn to speculate
How this thing might be managed and how that,
And none the wiser. Carey thought himself
So safe, he laughed and puffed his cigarette
Leaving the prison van. Well, what he did
At last was right.
             And what were right for me
To do at this conjuncture? Openly
Avow my sorrow that untimely words
Escaped me which some miscreant might wrest
To implication of assent to crime?
That were heroic, that were right indeed;
My conscience so inclines. I would not bear
The blame of giving entrance, thoughtlessly,

To wicked thoughts in other minds. For none
Amongst my hearers, thinking I approved,
But well might set his wits imagining
How he would carry on his private war
Were he Avenger: how he should procure
His stuffs; how keep a good face to the world;
And think it easy since a single man
Risking no more than his particular life.
With fairly even chances of escape,
Might carry half a town's destruction packed
In greatcoat-pockets or a Gladstone bag;
Or dowdy woman drop her petticoat
And wreck a nation's palace, and walk off
Slim and secure; or gleeful speculate
What were the outraged Briton's sentiments
And attitude regarding Ireland's right,
Should some fine morning show Westminster Bridge
Half discontinuous, or Victoria Tower
Hanging side-rent and ready to come down
Lengthwise along the roof of the House of Lords?
Or should some *quasi* city shopkeeper
Have tunnelled till he got below the Bank,
And sent the gold he scorned to touch sky-high
Far as the Strand? and think within himself
That Pharaoh, when he heard the mourning cry
For Egypt's first-born, were not more in haste
To let the Jews go than the Irish they.
       More I could fancy; but immoral thoughts
Fancied in others might infect myself
And that were what our guides in ethics call
Morosa delectatio, and a sin:
Sin's punishment, besides; for greater pain
Hardly attends the damned than have their minds
Compelled to dwell, whether they will or no,
On thoughts they know are evil. What to these
Were Carey's worst imaginings? Two or three
Men in high office, well-instructed men,
Who knew the perils that attend on place,

And, haply, were not wholly unprepared—
What these, compared with casual multitudes
Of young and old sent indiscriminate
To death and pain? Or what the finished Law
On those poor self-imagined Brutuses.
To rage of angered cities, when the arm
Of civil power is impotent to stay
A people's fury bent on massacre,
On bloody vengance, fire and banishment?
     Yes, here he waited till the man in grey
Should show himself approaching. Here his fate
Turned on the central pivot, once for all.
Had Carey, then, but walked the other way,
And meeting Under-secretary Burke,
Said, "Sir, I would not have you walk alone
Further, just now," it might have all been stopped,
And no blood spilt, and no necks stretched over there.
But here he stood, and had his chance, and chose
To walk in front and show the handkerchief:
And, in his pausing footsteps, here stand I
Still free to turn whichever way I will."

Sir Samuel Ferguson

Lady M. C. Ferguson, *Sir Samuel Ferguson in the Ireland of his day* vol. 1, (London, 1896), pp 263-7.
Written in early 1886, this poem was one of Sir Samuel Ferguson's last. In it he imagined himself following the steps of James Carey, one of the men who murdered chief-secretary Lord Frederick Cavendish and under-secretary T. H. Burke, May 1882, in Dublin's Phoenix Park.

Sir Samuel Ferguson (Royal Irish Academy)

Sir Samuel Ferguson was probably the most prominent Irish poet of the nineteenth century. Born in Belfast in 1810 he was educated at the Royal Belfast Academical Institution. After following a legal career until 1867 he became deputy-keeper of the public records of Ireland. In 1878 he was knighted for his work in reorganising the Irish records. From early days in Belfast he contributed verse to literary magazines including *Blackwoods*. Although most of his life was spent outside Ulster many of his poems call on the Ulster countryside and past: the ballad 'Anna Grace' is perhaps the best known of these. Ferguson developed a deep knowledge of early Irish legends and literature and his various long poems based on stories of the Irish past played an important role in the literary and cultural revival which occurred at the end of the century. For some this movement was to have nationalist overtones but not for Sir Samuel who, after a brief encounter with the repeal movement in the late 1840s became a strong believer in the union with Great Britain. He died in 1886. His wife, Lady Mary Catherine Ferguson, wrote a biography of him and it is from this that the poem on the other page is taken. Several collected editions of his work have been produced, the most recent being *Poems of Sir Samuel Ferguson* (Dublin, 1963), introduced by Padraic Colum.

107

The end of an era, Ulster affairs over-shadowed by events in Europe—the outbreak of the First World War. This photograph shows soldiers of the 36th (Ulster) Division marching past through Donegall Square, Belfast, shortly before embarkation for France. (Public Record Office of Northern Ireland)

Left: Sightseers at the Giant's Causeway, c. 1900 (Marcus Patton Collection, Belfast).

Right: Legananny dolmen, near Castlewellan, Co. Down (Linenhall Library).

Flooding in Donegall Square North, Belfast, 1895 (Public Record Office of Northern Ireland)

Connacht

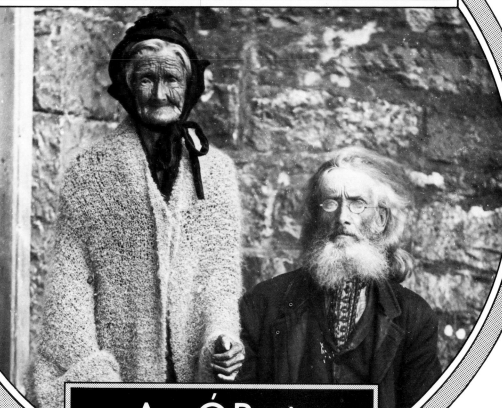

Book Two

Art Ó Broin
& Seán McMahon

Preface

OUR THANKS ARE DUE to the National Library of Ireland; the staff of the Library of the Institute of Continuing Education (NUU), Magee College, Derry, especially Alan Roberts; the staff of the Belfast Central Library; Peter Folan of the Library of UCG; Nora Niland and Hubert Geelan of the Sligo County Library and Museum; Desmond Wynne of Castlebar; Mother M. Enda, Sr Teresa Margaret, Seamus Sherry and John Heneghan of Foxford; Ronnie O'Gorman, Tom Kenny, Maurice Semple of Galway; the Lynches of Lisdoonvarna; Declan Bree, Eileen Lambert of Sligo; Rev Martin Coen of Craughwell; Annie Giblin of Castlerea; Rosaleen Conifrey of Leitrim Co Library; Kay O'Connor, Ballinrobe; Eileen Higgins and Eamon O'Boyle of Claremorris; Jackie Clarke of Ballina; Gregóir Ó Dughaill and Frank Corr of the State Paper Office, Dublin Castle; George Thompson and Nicholas Love of Manorhamilton; P. Keaney of Carrick-on-Shannon; James Finn and Miss Gavin of Roscommon; Liam Jordan of Ballinasloe, Brian Walker of Belfast and Jim Craig and Frank D'Arcy of Derry.

Introduction

This book is a record in picture and literary excerpt of life in the west of Ireland on both sides of the century's turn. It is hard, almost impossible, to imagine the quality of life then (or in any past era) and conventional histories however excellent cannot hope to give us this sense of past time. We may well ask if we can ever understand or truly imagine what people like ourselves felt in those days. The world of our great-grandfathers exists if at all in the already failing memories of our own grandparents (and it takes a considerable effort on our part to realise that they too were once young). Yet there is a way to reach in imagination towards some concept of the lives that people lived then.

At Black Head, Co Clare 1914 (Lynch Collection Lisdoonvarna)

Thanks to photography, the new toy, we have permanent images of the past, perhaps a little stiff, deliberately posed often, but certainly in some way authentic. And if we add to these pictorial images other images from the imaginative writings of the time we can arrive at an acceptable version which will be true for us and not too false of them.

Unlike Ulster, Connacht had no city, no urban literary tradition and no theatre. The occasional writings, sketches, lampoons, one-act plays that the period provided in abundance in Belfast and the stout northern towns were simply not there but by the law of unreasonable compensation the west provided most of the giants of the Irish literary revival. Lady Gregory, Edward Martyn, George Moore and of course, Yeats and Synge all had the strongest of connections with Connacht.

It was a region in which heavy industry, proletarian urban life and sociological anomie played little part in the life of people; there were peasants, small shopkeepers, half-mounted gentry and a rapidly increasing number of tourists. Our period, 1875 to 1925, was one of considerable change, socially and politically but it seemed to have a more muted effect upon the west than other places. What did produce by western standards a revolutionary change was the Plan of Campaign — the Land League's answer to Castle Rackrent. And it did have its meteors: the names of Michael Davitt and Captain Boycott are part of Connacht mythology, and so is that of Constance Markiewicz. The feeling of life, the sense of space, loneliness, hard work and distances painfully travelled is captured best in the literature of the time. The photographs, in their formal way, show with equal effect the contrast between peasant cabin and Big House - the wildness and beauty of the terrain setting off the greatness of the houses, the opulence of the better hotels, and on the permanent way the elaboration of stonework and steel.

While we cannot question the deliberate artistry of the writer we might wonder if the photographer saw himself as more than a journeyman. Certainly in the one excerpt that we could find where a photographer is mentioned he is portrayed with less than respect. It is most likely that our two chief photographers were too concerned to get on with their jobs to worry unduly about their art, if indeed they considered it at all. The round of

Promenade, Salthill
(Lawrence Collection, National Library)

Tourist Boat on the River Shannon (Lawrence Collection, National Library of Ireland)

events: christenings, weddings, sports days, staff outings, visits by Personages filled their days. A Boycott Expedition or a Land League riot was an event rarely captured except by happy accident. As their work shows they were fine photographers but they would have been startled had anyone suggested that they were creative artists.

Robert French, the chief photographer who took the pictures for the Dublin firm of Lawrence, was born in Dublin in 1841 and after an early career which included service in the RIC, began to take photographs around 1880. Thomas J Wynne, a contemporary and friend of French (they frequently exchanged albums), is thought by his grandson, Desmond Wynne of Castlebar to have been born in America in 1838 but he afterwards settled in Castlebar. His collection is a fascinating record of life in Mayo in our period, with portfolios on the Lucan family, the Boycott affair, evictions, politics, amateur theatre and the events of life in a self-contained part of the country. He died in 1900 but not before he had established through his sons, branches in Loughrea, Tipperary and Portarlington. One further notable collection, that of Thady Kilgannon of Sligo perished in the town dump in 1951 — a fate which seems to have overtaken several other collections. Kilgannon logically enough extended his interest to moving pictures and became the proprietor of Sligo's two cinemas.

Our two viewpoints, those of writer and photographer, are necessarily different, and not just because of their different media. Often, surprisingly it is the photographer who gives the more romantic picture. Compare, for example, Jane Barlow's realistic description of peasant life with French's version of the girl and the donkey, which with Hinde-sight might be found on any modern revolving card-stand. His Galway women, too, seem too serene to engage in the fish-wife vituperation recorded by Somerville and Ross in *The Real Charlotte*. We can grasp little of the misery of Seumas O'Kelly's turf-seller in French's

9

study of the sturdy farmer with his load of turf in Ballinrobe. Then, of course, most of French's photographs are the perfect complement to Guinan's description. In the case of Lissadell House the photographer was more accurate than the poet: Yeat's 'great windows open to the south', maybe, but to the cold eye of the camera the place seems lumpish and illproportioned. One outstanding writer, perhaps in his optimisti

Lissadell House, Sligo (Lawrence Collection, National Library of Ireland)

way the most representative of the time, was Percy French who best came to terms for all his genial mocking, with the artifacts of the New Age. His songs of aeroplanes, motor-cars, bicycles were as commercially successful as the photographs. In general we have matched picture and text. The connection may not always be obvious but it does exist. We are responsible for selection but we hope that photograph and excerpt combined give an acceptable and not entirely subjective account of the west of Ireland of fifty to a hundred years ago.

Art Byrne & Sean McMahon

On Inisheer (*Synge Collection, Trinity College*)

The Pier, Inishmore, Aran (Lawrence Collection, National Library of Ireland).

"FRIENDS," BEGAN O'MALLEY in Irish, addressing his peasant followers. "I am **glad to have an** opportunity to speak here to-day to these gentlemen who have come from the mainland. I am going to address these gentlemen in English since they do not understand their own native language, but I ask you as the descendants of the ancient clansmen of the O'Malleys to see that I get a hearing. If anybody wants to create a disturbance in order to prevent me from saying what I have to say, let us see to it that he will get the worst of the argument. We ruled this island for centuries before the foreigner came with their yardsticks and their beer measures to rob us of our birthright, but we are not conquered yet and we will to-day make that clear to them."

There were loud cries of "O'Mailleach Abu" and waving of blackthorn sticks, and then O'Malley turned to the important people on the platform and, clearing his throat, spoke in English.

"I am speaking now to you priests and politicians, and the deluded people who follow you. You have come here to-day to hold a meeting, to try and foist your Home Rule programme on the natives of Inverara. As an O'Malley and the descendant of the chiefs who ruled over this island, I came to utter a protest. You priests and you politicians are the curse of this country" (here there were cries of protest, but the cries of protest were drowned in shouts of "Mailleach Abu," and Fr. O'Reilly raised his hand for silence, although the pimple on his nose was swelling and appeared to be on the point of bursting). "Ireland needs to be rid of her 'Gentry', to be rid of those descendants of adventurers, who were picked by marauding English generals from the London brothels and foisted on this country as 'gentlemen'. Ireland needs to be rid of those dissolute, roystering, ignorant scoundrels, who have never done anything for the country but rob it, except when once and again the dung of their stables has been raked by the hand of fate and they have produced a Moore or a Parnell.

"And after them, Ireland wants to be rid of her priests and politicians" (renewed cries of protest, which threatened this time to end in blows, but the parish priest again came to the rescue, even though he himself was trembling with wrath, and Fr. Considine's face was hidden behind his red silk handkerchief to hide his anger). "Ireland needs to be rid of her priests and politicians, for they are the two main forces that are keeping the country in ignorance. When she is free of these three scourges she can advance.

"And I want to point out," he continued, raising his voice, "that this objective cannot be gained by begging from British Kings, or by prayer to God, or by speeches. It can only be gained by the same methods by which the Land League men won the land, by reliance on our own brawn and muscle, and by our willingness to die for the mother that gave us all birth" (here there was a cheer even from the natives of Kilmurrage, and the young man in the grey tweed suit and the straw hat, who was now standing beside Cissy Carmody, waved his hat in the air and shouted "To hell with the King").

Liam O'Flaherty, *Thy Neighbour's Wife,* (London, 1923) pp73-75

LIAM O'FLAHERTY was born on Inishmore, Aran in 1897. After a spell at a seminary in Dublin he left to become an undergraduate at UCD. When the war started he joined the Irish Guards and was shell-shocked and invalided out. His experiences in the war provided the background for one of his lesser known but effective novels. *The Return of the Brute* (1929). His active period as a socialist revolutionary was short but he has remained true to the socialist ideal. Popularly known as the author of *The Informer* (1925), his fame will rest on his short stories both in English and in Irish. *Duil* (1953) contained the best of his writing in Irish. His autobiography, *Shame The Devil* (1934) deserves reprinting.

... so I sat down on the slip and drew out my wallet of photographs. In an instant I had the whole band clambering round me, in their ordinary mood.'

J M Synge, *The Aran Islands*, (Dublin, 1907)

Synge left his photographs and camera to his nephew, Edward M. Stephens, and they were eventually published with his wife, Lilo's permission in 1971. The camera was a Klito, a plate-changing model made by Haughton's of London.

A currach by the pier at Inishmaan [*Synge Collection, Trinity College*].

THE grand road from the mountain goes shining to the sea,
  And there is traffic in it and many a horse and cart,
But the little roads of Cloonagh are dearer far to me,
  And the little roads of Cloonagh go rambling through my heart.
A great storm from the ocean goes shouting o'er the hill,
  And there is a glory in it and terror on the wind,
But the haunted air of twilight is very strange and still,
  And the little winds of twilight are dearer to my mind.
The great waves of the Atlantic sweep storming on the way,
  Shining green and silver with the hidden herring shoal,
But the Little Waves of Breffny have drenched my heart in spray,
  And the Little Waves of Breffny go stumbling through my soul.

Eva Gore-Booth, 'The Little Waves of Breffny', from *Selected Poems* (Dublin, undated)

EVA GORE-BOOTH was the younger sister of Constance Marciewicz and in her quiet way just as politically concerned as her more flamboyant sister. Born at Lissadell in 1870 her poetry was quasi-philosophical and mystical. '*The Little Waves of Breffny*' is a favourite anthology piece. She died in 1926.

ACHILL, much the largest of the off-shore islands, became a tourist centre in the eighteen nineties with the building of an iron swivel-bridge. Till then its main source of revenue was fishing, which was profuse but unorganised, a fact which irritated many economically minded Victorian visitors. A Mr. J. G. V. Porter suggested it as the site for a 'magnificent imperial sea-fish aquarium; but, characteristically nothing came of it.'

Achill People (Lawrence Collection, National Library of Ireland)

THE "ISLAND CHAPEL," as everyone called it, was an old-fashioned, cruciform building, wide, squat and low, unlovely in its architecture and furnished in the plainest and poorest style. It had two gloomy galleries, entered from the outside by means of big, ungainly stone stairs, whose rough-hewn steps were worn thin by the feet of generation after generation of devout worshippers. Everything, in a word, in and about the "Island Chapel" was antiquated, dim and faded, unmistakably proclaiming that it was a poor man's church. Not that it was not always clean and neat, for Susan Conrahy never allowed a speck of dust or rust to rest on anything. All the same, in spite of her oft repeated washing, scrubbing and scouring, she was unable to counteract the wear and tear of time. Indeed, the people somehow liked their old chapel all the better for its congenial poverty, and those of them who occasionally heard Mass in grander churches used to say that they felt much more at home in their own dear, dingy "Island Chapel," and could pray far better in it, as there was no grandeur there to distract their thoughts.

Although it was the principal parochial church, everyone spoke of it as the "Island Chapel." When Father Devoy came to the parish, he began to call it "the Island Church;" but he soon found he was constantly misunderstood, as that term was exclusively applied to the Protestant place of worship in the district, a dismal-looking structure, attended on Sunday afternoons by about a dozen people, or thereabouts. However, although he frequently protested against the popular misapplication of the term, "church", in this connection, he could not wean his people from calling their place of worship by the more homely and familiar name of "the chapel", and was, consequently, obliged to fall in with custom himself.

Joseph Guinan, *The Island Parish*, (Dublin, 1908) pp 115-116

THE REV. JOSEPH GUINAN, famous as the author of *The Soggarth Aroon* (1905), a title cribbed from John Banim. His accounts of life among the poor peasants of the West are based upon first-hand experience but are a little sentimental and emotional by to-day's standards.

Below: *Bannacurry Monastery, Achill (Lawrence Collection, National Library of Ireland*

THE YOUNG MAN has been buried, and his funeral was one of the strangest scenes I have met with. People could be seen going down to his house from early in the day, yet when I went there with the old man about the middle of the afternoon, the coffin was still lying in front of the door, with the men and women of the family standing round beating it, and keening over it, in a great crowd of people. A little later every one knelt down and a last prayer was said. Then the cousins of the dead man got ready two oars and some pieces of rope - the men of his own family seemed too broken with grief to know what they were doing - the coffin was tied up, and the procession began. The old women walked close behind the coffin, and I happened to take a place just after them, among the first of the men. The rough lane to the graveyard slopes away towards the east, and the crowd of women going down before me in their red dresses, cloaked with red petti-coats, with the waistband that is held round the head just seen from behind, had a strange effect, to which the white coffin and the unity of colour gave a nearly cloistral quietness.

This time the graveyard was filled with withered grass and bracken instead of the early ferns that were to be seen everywhere at the other funeral I have spoken of, and the grief of the people was of a different kind, as they had come to bury a young man who had died in his first manhood, instead of an old woman of eighty. For this reason the keen lost a part of its formal nature, and was recited as the expression of intense personal grief by the young men and women of the man's own family.

When the coffin had been laid down, near the grave that was to be opened, two long switches were cut from the brambles among the rocks, and the length and breadth of the coffin were marked on them. Then the men began their work, clearing off stones and thin layers of earth, and breaking up an old coffin that was in the place into which the new one had to be lowered. When a number of blackened boards and pieces of bone had been thrown up with the clay, a skull was lifted out, and placed upon a gravestone. Immediately the old woman, the mother of the dead man, took it up in her hands, and carried it away be herself. Then she sat down and put it in her lap - it was the skull of her own mother - and began keening and shrieking over it with the wildest lamentation.

As the pile of mouldering clay got higher beside the grave a heavy smell began to rise from it, and the men hurried with their work, measuring the hole repeat-edly with the two rods of bramble. When it was nearly deep enough the old woman got up and came back to the coffin, and began to beat on it, holding the skull in her left hand. This last moment of grief was the most terrible of all. The young women were nearly lying among the stones, worn out with their passion of grief, yet raising themselves every few moments to beat with magnificent gestures on the boards of the coffin. The young men were worn out also, and their voices cracked continually in the wail of the keen.

When everything was ready the sheet was unpinned from the coffin, and it was lowered into its place. Then an old man took a wooden vessel with holy water in it, and a wisp of bracken, and the people crowded round him while he splashed the water over them. They seemed eager to get as much of it as possible, more than one old woman crying out with a humor-ous voice - 'Tabhair dham braon eile, a Mhourteen.' ('Give me another drop, Martin.')

When the grave was half filled in, I wandered round towards the north watching two seals that were chasing each other near the surf. I reached the Sandy Head as the light began to fail, and found some of the men I knew best fishing there with a sort of drag-net. It is a tedious process, and I sat for a long time on the sand watching the net being put out, and then drawn in again by eight men working together with a slow rhythmical movement.

As they talked to me and gave me a little poteen and a little bread when they thought I was hungry, I could not help feeling that I was talking with men who were under a judgement of death. I knew that every one of them would be drowned in the sea in a few years and battered naked on the rocks, or would die in his own cottage and be buried with another fearful scene in the graveyard I had come from.

J.M. SYNGE, *The Aran Islands* (Dublin, 1907)

ACHILL DISASTER: Twenty-three out of a hundred migrant workers were drowned when the hooker taking them from Daly's Point to Westport capsized. They were mostly in their teens and indeed for many it was their first trip to Scotland for the harvest. What seems to have happened was that in their excitement at seeing the Glasgow steamer for the first time they stood up and caused the boat to overturn. Many more would have been lost but for the action of the crew of the steamer. The bodies were brought as far as Mallaranny by train on the new line that was being built from Westport to Achill Sound.

SYNGE'S GENIUS as a dramatist has tended to obscure his talent as prose writer. It is probably true that he needed the time on Aran to organise his gifts, though the results were by no means as magical as Yeats might have boasted. Anyway the account of his Aran sojourns and of his wanderings in Wicklow, Kerry and Connemara is written in prose of the highest quality.

The Aftermath of the Achill Disaster, June 1894 (Wynne Collection, Castlebar)

Fish Curing at Clare Island [Lawrence Collection National Library of Ireland]

THE top o' the mornin' to you, Mick,
  Isn't it fine an' dhry an' still?
Just an elegant day, avic,
  To stick the toleys on Tullagh hill.
The field is turned, an' every clod
  In ridge an' furrow is fresh an' brown;
So let's away, with the help o' God,
  By the heel o' the evenin' we'll have them down.

    As long as there's plenty o' milk to churn,
      An' plenty o' pyaties in ridge an' furrow,
    By the winter fire we'll laugh to scorn
      The frown o' famine an' scowl o' sorrow.

There's a time to work, an' a time to talk;
  So, Patsy, my boy, your pratin' shtop!
By Midsummer Day, blossom an' stalk,
  We'll feast our eyes on a right good crop.
Oh, the purple blossoms, so full o' joy,
  Burstin' up from our Irish loam,
They're betther than gold to the peasant, boy;
  They crown him king in his Irish home!

    As long as the cows have milk to churn,
      With plenty o' pyaties in ridge an' furrow,
    By the winter hearth we'll laugh to scorn
      The frown o' famine an' scowl o' sorrow.

PATRICK J COLEMAN, 'Seedtime', in Brooke and
Rolleston, *A Treasury of Irish Poetry* (London, 1900)
p.403.

PATRICK JAMES COLEMAN was born in Ballaghadereen, Co. Mayo in 1867. Educated at Stonyhurst and London
University he took an MA at La Salle College, Philadelphia where he had gone to teach Classics. He was a frequent
contributor to American Catholic journals of which there were many in those lush days.

22 Right: *Harvest Time [Lawrence Collection, The National Library of Ireland]*

GRACE RHYS (NEE LITTLE) was born in Boyle, Co. Roscommon in 1865. Best known as writer of historical romances such as *The Charming of Estercel* (1913), set in the period of Essex and O'Neill. She also wrote pastoral lyrics with a West of Ireland background, one of which 'Wild Pastures', she included in her anthology on Celtic Literature, (1927), She married Ernest Rhys, the founder of the Everyman Library, in 1891.

Lough Nafooey, Co. Galway [*Lawrence Collection, National Library of Ireland*]

MY black flocks wander on the bitter salt marshes;
  In the mist they feed and drink:
They pick at the sea-holly and and rough plants and grasses
  At the harsh water's brink.

My white flocks stray about the landward meadows: Their fleeces shine;
With lowered heads they feed on the tender herbs and grasses
  Tasting their honey-wine.

But my horned sheep spring and go upon the mountains
  Lifting their heads to the wind;
Out on the crags they stand; they drink of the running water,
  In the way of their kind.

Grace Rhys, 'Wild Pastures from (A Celtic
Anthology, London, 1927) p132.

Connemara Girls (Lawrence Collection, National Library of Ireland).

AT THE DUFFCLANE END a donkey may now and then be met carrying a tall pyramid of chocolate-brown turf-sods, based on two pendant panniers, between which his large head bobs patiently, while beneath the load his slender, tottering legs take quick staccato steps, each scarcely the length of one of his own ears; or an old woman comes by with a creel projecting quaintly under her dark-blue cloak; or a girl saunters barefooted after a single file of gabbling geese, knitting along grey stocking as she goes, and never seeming to lift her eyes from the twinkle of her needles. But after you have gone a short way the chances are that you will meet nothing more civilised and conversable than wild birds and very large gnats, until you come in sight of Lisconnel.

Just before that, the road starts abruptly, as if it had suddenly taken fright at its own loneliness, and dips down a steepish slope, but quickly pulls itself up, finding that escape is impossible. The hill, whose spur it has thus crossed, is very insignificant, only a knoll-like *knockawn*, prolonged on the left hand as a low ridge, soon dwindling into a mere bank, and imperceptibly ceasing from the face of the resurgent bog. Yet it probably fixed the site of Lisconnel, because it offered some protection from the full sweep of the west wind, and because its boulder-strewn slopes, and a narrow strip at their foot, have a covering of poor light soil in which potatoes can be set. Such advantages seldom recur within a radius of several miles. For when I spoke of the spaciousness of Lisconnel I did not mean that there is much room in it for you or me, or anybody who must needs have "a bit of lan" to live on. The craggy ridge is surmounted by a few weather-worn thorn bushes, and one ash tree, so strongly warped to the eastward that a glance at it on the stillest day creates an impression of blasts blowing roughly. Also, after the manner of trees thus situated, it seems to draw down and diffuse the very spirit of the desolate surrounding solitudes. The cabins themselves look somehow as if they felt its spell, and were huddling together for company. Three in a row on one side of the road, a couple fast by on the other - not exactly facing them, because of a swampy patch - two more a few paces further on, with "Ody Rafferty's" and "the widow M'Gurk's", which stand "a trifle back o' the road" up the hillslopes, climbing down to join the group. That is all Lisconnel, unless we count in the O'Driscolls' old dwelling, whose roof has long since top-dressed a neighbouring field, and whose walls are in some places peered over by the nettles.

Cabin walls in Lisconnel are built of rough stones with no mortar, and not mud enough to preclude a great deal of unscientific ventilation, which, maybe, has its advantages, dearly paid for through many a shivering night. All its roofs are thatched, but none of them with straw, which is too scarce for such a use. Rushes serve instead, not quite satisfactorily, being neither so warm nor so durable, nor even so picturesque, for their pale grey-green looks crude and cold, and the weather only bleaches it into a more colourless drab, when straw would be mellowly golden and russet. A thick fringe of stones must hang along the eaves, or roof and rafters would part company the first time the wind got a fair undergrip of the thatch.

Jane Barlow, *Irish Idylls* (London, 1892) pp 5-7

JANE BARLOW was born in Clontarf in 1857, daughter of the Rev. James Barlow who became Vice-Provost of Trinity College Dublin. Though she wrote poems her prose writings are superior. *Irish Idylls* (1892) shows a remarkable understanding and appreciation of peasant life in the West where all of her work is set. She died in 1917.

(Séachaideann fear maide dhó, cuireann sé sop féir timchioll air; tosaigheann se dh'á chasadh, agus Síghle ag tabhairt amach an fhéir dó.)

MAC UI h-ANN. (ag gabhail) -

Ta péarla mná 'tabhairt soluis dúinn,
Is í mo ghrádh, is í mo rún,
'Sí Úna bhán, an righ-bhean   chiuin,
'S ni thuigid na Muimhnigh leath a stuaim.

Atá na Muimhnigh seo dallta ag Dia,
Ni aithnighid eala thar lacha liath,
Acht tiucfaidh sí liom-sa, mo Hélen bhreágh

McKeown's Industry, Leenane. (Lawrence Collection, National Library of Ireland).

Mar a molfar a pearsa 's a sgéimh go bráth.

Ara! mhuise! mhuise! Nach é seo an baile breágh lághach, nach é
seo an baile thar bárr, an baile a mbíonn an oiread sin rógaire crochta ann
nach mbíonn aon easbhuidh rópa ar na daoinibh, leis an méad rópa
ghoideann siad ó'n gcrochaire. Cráidhteacháin atá ionnta. Tá na rópaidh
aca agus ní thugann siad uatha iad - acht go gcuireann siad an
Connachtach bocht ag casadh sugáin dóibh! Nior chas siad sugán féir in
san mbaile seo ariamh - agus an méad sughán cnáibe ata aca de bhárr an
chrochaire!

Gnidheann Connachtach ciallmhar
Rópa dhó féin,
Acht goideann an Muimhneach
Ó'n gcrochaire é!
Go bhfeicidh mé rópa
Breágh cnáibe go fóill
D'á fhásgadh ar sgóigibh
Gach aoinne ann so!

Mar gheall ar aon mhnaoi amháin d'imthigheadar na Gréagaigh, agus
níor stopadar agus níor mhór-chómnuigheadar no gur sgriosadar an
Traoi, agus mar gheall ar aon mhnaoi amháin béidh an baile seo
damanta go deó na ndeór agus go bruinne an bhrátha, le Dia na ngrás, go
síorruidhe suthain, nuair nár thuigeadar gur ab í Una ní Ríogáin an dara
Helen do rugadh in a measg, agus go rug sí bárr áille ar Helen agus ar
Bhénus, ar a dtáinig riompi agus ar dtiucfas 'na diaigh.

Acht tiucfaidh sí liom mo phéarla mná
Go cúige Connacht na ndaoine breágh;
Gheobhaidh sí féasta fíon a's feóil,
Rinnceanna árda, spórt a's ceól.

O! mhuise! mhuise! nár éirighidh an ghrian ar an mbaile seo, agus nár
lasaidh réalta air, agus nár -

(Tá sé san am so amuigh thar an dorus. Eirigheann na fir uile
agus dúnaid é d'aon ruaig amháin air. Tugann Una léim chum an
doruis, acht beirid na mná uirri. Téidheann Séamus anonn chuici.)

Dubhglas De hÍde, ''Casadh an tSúgáin'' Samhain 1901. ltn. 28,29.

DOUGLAS HYDE, 'An Craoibhín Aoibhinn' was born on January 17, 1862, in Co. Roscommon but spent most of his youth and early manhood at Frenchpark in the same county where his father was minister. Educated at home he learned Irish locally, a fact which turned him from two likely careers in the Church and the Law. His paper, 'The Necessity for De-Anglicising Ireland' on November 25, 1892 was followed the next summer by the founding with Eoin MacNeill of the Gaelic League. His best known books are *The Love Songs of Connacht* (1893) and *Mise agus an Conradh* (1937). He became first president of the state whose culture he helped to form. He died in 1949.

Casadh an tSúgáin (*The Twisting of the Rope*) was based upon a West of Ireland folktale. It tells how a wandering Connacht poet drives to distraction the decent people of a Munster house by his greed, railing and boasting. Hospitality prevents them from ejecting him but one evening while the family are making straw ropes for thatching he demonstrates his skill and twists himself out of the house. The piece printed describes the final exorcism. It was the first play in modern Irish and was first performed on October 21, 1901 at the Gaiety Theatre, Dublin.

Ropemaking on Aran [Synge Collection, Trinity College]

In ropemaking, two men usually sat together, one of them hammering the straw with a heavy block of wood to make it more pliable, the other forming the untwisted rope. The actual twisting was done by a boy or girl with a bent stick. The boastfulness of the poet in Hyde's play is all the more contemptible since the work of twisting was inappropriate for a man.

TRANSPORT & TOURISM

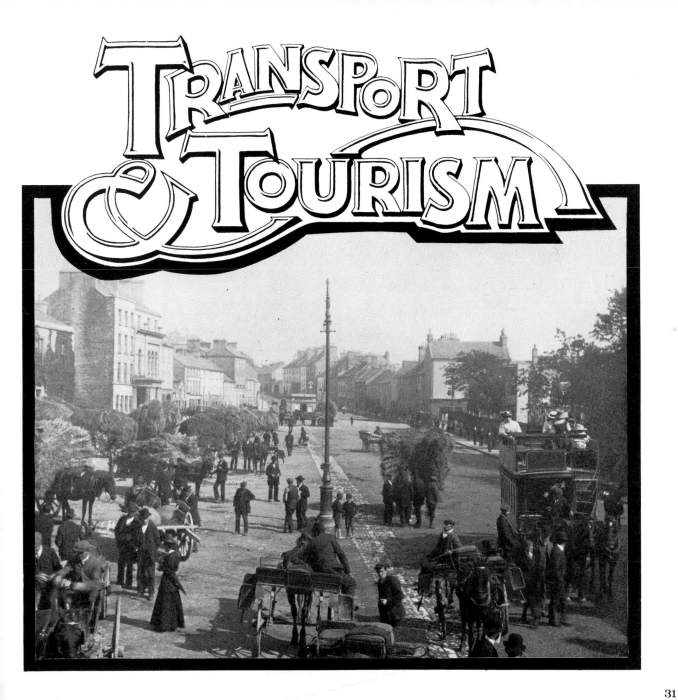

SOMEWHERE about forty years ago, when old gentlemen had faint recollections of their grandfathers wearing swords, and fast young gentlemen sneered at the "old square-toes" for doing so; before steam had puffed out all recollection of those barbarous days, when a gentleman's honor was deemed of more value than his bond, and some few years before the laying down of the electric telegraph, or the raising up of 18,B, * on a fine evening in the month of August, 18—, the "Tallyho" day coach, running between Dublin and L——, was seen passing through the principal entrance of Dalystown, a fine old place, situate and being, (as my friends of the legal profession would say,) in the county of Galway, and bordering the counties of Mayo and Roscommon.

This invasion of private property, on the part of the Tallyho, was accounted for by the coachman, who informed one of his passengers that by getting in at this gate, driving right through the demesne, and coming out on the opposite side, they avoided the half circle which the public road made, and shortened the distance fully a mile.

It was much pleasanter too, to bowl along the smooth gravelled avenue, than to travel the hilly, rutty road. So he was very glad to avail himself of the privilege of passing through the demesne, kindly given to him by the owner.

As the coach came in view of the house, and elderly gentleman and a young girl were seen standing at the hall door, anxiously watching its approach, while a number of domestics and laborers were grouped around the entrance to the stables and farm yard, evincing, by their eager looks, that the approach of the Tallyho was watched, on this evening, with unusual interest.

Suddenly a man, dressed in an old, faded hunting coat, tattered corduroys, his feet and legs free from the innovations of shoes and stockings, jumped up from the grass on which he had been lying, and as the coach came within a few yards of him, he cast a keen look up at its roof, then flinging an old hunting cap high in the air, he shouted, as he headed the coach, "Yoicks, Tallyho! here he comes, master, Mr. Henry himself, there's his handsome face, behind Joe. Yoicks, Tallyho".

Dillon O'Brien, *The Dalys of Dalystown* (St Paul, 1866) pp 10,11

Salthill, Galway [Lawrence Collection, The National Library of Ireland]

DILLON O'BRIEN was born at Kilmore, Co. Roscommon in 1817 and became Government teacher at the Indian Mission at La Pointe, Minnesota. He later settled in St. Paul and began to write what are literally Irish-American novels since the action takes place in both countries. As one who did well in the States he tends to use them as the source of *Di ex Machinis* to resolve the problems of his Irish characters. *The Dalys of Dalystown* (1866) is his best known novel and here typically money earned in America enables the hero, young Daly, to buy back the family estates and resume benevolent landlordism.

"We left Galway for Clifden at 9.30 next morning. The public conveyance is a large-paper edition of the outside car, with an elevated seat for the driver. There is one place to be avoided on some of these vehicles, that nearest to the horses on the offside, on account of the iron bar of the drag, which operates from time to time very disagreeably on the back and shoulders of the contiguous traveller."

S Reynold Hole: *A Little Tour of Ireland* (London 1896)
Below: *A Galway Mail Car* (*Lawrence Collection, National Library of Ireland*)

Left: The Galway and Salthill Tramway was constructed in 1879. It was horsedrawn and ran from Eyre Square through the city to Salthill. Labour troubles and the war killed the company and petrol buses came in 1919. **33**

The station in Galway was built in 1851 at the height of the great railway expansion. The line from Westport to Achill Sound built in the mid-1890's was really the twilight of this enterprise. The photograph shows the building of a traditional stone-bridge, which is rather unusual since by then most railway bridges were being built of iron.

Railway Station, Galway [Lawrence Collection, The National Library of Ireland]

Right: *Building the railway bridge at Newport in the eighteen-nineties (Wynne Collection, Castlebar)*

IT WAS THE EVE of the Parnell celebration in Dublin, and the town was full of excursionists waiting for a train which was to start at midnight. When Michael left me I spent some time in an hotel, and then wandered down to the railway.

A wild crowd was on the platform, surging round the train in every stage of intoxication. It gave me a better instance than I had yet seen of the half-savage temperament of Connaught. The tension of human excitement seemed greater in this insignificant crowd than anything I have felt among enormous mobs in Rome or Paris.

There were a few people from the islands on the platform, and I got in along with them to a third-class carriage. One of the women of the party had her niece with her, a young girl from Connaught who was put beside me; at the other end of the carriage there were some old men who were talking in Irish, and a young man who had been a sailor.

When the train started there were wild cheers and cries on the platform, and in the train itself the noise was intense; men and women shrieking and singing and beating their sticks on the partitions. At several stations there was a rush to the bar, so th excitement increased as we proceeded.

At Ballinasloe there were some soldiers on the platform looking for places. The sailor in our compartment had a dispute with one of them, and in an instant the door was flung open and the compartment was filled with reeling uniforms and sticks. Peace was made after a moment of uproar and the soldiers got out, but as they did so a pack of their women followers thrust their bare heads and arms into the doorway, cursing and blaspheming with extraordinary rage.

As the train moved away a moment later, these women set up a frantic lamentation. I looked out and caught a glimpse of the wildest heads and figures I have ever seen, shrieking and screaming and waving their naked arms in the light of the lanterns.

As the night went on girls began crying out in the carriage next to us, and I could hear the words of obscene songs when the train stopped at a station.

In our own compartment the sailor would allow no one to sleep, and talked all night with sometimes a touch of wit or brutality, and always with a wonderful fluency with wild temperament behind it.

The old men in the corner, dressed in black coats that had something of the antiquity of heirlooms, talked all night among themselves in Gaelic. The young girl beside me lost her shyness after a while, and let me point out the features of the country that were beginning to appear through the dawn as we drew near Dublin. She was delighted with the shadows of the trees - trees are rare in Connaught - and with the canal, which was beginning to reflect the morning light. Every time I showed her some new shadow she cried out with naïve excitement

'Oh, it's lovely, but I can't see it.'

This presence at my side contrasted curiously with the brutality that shook the barrier behind us. The whole spirit of the west of Ireland, with its strange wildness and reserve, seemed moving in this single train to pay a last homage to the dead statesman of the east.

J. M. SYNGE *The Aran Islands*
(Dublin, 1907)

"WHERE TO NOW"

"WHERE TO NOW, your Excellency?" he inquired, dismally enough.

"To bl—zes!" answered his Excellency.

It was the first time the smooth, smiling lips of Lord Carlisle had shaped a profane syllable. Before decorum could stop the words they were out. But decorum resumed command the next instant.

"Ay, to blazes, to be sure," he continued, in quite an altered tone of voice, with a look of mild reproach at the tittering *aide-de-camp*. "But what blazes? that is the question. The blazing fire that this morning browned our toast in the best parlor of Mack's Hotel in Galway, or the blazes that are perhaps kindly cooking our dinners in Cong? Any blazes, or, at least, almost any blazes, were welcome on such an evening as this." He gazed as he spoke, with a half shudder, at the rain-blotted landscape, and smiled a sickly smile at his own sickly pleasantries.

"Cong is the nearest refuge — perhaps, I should rather say Galway is the farther of the two, your Excellency," interposed the private secretary.

"Then to Cong let it be," said Lord Carlisle, leaning back in his carriage, with a look of patient resignation.

Unlike the hotel from which they parted a good three hours ago, at Maam, the house is ablaze with light, and redolent with savoury odors. Now and again, from inside, a burst of jolly laughter drowns the fretful whining of the wind.

The very look of the place seemed to bid a cordial welcome to the wet, weary, and hungry travelers. A smile began to dawn on the pale face of this Excellency, as eyes, ears, nostrils gave him promise of a pleasant fare and comfortable quarters. The flickering smile disappeared in black despair when the host, whom a thundering peal upon the knocker brought to the door, spoke almost the same words as the churl of Maam, "No room for you here."

The Lord Carlisle's dignity yielded to his despair "I am the Lord Lieutenant!" he cried from his carriage.

"I could not let you in if you were the King," retorted the other. "Not even if you were the Pope of Rome, could you get in without leave.

"Who says a word against my good friend, his Holiness?" cried a rich jovial voice behind them, and the host drew aside respectfully, as a tall, burly figure, with a big face, as full of good humour as the sun is of light at midday, came striding down the passage and met the Viceroy face to face at the door.

"Big Joe!" cried Lord Carlisle in delighted amazement.

"Your Excellency," responded the other, with old-fashioned courtesy, "now and always at your service."

"Never needed it more, Joe," responded Lord Carlisle pitifully. I'd give my Garter for a dinner and bed. I have been turned like a beggarman out of all the hotels in Connemara."

"I'm afraid you will find it hard to get in here," said Big Joe, "You see, you are not the kind of guest that was expected, and I don't think you would like the company any more than they'd like you."

"Any company is good enough for me," said the other entreatingly, "if Big Joe M'Donnell is amongst them. But a good dinner would make the worst company in the world pleasant to me now."

Big Joe was silent for a moment. "I'll tell you the whole truth," he said, "and nothing but the truth. We hold our Patrick's day dinner here to-night. Every man is bound to tell a story or drink a quart of salt water; so there will be a good many stories," he added, with humorous twinkles in his eyes, "and they might not all suit the ears of his Excellency."

"His Excellency's ears are neither as long nor as tender as a donkey's" was the curt reply, "and his Excellency's teeth are as hungry as a wolf's."

"Well, if they don't mind hearing they might mind telling," said Joe. "There is very little Castle company amongst us to-night, and some of the yarns spun might be twisted into a hemp cravat for the neck of the spinner."

Lord Carlisle drew himself up haughtily, with an indignant flush upon his handsom old face. "I have sat at your table," he said, "and you have sat at mine. I did not expect that insinuation from Joe M'Donnell. There is some honor yet left even amongst Irish Lord Lieutenants."

Mathias McDonnell Bodkin *The Lord Lieutenant's Adventure*.

Railway Hotel, Westport [Lawrence Collection The National Library of Ireland]

MATHIAS McDONNELL BODKIN was born in Tuam in 1849. He was Nationalist MP for North Roscommon and later a County Court Judge in Clare. His experiences as a judge provided him with much of his humorous material. He wrote plays under the pseudonym 'Crom a boo'. *The Lord Lieutenant's Adventure* is in its wildness and farcicality straight out of the Somerville and Ross stable, however much the Nationalist author might have wished to disclaim it.

THE RAILWAY HOTELS followed the building of the stations and were developed both for commercial reasons and for the ever-growing tourist trade. When the Galway-Clifden line was opened in 1895 the company organised a two-way omnibus service between Clifden and Westport so that these same tourists might do the wilds of Connemara in style and reasonable comfort. A 'Tourist Train' which took passengers from Dublin direct to Clifden ran from 1903 to 1906.

WHO were the builders? Question not the silence
That settles on the lake for evermore,
Save when the sea-bird screams and to the islands
The echo answers from the steep-cliffed shore.

O half-remaining ruin, in the lore
Of human life a gap shall all deplore
Beholding thee; since thou art like the dead
Found slain, no token to reveal the why,
The name, the story. Some one murder'd

We know, we guess, and gazing upon thee,
And, filled by the long silence of reply,
We guess some garnered sheaf of tragedy;—
Of tribe or nation slain so utterly

That even their ghosts are dead, and on their grave
Springeth no bloom of legend in its wilderness;
And age by age weak washing round the islands
No faintest sigh of story lisps the wave.

William Larminie, The Nameless Ruin, in *The Dublin Book of Irish Verse* (Dublin 1909) pp. 498-9

WILLIAM LARMINIE was born in Castlebar in 1850. Unlike his Irish Renaissance colleagues, John Todhunter, Katherine Tynan and T W Rolleston, he preferred epic narrative poems to lyrics. He lived in England, working as a civil servant till an early retirement due to ill-health in 1888. Two years later he produced *Glanlua and Other Poems*. He was strongly influenced by heroic Irish themes and Gaelic prosody and his comparatively early death at Bray in 1900 may well have removed Yeat's one poetic rival.

Left: *Pigeon Hole, Cong. (Lawrence Collection, National Library of Ireland)*

"Lough Mask which is thirty-six feet higher than Lough Corrib, sends its surplus waters to the latter through one of those subterraneous channels common to the limestone formation, untill close to Cong, where the river rises, and soon after turns a corn mill. The stream is visible in several places on the passage; but the most remarkable opening is the Pigeon Hole, which is about a mile from Cong. The descent, about sixty feet, is not difficult; and by the assistance of a light the course of the stream can be traced in its caverned bed for a considerable distance. Taking the advantages of lake and mountain scenery which this place enjoys, together with its site, we cannot but regret that such a miserable village as Cong should occupy so important a position."
James Frazer: A Handbook for Travellers in Ireland (Dublin 1844)

THE CLADDAGH was an old fishing village on the far bank of the Corrib from Galway City. Its inhabitants had the sole right to fish in Galway Bay, hence its mention in the song Galway Bay. Originally the native Irish without the walls of the Norman city, they developed a rich tradition of separate life. The most famous relic of this tradition is the Claddagh Ring, consisting of two hands clasping a crowned heart, which has at present a certain chic as a wedding ring. Fishing was the prime-feature of life: the Dominican fathers established a 'piscatorial school' as early as 1846. All the nineteenth-century guide books are eloquent about the colour and life of the community. In 1934 it was demolished and replaced by modern houses. The word claddagh in Irish means 'sea-shore'.

Below and right: *The Claddagh, Galway (Lawrence Collection, National Library of Ireland)*

O! my boat can safely float in the teeth of wind and weather,
   And out-race the fastest hooker between Galway and Kinsale;
When the black floor of the ocean and the white foam rush together,
   High she rides, in her pride, like a sea-gull through the gale.

    O! she's neat, oh, she's sweet, she's a beauty ev'ry line!
    The "Queen of Connemara" is that bounding bark of mine.
When she's loaded down with fish till the water lips the gunwale,
   Not a drop she'll take on board her that would wash a fly away;
From the fleet she'll slip out swiftly like a greyhound from her kennel,
   And she'll land her silver store the first at ould Kinvara quay.

    O! she's neat, etc.
"Heart of stone, grim and lone, o'er the boiling breakers foaming
   Have you ever all your days seen a boat to equal mine?"
"O! by all the keels I've stove in, and the wild cries of the drowning
   But she beats the bravest bark ever breast the bursting brine."

    O! she's neat, etc.
There's a light shines out afar, and it keeps me from dismaying,
   When the skies are ink above us, and the sea runs white with foam,
In a cot in Connemara, there's a wife and wee one praying
   To the One who walked the waters once, to send us safely home.

    O! she's neat, oh, she's sweet, she's a beauty ev'ry line!

Francis A Fahy, 'The Queen of Connemara', from *The Ould Plaid Shawl & Other Songs*, Ed. P.S. O'Hegarty (Dublin, 1949)

Piers and Cliff, Enniscrone, Co. Sligo
(*Lawrence Collection, National Library of Ireland*)

Typical of the comic writing of the period, this was reprinted (from *The Jarvey*) because of its local interest, in the Sligo Independent of August 17, 1889. It is almost certainly by Percy French.

WILL WAGTAIL'S ACCOUNT OF HIS VISIT TO MULLAGHMORE

This pleasant little watering place, like many other another more pretentious seaside resort, is situated on the margin of the treacherous ocean.

The "loan of a fill of tobacco" to an old coastguardsman, elicited the information that it was the Atlantic ocean, and "there was no land nearther nor America."

A vehicle called "the long car" brings you and your luggage (if you have any) to Mullaghmore, but be careful not to say to any of the obsequious natives "Carry my luggage to the best hotel, my good man," as there is no hotel, and the remark shows you to be a stranger and a tourist.

The head landlord, the Hon. Evelyn Ashley, might convert his "palatial home" (good phrase) into "The Evelyn Arms," and drive a good business. An advertisement in *The Jarvey* and *Irish Cyclist* would be a wise beginning, but the scheme should be undertaken in a spirit of enterprise and industry to ensure success.

I forgot the name of the shop which provides Mullaghmore with the necessaries of life, but as there is only one emporium at present you are bound to patronise it.

There is not the slightest use bringing any illness or disease to this backward locality, as there is no doctor to tell you what to do under the circumstances.

As a natural consequence, there are no deaths, though births and marriages are recognised institutions.

I was so surprised to hear this (from the oldest inhabitant, too), that I went and interviewed the sexton. He assured me it was quite true, and that he himself was a mere amateur, and had never performed in public.

There is a very good sea fishing to be had, and the prices charged by the local dealers would fill the gay deceivers of Baggot Street or William Street with horror and despair, but not, I fear, with remorse.

The bathing is good, but the accommodation isn't, at least for ladies, as there are only a few bathing-boxes scattered along the coast.

For men, a well-aired roof is considered sufficient as a tiring chamber.

In my character of Official Lyre I thought it well to imbibe some poetical inspiration by watching some sea nymphs at their gambols in the "buoyant blue."

The lines underneath will show the hour was not a propitious one.

I insert here some spirited verses which I found carved in relief in a friend's note-book:

LINES ON MULLAGHMORE

Of all bewcheous situations
For tourists' recreations,
(I made these observations
   As I walk along the shore;)
The finest naval cinther
The Atlantic waves can inther,
In summer or in winther,
   Is lovely Mullaghmore.

And the valiant population,
They take their recreation
In pleasant conversation,
   Making bargains at the door;
Or maybe 'tis their pleasure,
In sport to pass their leisure,
For time has ne'er a measure
   At lovely Mullaghmore.

But I'm getting to dominions
Where the unambitious pinions
Of the Paygasus can niver
   Unaided hope to soar;
Och, while the rain's a-pourin',
And the ocean waves are roarin',
Who'd be thinkin' of Bundoran
   To compare with Mullaghmore.

43

LISDOONVARNA became known as Ireland's Premier Spa in the last quarter of the nineteenth-century. People flocked to take the waters from all over the country. The twin wells were of iron and magnesium and there was a sulphur well about a mile away. It early became a popular resort for the clergy where they felt themselves able to relax, as even a French traveller noticed:

"Je me rappelle, dans le vaste salon de l'hotel de l'Aigle, une quinzaine de ces révérends pères, — ainsi les appelle-t-on — buvant du punch au whisky et chantant à tour de rôle des chansons comiques bêtes à pleurer, et des romances sentimentales en facon de complainte d'aveugle."
Marie-Anne de Bovet, *Trois Mois en Irlande* (Paris, 1908)

FRANCIS ARTHUR FAHY was born in Kinvara, Co Galway in 1854. Famous for his song-lyrics which many thought were traditional (a fate he shared with Joseph Campbell and Padraic Colum), he lived in London from 1873 till his death in 1935. He was one of the founders of the London Branch of the Gaelic League and wrote books for children on Irish heritage including an *Irish History in Rhyme*. Though not so well known as some of his other pieces, such as 'Haste to the Wedding' and 'The Ould Plaid Shawl', 'The Bog Road, Lisdoonvarna' is typical of his work.

Twin Wells, Lisdoonvarna [Lawrence Collection, The National Library of Ireland]

THE BOG ROAD

Could I travel afar now
From Bantry to Barna,
'Tis to Lisdoonvarna
    My way I would find;
For there, one bright summer,
Myself, a new-comer,
Found mirth, fun, and humour
    That ne'er leaves my mind.
O! those who each season,
Without rhyme or reason,
Cross far foreign seas on
    To light the heart's load,
Know nought of the pleasure,
Without stint or measure,
That waits them with leisure
    Along the Bog Road.

'Tis there every morning,
Dull drowsiness scorning,
Stout lads without warning
    Roam over the hills,
While matron and widdy
(Lamenting "poor Biddy")
Take draughts that would rid ye
    'Tis said, from all ills.
There farmers together
Discuss on the heather
The markets, the weather,
    The last crops they sowed;
While children are sporting,
Young couples resorting
Are cosily courting
    Along the Bog Road.

Francis A. Fahy, 'The Bog Road, Lisdoonvarna' from *The Ould Plaid Shawl and Other Songs* (Dublin, 1949)

Here wild roses grow 'mid the sweet mountain heather,
The blue-bell and fern in profusion together,
With mountain lambs bleating high up on the bar,
O, where is the valley can equal Glencar?

O, Glencar, dear Glencar, my mind still is tracing
Thy bright sylvan glades with flowers interlacing;
My heart wanders back to thy valleys and braes,
And rests 'mid the charms of thy hills and pathways.

Denis Johnston, 'Glencar', in *Modern Irish Poets II*
(Belfast, 1897)

Glencar Lake [Lawrence Collection, The National Library of Ireland]

DENIS JOHNSTON was born in Dromahair, Co Sligo in 1869. The poem 'Glencar' is included in *Modern Irish Poets II* published by W J Paul in Belfast in 1897. Apart from a stated preference for Byron, Scott and Burns little is known about him.

GLENCAR was very popular with the tourists of the period. The guide-book writers were fond of describing it as 'Ireland's Swiss Valley'; there was even an open-air tea-house in the heart of the glen.

45

UNLIKE MOST IRISH TOWNS which just growed, Clifden was practically the invention of an entrepreneur called D'Arcy; so that a site which 'so late as 1845' had scarcely a house on it, had in the words of one visitor, 'a town of some 1300 inhabitants with many good shops, a well-attended market and a considerable export trade in corn'. D'Arcy also had established an Irish Church Mission school which earned the comment from our guide, W F Wakeman, that the poor of the area would be the best educated in the country.

Clifden, Co. Galway [Lawrence Collection, National Library of Ireland]

BHÍ AN TEASPAG ina chodladh. Ní raibh le feiceáil ach a shrón, a bhéal, a smig agus leathshúil leis nuair a d'fhéach an fear aimsire, tiománaí an ghluaisteáin, isteach trí na fuinneoga air. Bhí faoi insint dó go gcaithfeadh sé moill a chur air, go raibh rud éigin cearr le hinneall an chairr, ach nuair a thug sé faoi deara sa chúinne é, agus a raibh de chótaí móra agus eile a bhí aige timpeall air, shíll sé gurbh fhearr dó féin gan bacadh leis go gcuirfeadh sé caoi ar an inneall diabhalta sin gan mhaith.

Scar sé a chóta mór féin ar an mbóthar faoin gcarr, agus isteach leis faoi, ag snámháil ar a bholg, ar nós péiste. Bhí solas deas ó na réaltaí, ach b'fhearr ná sin an solas a bhí aige ó dhá lampa cinn an ghluaisteáin. Nuair a chonaic sé cén obair mhór a bhí roimhe, agus deis a chur ar an inneall, thug sé trí mhionn agus d'fhan achar beag ar a leathuillinn ag féachaint suas uaidh ar thóin an ghluaisteáin agus ar na rothaí aimhréidhe a bhí istigh i mbolg an innill.

Nach ar an easpag a bhí an tubaiste agus a leithéid de ghluaisteán a cheannach! Fuair sé an gluaisteán saor go maith - ach cén mhaith a bhí i ngluaisteán saor mura ngluaisfeadh sé? Nach é a bhí ceanndána nár ghlac sé comhairle leis féin - ach ar ndóigh, ní ar an easpag a bheadh an t-inneall gan mhaith sin a leigheas! D'fhéadfadh an t-easpag fanacht ar a sháimhín só istigh sa charr, agus é féin ar a bholg ar an mbóthar fuar fliuch ag iarraidh caoi a chur ar an diabhal sin d'inneall!

Rug sé ar a chuid uirlisí. Bhain sé slabhra beag amach as an inneall. Bhain roth beag cruach as áit éigin eile. Chroch sé suas ceann de na lampaí móra, gur dhearc sé isteach i ndiamhair an innealra. Thug sé trí mhionn eile ansin, agus bhagair sé a dhorn ar an easpag, nó ar an áit a shíl sé an t-easpag a bheith ina chodladh istigh sa charr.

Is iomaí sin easpag ar chuir sé aithne air ó chuaigh sé ar aimsir ag an gcléir, i dtosach, ach diabhal easpag acu a bhí chomh ceanndána leis an easpag a bhí ina chodladh os a chionn. Cén meas a d'fhéadfadh a bheith ar dhuine a cheannaigh gluaisteán den déanamh sin? Bhí fonn air an t-inneall a bhaint ó chéile ar fad: gan bior, barra ná bís a fhágáil ann-céard a déarfadh an t-easpag ansin nuair a bheadh air iad a chur ina n-ionad ceart féin arís? ' Cheap an tiománaí gur mhór an spórt a bheith ag féachaint ar an easpag ina luí ar an mbóthar fliuch agus é ag iarraidh an t-inneall bradach diabhalta a chur le chéile arís!

Ní hé sin a rinne sé. Thosaigh sé ag obair ar a dhícheall. Thosaigh sé ag eascainí ar a dhícheall. Ag eascainí ar an easpag a bhí istigh sa charr a bhí sé, agus ar gach uile easpag eile a bhí chomh ceanndána is nach nglacfadh comhairle faoi ghluaisteán. A leithéid de ghíoscán agus d'eascainí is a bhí le cloisteáil istigh faoin gcarr!

Pádraic Ó Conaire, *Seacht mBua an Eirí amach* (Baile Átha Cliath, 1918). ltn. 101, 102.

PÁDRAIC Ó CONAIRE was born in Galway in 1883 but spent most of his young manhood in England. He began writing in Irish in 1904 when he won the Gaelic League Oireachtas prize, which he won again in 1907. He lived in Ireland from 1914 till his death in 1928. His best known books are *M'Asal Beag Dubh*, *Síol Éabha* and *Seacht mBua an Eirí Amach* (1918). Ó Conaire wrote Irish like an angel but current translations catch neither the quality of the language nor the spirit of the man.

The excerpt concerns the tribulations of a chauffeur coping with one of the breakdowns that was so characteristic of the early days of motoring. The fact that his master was a bishop, so episcopal that throughout all the 'mechanicking' he stayed sleeping, adds to the satirical element in the piece.

Corner of Grattan and Teeling Streets, Sligo. The pillion passenger may have been a Kilgannon. (Sligo Museum)

THE BIG HOUSE

HE NOT ONLY KNEW every hound in his pack, but he knew their ages, their sires and their dams; and the sires and the dams of most of their sires and dams. He knew the constitution of each, and to what extent their noses were to be trusted. 'It's a very heavy scent to-day,' he would say, 'because Gaylap carries it over the plough. It's only a catching scent because the drops don't hang on the bushes.' His lore on all such matters was incredible, but he would never listen to any argument. A man had a right to his own opinion; but then the man who differed from him knew nothing. He gave out his little laws to favoured individuals; not by way of conversation, for which he cared nothing, but because it might be well that the favoured individual should know the truth on that occasion.

As a man to ride he was a complete master of his art. There was nothing which a horse could do with a man on his back, which Daly could not make him do; and when he had ridden a horse he would know exactly what was within his power. But there was no desire with him for the showing off of a horse. He often rode to sell a horse, but he never seemed to do so. He never rode at difficult places unless driven to do so by the exigencies of the moment. He was always quiet in the field, unless when driven to express himself as to the faults of some young man. Then he could blaze forth in his anger with great power. He was constantly to be seen trotting along a road when hounds were running, because he had no desire to achieve for himself a character for hard riding. But he was always with his hounds when he was wanted, and it was boasted of him that he had ridden four days a week through the season on three horses, and had never lamed one of them. He was rarely known to have a second horse out, and when he did so, it was for some purpose peculiar to the day's work. On such days he had generally a horse to sell.

It is hardly necessary to say that Black Daly was an unmarried man. No one who knew him could conceive that he should have had a wife. His hounds were his children, and he could have taught no wife to assist him in looking after them, with the constant attention and tender care which was given to them by Barney Smith, his hunstman. A wife, had she seen to the feeding of the numerous babies, would have given them too much to eat, and had she not undertaken this care, she would have been useless at Daly's Bridge. But Barney Smith was invaluable; double the amount of work got usually from a huntsman was done by him. There was no kennel man, no second horseman, no stud-groom at the Ahaseragh kennels. It may be said that Black Daly filled all these positions himself, and that in each Barney Smith was his first lieutenant. Circumstances had given him the use of the Ahaseragh kennels, which had been the property of his cousin, and circumstances had not enabled him to build others at Daly's Bridge. Gradually he had found it easier to move himself than the hounds. And so it had come to pass that two rooms had been prepared for him close to the kennels,

Previous page: *Capt. Blake, Tower Hill, Co Mayo* [*Wynne Collection, Castlebar*]

The Meet, Co Mayo [*Wynne Collection, Castlebar*]

and that Mr. Barney Smith gave him such attendance as was necessary. Of strictly personal attendance Black Daly wanted very little; but the discomforts of that home, while one pair of breeches were supposed to be at Daly's Bridge, and the others at Ahaseragh, were presumed by the world at large to be very grievous.

But the personal appearance of Mr. Daly on hunting mornings, was not a matter of indifference. It was not that he wore beautiful pink tops, or came out guarded from the dust by little aprons, or had his cravat just out of the bandbox, or his scarlet coat always new, and in the latest fashion, nor had his hat just come from the shop in Piccadilly with the newest twist to its rim. But there was something manly, and even powerful about his whole apparel. He was always the same, so that by men even in his own county, he would hardly have been known in other garments. The strong, broad-brimmed high hat, with the cord passing down his back beneath his coat, that had known the weather of various winters; the dark, red coat, with long swallow tails, which had grown nearly black under many storms; the dark, buff striped waistcoat, with the stripes running downwards, long, so as to come well down over his breeches; the breeches themselves, which were always of leather, but which had become nearly brown under the hands of Barney Smith or his wife, and the mahogany top-boots, of which the tops seemed to be a foot in length, could none of them have been worn by any but Black Daly. His very spurs must have surely been made for him, they were in length and weight, and general strength of leather, so peculiarly his own. He was unlike other masters of hounds in this, that he never carried a horn; but he spoke to his hounds in a chirruping voice, which all County Galway believed to be understood by every hound in the pack.

Anthony Trollope, *The Land-leaguers*, (London, 1883)

ANTHONY TROLLOPE (1815-1882) Trollope's first writing was done in Ireland when as postal surveyor he was responsible for the provision of Ireland's first pillar-boxes. *The Landleaguers*, published postumously in 1883 is set in Galway.

The Anglo-Irish tradition of hunting packs was established in the mid-eighteenth-century. It was particularly popular in East Galway where the loose stone walls provided good sport. The most famous hunt was The Galway Blazers (the County Galway Hunt) who may have got their name from the time they set fire to Dooly's Hotel in Birr, when they were the guests of the Ormond Hunt.

THE May fire once on every dreaming hill
All the fair land with burning bloom would fill:
All the fair land, at visionary night,
Gave loving glory to the Lord of Light.
Have we no leaping flames of Beltaine praise
To kindle in the joyous ancient ways;
No fire of song, of vision, of white dream,
Fit for the Master of the Heavenly Gleam;
For him who first made Ireland move in chime,
Musical from the misty dawn of time?

Ah, yes: for sacrifice this night we bring
The passion of a lost soul's triumphing:
All rich with faery airs that, wandering long
Uncaught, here gather into Irish song;
Sweet as the old remembering winds that wail
From hill to hill of gracious Inisfail;
Sad as the unforgetting winds that pass
Over her children in her holy grass
At home, and sleeping well upon her breast,
Where snowy Déidre and her sorrows rest.

Another tale we tell you: how a man,
Filled with high dreams, his race of longing ran,
Haunted by fair and infinite desire;
Whose life was music, yet a wounding fire.
Stern is the story: welcome it no less,
Aching and lofty in its loveliness.
Come, then, and keep with us an Irish feast,
Wherein the Lord of Light and Song is priest;
Now, at this opening of the gentle May,
Watch warring passions at their storm and play;
Wrought with the flaming ecstasy of art,
Sprung from the dreaming of an Irish heart.

Lionel Johnson

The stables, Rockingham [Lawrence Collection, National Library of Ireland]

Prologue to *The Countess Cathleen* and *The Heather Field, in Beltaine*: The organ of the Irish Literary Theatre
52 (Dublin 1899) p.5.

LIONEL JOHNSON was born in Broadstairs, Kent in 1867. A friend of Yeats from Rhymers' Club days, he lived up to the fin-de-siécle reputation of dying young, a catholic, and of drink (1902). Influenced by Yeats and West of Ireland atmosphere, he was the appropriate man to write the verse prologue to the first programme of the Irish Literary Theatre which presented on May 8, 1899, *The Countess Cathleen* by Mr Yeats and on May 9 *The Heather Field* by Mr Martyn.

Moore Hall, burned down in the Civil War was the home of George Henry Moore, the father of the famous George Augustus, part of whose contribution to the Irish Literary Theatre was the 'doctoring' of Edward Martyn's rather ungainly plays for the stage. The father was that rather anomalous creature a catholic landlord who was able to nurse his tenants through the famine years when they could not pay rents because of his winning £10,000 on his horse Coranna in the Chester Cup in 1846. HIs mercurial son was a very special kind of absentee landlord, refusing to forsake the artists colony in Paris for his paternal acres in Mayo.

53

The light of evening, Lissadell,
Great windows, open to the south,
Two girls in silk kimonos, both
Beautiful, one a gazelle.
But a raving autumn shears
Blossom from the summer's wreath;
The older is condemned to death,
Pardoned, drags out lonely years
Conspiring among the ignorant.
I know not what the younger dreams —
Some vague Utopia — and she seems,
When withered old and skeleton-gaunt,
An image of such politics.
Many a time I think to seek
One or the other out and speak
Of that old Georgian mansion, mix
Pictures of the mind, recall
That table and the talk of youth,
Two girls in silk kimonos, both
Beautiful, one a gazelle.

Dear shadows, now you know it all,
All the folly of a fight
With a common wrong or right.
The innocent and the beautiful
Have no enemy but time;
Arise and bid me strike a match
And strike another till time catch;
Should the conflagration climb,
Run till all the sages know.
We the great gazebo built,
They convicted us of guilt;
Bid me strike a match and blow.

October 1927

W. B. Yeats, In memory of Eva Gore-Booth and Con Markiewicz, from *The Winding Stair and Other Poems* (London 1933)

THE POLLEXFENS were at best small gentry so the young Yeats would not have visited Lissadell House as part of his social round, but he had always admired the house which he could see from Rosses Point. When in 1894 he was invited to lecture at the school house on the estate, he met Eva Gore-Booth and her even more beautiful sister Con, whom he fancied looked like Maud Gonne. The pleasure of those days when he had his first taste of the 'accustomed, ceremonious' life remained with him always so that thirty years afterwards he could still remember these 'comets'.

54 Certainly they influenced his life and work and led him to take the first steps on the road to Coole.

Eva and Constance Gore-Booth Co-operating. (*Kilgannon Collection, Sligo Museum*)

ONE REMEMBERS EVERYTHING better than the moment of ecstasy - the colour of the rooms, their shapes, the furniture, all is seen by me to-day as truly as if the reality were before me; the very wood we burned in the great fireplace, the shapes of one log, how it fell into ashes at one end leaving a great knotted stump at the other, the moving of the candles into shadowy places so that the light should not fall upon our eyes - all these details are remembered, only the moment of ecstasy is forgotten. It is a pity that this is so. But I remember how I stood at the foot of the bed bidding her good-night, for the moment comes when all lovers must part, unless indeed they are married folk 'who occupy the same room.' The occupation of the same room, one of the most important questions in love's economy, was being treated when the pink waiter brought in our dinner; and the reader will remember that I was telling Doris how those learned in love had told me that he who has not waked up in the morning with his beloved seeing the sunlight in the window, hearing the birds in the branches, does not know the rapture of love, the enchantment of its intimacy. The sympathetic reader will not have forgotten this avowal, and his instinct leaping forward he will have seen me standing triumphant on the summit of all earthly love; therefore the admission that, feeling myself falling asleep, I bade Doris good-night at the foot of the bed will have cast him into the slough of despond from which my narrative, however lively it may prove, may fail to lift him. But though I did not realise the sacred moment at Orelay, and consequently will never realise it, in this world at least, that moment which, with the music of harps, Wagner depicts so completely, when Siegfried's kiss awakes Brunnhilde and she opens her eyes to the beauty of the world, I learned nevertheless at Orelay that my friend who said I was but a novice, a mere acolyte in Love's service, was not wholly wrong in his criticism of my life, for waking suddenly after sleeping for some hours, I heard Doris trying the handle of my door, and I called to ask her if she were seeking anything. She said she wished to know the time; there was no clock in her room, but there was one on my chimney-piece. It seemed so kind of her to come to my room that I could not refrain from taking her in my arms, and I told her that I had never seen a woman so early in the morning before. This pleased her, for she did not wish our love to be sullied with memories of other women. She shed such a delight about me that morning that I sought her the following morning in her room, and that visit, too, is remembered, though it is less distinct in my mind than her visit to my room. When I left her to dress myself she came running in to tell me something she had forgotten to tell me, and she sat watching me while I shaved, laughing at the absurdity, for it was absurd that she should always have something to say to me. No sooner had she gone than something awoke in my mind too, something I had unfortunately forgotten to say, and I had to rush back and to beg of her to let me open the door, though she was in her bath.

56

Right: *The Library, Renvyle Hotel, Co. Galway*

GEORGE AUGUSTUS MOORE was born at his father's house Moore Hall, Lough Carra, Co. Mayo in 1852. *Enfant terrible* of the Irish Renaissance, gadfly of 'dear Edward' Martyn, his account of his Irish adventure in *Hail and Farewell* (1914) makes very entertaining if scandalously inaccurate reading. His most significant Irish works are *The Untilled Field* (1902) — a seminal collection of short-stories, deliberate models for the new Irish writers, and *The Lake* (1905).

In his preface to the 1914 edition of *The Untilled Field* he writes, 'It must have been somewhere at the end of the nineties, not unlikely in ninety-nine, that dear Edward said to me in the Temple: 'I should like to write my plays in Irish.' And it was not long afterwards, in the beginning of 1900, that Yeats persuaded him to come to Ireland to found a literary theatre. In search of a third person, they called on me in

I know a statue of a woman leaning forward wiping her thighs, and that was the movement I discovered Doris in. The statue is a stupid thing, lacking in personal observation; all that the sculptor had omitted I perceived in Doris, but the comparison only floated across my mind; the delight of seeing her naked absorbed me, and I thought of other things, of Fragonard, for Fragonard realised what a little thing a woman is compared with a man, and this was just the idea that Doris conveyed; her great mass of hair made her look smaller than she really was, her head seemed too large for her body, yet this seeming, for it was no more than a seeming, did not detract from her beauty; she was as charming as if she had looked the regulation seven-and-a-half heads, for she was a Fragonard - an eighteenth century bedfellow, that is what she was . . . She bid me away. No one had ever seen her in her bath before; she did not like it; no, she did not! And thinking how charming these subterfuges were, how little love would be without them, I heard her calling, saying that she would be with me in ten minutes, that I was to ring and tell the waiter to bring up our first breakfast.

George Moore, *Memoirs of my Dead Life*, (London, 1906), pp 207-8

Victoria Street, and it is related in *Ave** how we packed our bags and went away to do something. We all did something, but none did what he set out to do. Yeats founded a realistic theatre, Edward emptied two churches — he and Palestrina between them — and I wrote *The Untilled Field*, a book written in the beginning out of no desire of self-expression, but in the hope of furnishing the young Irish of the future with models.'

The Lake is less naturalistic and much more consciously symbolic. When the priest-hero dives in the lake to come out on the other bank lay and free, it is obviously Ireland he is washing off him as much as his celibacy. Even here Moore's sense of mischief did not desert him; he called his hero Oliver Gogarty, another oblique claim to literary fame for the Buck Mulligan of *Ulysses*. He died on January 21, 1933 in his famous Ebury Street house in Victoria.

*The first of the three volume, Ave, Salve, Vale of *Hail and Farewell*   **57**

LORD SHRULE, *an elderly benevolent-looking man dressed in a somewhat old-fashioned riding costume*, MILES TYRRELL, *and* CARDEN TYRRELL *enter by the door at right.*

LORD SHRULE: Now that the inspector has gone out again to his work, I must say, my dear Carden, I am astounded at hearing of this new expenditure you contemplate. I did not like to speak before him — Ah, Ussher, how do you do? (*To* KIT.) And how is my little man?

KIT: (*Holding out his hand.*): Very well, thanks —

LORD SHRULE: That's right, that's right. I was saying, my dear Carden, your fresh project of expenditure fills me with amazement. Have you heard about it, Ussher?

USSHER: I have indeed.

LORD SHRULE: Well, does it not seem to you extremely imprudent — nay, reckless?

USSHER: Oh, you must not ask me, Lord Shrule. Carden seems determined. And, after all, he is the best judge of his own affairs.

TYRRELL: Yes, Barry, that is just it.

LORD SHRULE: Come, come, Carden, you will not mind the advice of an old man who has a long experience in the management of land. Your father and I were always fast friends, and I naturally take a great interest in you and your family.

TYRRELL: I know you have always been very kind, Lord Shrule. Forgive me if I have spoken hastily. I did not mean —

LORD SHRULE: Of course not, my dear Carden — I quite understand you. I fear indeed you must think it rather impertinent of your friends to interfere in your business. But then, as I have said, I consider myself privileged.

TYRRELL: You may be quite sure, Lord Shrule, I could not take anything from you except in good part.

LORD SHRULE: I thought so. Well, let me implore of you, if only for the sake of your family, to desist. This is certainly the wildest scheme I ever heard of, and couldn't pay, even if the drainage were to turn out a success.

TYRRELL: But you forget it is necessary now that the drainage of the heather field falls into this land. There is the cutting through it for the water to get to the sea. Now, what is easier than to reclaim the land through which this cutting goes?

LORD SHRULE: My dear Carden, don't mind the cutting — don't mind the heather field. What you have only got to think of is to cease altogether from loading your estate with an ever-growing burden of debt. For goodness' sake leave these works alone. If you continue them you will simply beggar yourself.

TYRRELL: (*Uneasily.*): I do not see that at all. The work will be very remunerative. It will double the value of the estate.

LORD SHRULE: Oh, Carden listen to me. I know well the nature of such works as you are carrying on. I have tried them myself — on a far smaller scale, of course. They never repay their expenditure.

TYRRELL: That is a mere assertion unsupported by argument. On the other hand, I have excellent reasons why I should believe that what I am about to undertake must have the best results. Look at the rich pasture now in the heather field. And am I to suppose that I shall not have the same in the valley when it is reclaimed? Until you can prove logically that I am mistaken, I must continue those works, which I clearly see are so profitable. Am I not right, Barry?

USSHER: I have said I shall never again discourage you, Carden.

LORD SHRULE: Ussher, upon my word I thought you knew better. But I suppose it is useless remonstrating with our friend about his experiments, which amount to seeming mania.

Edward Martyn, *The Heather Field* (produced Dublin, 1899)

EDWARD MARTYN was born at Masonbrook, Loughrea in 1859. He became co-founder and namer of the Irish Literary Theatre. Certainly the most generous and cultured of the group, his knowledge of European art and theatre was put at the disposal of his wilder colleagues, Moore and Yeats. Like Moore he was a catholic landlord with a house Tulira Castle in south Galway (an ancestor had been exempted from the Penal Laws) and he bore the expenses of launching the venture that was to become the Abbey Theatre. He was much more at the mercy of his conscience and consequently much more susceptible to attacks upon the 'immorality' of such plays as *The Countess Cathleen*. His own play (after Ibsen) *The Heather Field* followed *The Countess Cathleen* on the second night (May 9, 1899) as the first presentations of The Irish Literary Theatre at the Antient Concert Rooms in Brunswick (now Pearse) Street Dublin. When the Abbey went popular and realistic he founded his own amateur company, The Hardwicke Street Theatre where he staged the first Dublin productions of Chekov, Strindberg and Ibsen. His other great contribution to Irish cultural life was the advocacy of church music, especially that of Palestrina, and the establishment of the annual Féis Ceóil in 1897. He died in 1923 after willing his body for research.

The Earl of Lucan at Castlebar 1895
(*Wynne Collection*)

The Bingham family became Earls of Lucan in 1795 and took as their motto, 'Spes Mea Christus.' The subject of the photograph is the Third Earl who owned in all 60,000 acres in Mayo. A visiting journalist remarked in 1881 that he was absent too often, that his home farm was not well-managed and that his town of Castlebar was badly developed.

Hooker (centre picture) owned by the Healy brothers, Galway Harbour, 1894

TOWNS

"IF THESE are your views your mother will have to think of something else for you, Martha."

"I was up in Conarchy's shop yesterday," Martha Lee went on, "taking it all in. There were people there having themselves fitted out. Some of them were emigrants. I waited, observing the milliner attending them, imagining myself in her place. One party in a shawl, stout and with a little wobble in the walk - she came in like this" — Martha took a little comical trot down the room — "leaned across the counter and whispered to the milliner, and the milliner whispered back. They began to nod and smile and agree with each other, and I thought in the end they would fall into each other's arms and kiss. 'But the shape - what kind of a shape would we be saying?' the milliner asked sweetly at last. The stout party gave her a thump in the neck. 'You're a devil, I hear, for the Paris fashions,' says she, 'but you'll not make a show of me, for when I do wear a headpiece I do like to feel that it has a good hoult of me. Now give me out a nice bonnet with good jawstrings to it.'"

Ellen Noonan could not keep serious any longer. Martha Lee's mimicries were too good.

"When the stout party had gone with her handbox," Martha Lee went on, 'a couple of young chits from the town came fluttering in. They wore their hats on the last angle of their polls - airy pieces got up to look as if the next chance breeze that blew would waft them all up to the heavens. They were giggling, or trying to suppress giggling, as they stood at the counter. One of the party addressed the milliner in an accent that sounded as if the Reverend Mother had just handed it out over the wall of the most select boarding school in the land for young ladies of high breeding. They had to pull down all the boxes in the place for the inspection of the young ladies. The whole stock-in-trade of the shop was reviewed, and then they bought a pennyworth of elastic, and went giggling out of the shop. They were followed by a family which was sending one of its daughters to Philadelphia from her mountain home. Her face was as hard as a board, her light brown hair lay in little lumps about her head, wisps of it streeling down her face. She looked exactly as if her clothes were bundled about her and tied in the middle with a rope - a sack of a slovenly, pugnacious-looking agricultural apparition. It was the very devil to please her. She stood viewing herself in the mirror, a hat with a blaze of colours lying lop-sided on her head. 'Do you like it?' asked one of her friends. 'I do and I don't,' she said. 'I think I'd like something livelier.' Then her mother said: 'Julia, it's crooked. Give it a twisht more to the wesht.'"

Ellen Noonan laughed until the bed shook under her at the scathing tongue, the splendid acting of the other. Then she shook her head.

"You won't do as a milliner, Martha," she said.

Martha Lee paced up and down the room, her hands behind her back, a magnificent-looking, angry pantheress.

Seamus O'Kelly, *Wet Clay*, (Dublin, 1919) pp 118-19

Right.*Wynne's Photography Shop, Loughrea* Left: *House next door (Wynne Collection, Castlebar)*

(*A man carrying an antique camera with its trivet and black cloth enters through the gate. He has a beard and sharp eyes behind spectacles.*)

PHOTOGRAPHER (*to* CRILLY): I'm not mistaken, am I, in figuring that an important event is taking place here to-day? (*Leaving down the apparatus he takes a professional look at the yard and the persons.*) Confirmations, Confraternity Meetings, Ordinations, Weddings — I record them in my own special manner. Single photograph one shilling and sixpence, group two shillings and sixpence. I am Bartholomew Vincent Murann, Photographer to the Maharajah of Judpur.

CRILLY: That's a long way off.

MURANN: I travel. Recently I was where His Highness and suite were on a liner bound for the United States. They stepped on Irish ground. He gave me his patronage then. (*Turning to* CRILLY *with an album.*) You'll find the photographs there, sir. (CRILLY *takes album.*) I thought I might take the photograph here before the assembling of the First Communion class.

CRILLY: What photograph?

MURANN: The new Master of the Workhouse.

CRILLY: 'Pon my word, you fellows are ready for the drop kick! He has only been appointed.

MURANN: First day in office! Something to show in the parlour in after years! Ah, what a wonderful thing is the camera! What it can hand down to posterity! — And so reasonable in price!

TOURNOUR: I'll get my own likeness taken at the reasonable price of one and sixpence.

CRILLY: A picture of Tournour, no less!

TOURNOUR: To put in the Ward Master's office.

CRILLY: Office?

TOURNOUR: If there isn't an office, I'll get one.

CRILLY (*in disgust*): Give him the Workhouse!

MURANN: What a picturesque nook this is! A setting indeed! The grey old walls! The massive doorway! Something that's like . . . Well, well, who knows what it's like? If there was some figure there!

(THOMAS MUSKERRY *comes on the steps.* By Jove, that's it! That's it! The Master!

CRILLY: Not the Master you want.

MURANN (*to* MUSKERRY): Stay, sir! Don't move (MUSKERRY *in astonishment keeps his position.*)

CRILLY: HE's retired — he's not Master any more

MURANN: He's the proper figure for the Master standing there! Oh, sir, would you keep you stand just for a minute. A photograph of you i required!

(*He sets up his apparatus.*)

MUSKERRY: May I ask who you are, sir?

MURANN: Bartholomew Vincent Murann, photographer at large.

MUSKERRY: Has this been ordered?

(*The photographer is now busy getting blac cloth over his head and the camera.*)

MUSKERRY: The Guardians aren't as neglectful a I thought.

TOURNOUR: At one-and-sixpence to you, Miste Muskerry.

(MUSKERRY *notices him but says nothng* CRILLY *opens the album that had been give him.*)

MURANN: The Maharajah and his suite. An passengers from our port on the gangway.

CRILLY: Passengers! I'd like to see myself amongs them!

MURANN: Splendid position! Just a little to th right. I'll have you dominate the prospect.

(*Under the black cloth there are hurrie movements.* CHRISTY CLARKE *enters whee ing a barrow.* CRILLY *finds something in th album that startles him.*)

CRILLY: God in heaven! What am I looking at? I isn't Covey! On the gangway of a liner fc America! If that's him, it will be the end of me

(*The photographer comes from under the blac cloth.*)

MURANN: I'm proud, sir, proud of having th opportunity of obtaining such a striking photc graph. It will be looked on as a work of art. Ther you are, a majestic figure, if I may say so, wit the wall of the establishment you officiated in a your back. A worthy memento this will be!

MUSKERRY: The Board of Guardians can put under it what was publically stated — "The pattern of officials of Ireland."

TOURNOUR: Maybe they will and maybe they won't.

MUSKERRY (*coming to him*): Tournour!

TOURNOUR: Humbly asking the pardon of the retired Master of Garrisowen Workhouse!!

Padraic Colum, 'Thomas Muskerry' in *Plays* (Dublin 1966)

PADRAIC COLUM was born in Longford in 1881 and was son of the workhouse master of that town. Now known, perhaps unfortunately, as the author of such heavily-anthologised pieces as *The Old Woman of the Roads*, *A Drover*, and *Cradle Song*, since they have obscured his fame as dramatist and folklorist. He was one of the earliest of the Abbey playwrights and his play *Thomas Muskerry* (1909) was one of those which determined the theatre's future as a home of naturalistic drama. Most of his later life was spent in America. He died in 1972.

Castlebar Asylum Attendants, 1898 (Wynne Collection)

HE REACHED THE MARKET town while it was yet morning. He led the creel of turf through the straggling streets, where some people with the sleep in their eyes were moving about. The only sound he made was a low word of encouragement to the donkey.

"How much for the creel?" a man asked, standing at his shop door.

"Six shilling," Denis Donohoe replied, and waited, for it was above the business of a decent turf-seller to praise his wares or press for a sale.

"Good luck to you, son," said the merchant, "I hope you'll get it." He smiled, folded his hands one over the other, and retired to his shop.

Denis Donohoe moved on, saying in an undertone to the donkey, "Gee-up, Patsy. That old fellow is no good."

There were other inquiries, but nobody purchased. They said that money was very scarce. Denis Donohoe said nothing; money was too remote a thing for him to imagine how it could be ever anything else except scarce. He grew tired of going up and down past shops where there was no sign of business, so he drew the side streets and laneways, places where children screamed about the road, where there was a scent of soapy water, where women came to their doors and looked at him with eyes that expressed a slow resentment, their arms bare above the elbows, their hair hanging dankly about their ears, their voices, when they spoke, monotonous, and always sounding a note of tired complaint.

On the rise of a little bridge Denis Donohoe met a red-haired woman, a family of children skirmishing about her; there was a battle light in her wolfish eyes, her idle hands were folded over her stomach.

"How much, gossoon?" she asked.

"Six shilling."

"Six devils!" She walked over to the creel, handling some of the sods of turf. Denis Donohoe knew she was searching a constitutionally abusive mind for some word contemptuous of his wares. She found it at last, for she smacked her lips. It was in the Gaelic.

"*Spairteach*!" she cried - a word that was eloquent of bad turf, stuff dug from the first layer of the bog, a mere covering for the correct vein beneath it.

"It's good stone turf," Denis Donohoe protested, a little nettled.

The woman was joined by some people who were hanging about, anxious to take part in bargaining which involved no personal liability. They argued, made jokes, shouted, and finally began to bully Denis Donohoe, the woman leading, her voice half a scream, her stomach heaving, her eyes dancing with excitement, a yellow froth gathering at the corners of her angry mouth, her hand gripping a sod of the turf, for the only dissipation life now offered her was this haggling with and shouting down of turf sellers. Denis Donohoe stood immovable beside his cart, patient as his donkey, his swarthy face stolid under the shadow of his broad-brimmed black hat, his intelligent eyes quietly measuring his noisy antagonists. When the woman's anger had quite spent itself the turf was purchased for five shillings.

Séumas O'Kelly, *Waysiders* (Dublin, 1917) pp 42-45

SÉUMAS O'KELLY born in Loughrea Co. Galway in 1881, is chiefly remembered nowadays as the author of the story *The Weaver' Grave* which as a radio play by Micheal O hAodha won the Italia Prize in 1961, but in his time was an active Nationalist journalist, friend of Arthur Griffith, pre-Abbey realistic dramatist, short-story writer and novelist. His best play, The *Shuiler's Child* anticipates such melodramas as *The Year of the Hiker*. His death in November 1918, after harrassment by British soldiers, has caused him to be regarded as a martyr for the cause and he was honoured by a national funeral. *Wet Clay*, his best novel, was published posthumously in 1919.

Waysiders, subtitled 'Stories of Connacht', contains some of O'Kelly's best stories. Though a Nationalist in politics he had no illusions about the realities of Irish life and his clear view of the drudgery of farm life anticipates Brinsley MacNamara and Paddy Kavanagh.

'Tuam, once the Metropolitan See of Connaught, is a very ancient place; and if the residence of two archbishops, one of whom was generally associated with the aristocracy, and possessed of princely revenues, and each of whom had a numerous staff of clergy, could make a small town neat and prosperous, Tuam ought to be a model of comfort, order and beauty. But it has, unfortunately always been the reverse.'
J Godkin and J Walker, *Handbook of Ireland* (Dublin c. 1870)

The Square, Tuam (Lawrence Collection, The National Library of Ireland)

Castle Street, Sligo (Lawrence Collection, National Library of Ireland)

Mary Davenport O'Neill was the wife of Joseph O'Neill the novelist. Born in Galway in 1893 she has written verse plays as well as poetry. The poem 'Galway' is strictly speaking outside our period, but that part of the city is so timeless, and the poem so evocative, that we could not exclude it.

SWIFTLY WE GLIDE over the salt water estuary of Lough Athalia, into the great terminus of Galway, at 1.45 o'clock, and out through it into the enormous limestone hotel, built, 'regardless of expense' by the original directors of the railway; and from whence, 'after a bit and a sup', we emerge among the beggars into Eyre Square, surrounded by hotels, club-houses, banks, private residences and coach offices, where the great 'Bian' can forward us 'anywhere', and in which we can choose our newspaper according to our politics or polemics.''

Sir William Wilde: *Lough Corrib* (Dublin 1967)

Right: *Eyre Square, Galway (Lawrence Collection, National Library of Ireland)*

The monument is to Lord Dunkellin and was erected in 1873 and removed in 1922. As often, in 'spontaneous demonstration of affection', the tenants were forced by levy to contribute.

I KNOW a town tormented by the sea,
And there time goes slow
That the people see it flow
And watch it drowsily,
And growing older hour by hour they say,
'Please God, to-morrow!
Then we will work and play,'
And their tall houses crumble away.
This town is eaten through with memory
Of pride and thick red Spanish wine and gold
And of great come and go;
But the sea is cold,
And the spare, black trees
Crouch in the withering breeze
That blows from the sea,
And the land stands bare and alone,
For its warmth is turned away
And its strength held in hard cold grey-blue stone;
And the people are heard to say,
Through the raving of the jealous sea,
'Please God, to-morrow!
Then we will work and play.'

Mary Davenport O'Neill, 'Galway' from *Prometheus*
(Dublin, 1929)

Newport, Co. Mayo

S.S. Duras Galway (Lawrence Collection,
National Library of Ireland)

EDITH SOMERVILLE was born in Corfu in 1858 but apart from deliberately undertaken tours for the purposes of collecting copy spent most of her life in Munster and Connacht. She was the quintessential Anglo-Irish centaur and was the extravert partner of the two. *Violet Martin* was born at Ross, Co. Galway in 1862. More aware of John Bull's Other Ireland than Edith who lived in quasi-English close quarters in Castletownshend, Co. Cork, she supplied the depth, the gothic element and the self-critical humour. Their most famous books, *The Irish RM Stories* began simply as hunting sketches but developed into pieces of social history. Their finest novel, *The Real Charlotte* was published in three volumes in 1894. Edith continued to write after Violet's death of cancer in 1915 and still used the imprint Somerville and Ross, claiming that Violet's spirit was constantly with her. Attempts to form the same kind of non-physical passionate friendship with Dame Ethel Smyth did not succeed. She died at Castletownshend in 1949.

Market Day, Clifden, Lawrence Collection (National Library of Ireland)

"WHOEVER SAYS thim throuts isn't leppin' fresh out o' the lake he's a dom liar, and it's little I think of tellin' it t'ye up to yer nose! There's not one in the counthry but knows yer thricks and yer chat, and ye may go home out o' that, with yer bag sthrapped round ye, and ye can take the tay-leaves and the dhrippin' from the servants, and huxther thim to feed yer cats, but thanks be to God ye'll take nothing out o' my basket this day!"

There was a titter of horrified delight from the crowd.

"Ye never spoke a truer word than that, Mary Norris," replied a voice that sent a chill down Christopher's back; "When I come into Lismoyle, it's not to buy rotten fish from a drunken fish-fag, that'll be begging for crusts at my halldoor to-morrow. If I hear another word out of yer mouth I'll give you and your fish to the police, and the streets'll be rid of you and yer infernal tongue for a week, at all events, and the prison'll have a treat that it's pretty well used to!"

Another titter rewarded this sally, and Charlotte, well pleased, turned to walk away. As she did so, she caught sight of Christopher, looking at her with an expression from which he had not time to remove his emotions, and for a moment she wished that the earth would open and swallow her up. She reddened visibly, but recovered herself, and at once made her way out into the street towards him.

"How are you again, Mr. Dysart? You just came in time to get a specimen of the *res angusta domi*," she said, in a voice that contrasted almost ludicrously with her last utterances. "People like David, who talk about the advantages of poverty, have probably never tried buying fish in Lismoyle. It's always the way with these drunken old hags. They repay your charity by impudence and bad language, and one has to speak pretty strongly to them to make one's meaning penetrate to their minds."

Her eyes were still red and swollen from her violent crying at the funeral. But for them, Christopher could hardly have believed that this was the same being whom he had last seen on the sofa at Tally Ho, with the black gloves and the sal volataile.

"Oh yes, of course," he said vaguely; "everyone has to undergo Mary Norris some time or other. If you are going back to Tally Ho now, I can drive you there."

"No thank you, Mr Dysart. I'm not done my marketing yet, but Francie's at home and she'll give you tea. Don't wait for me. I've no appetite for anything to-day. I only came out to get a mouthful of fresh air, in hopes it might give me a better night, though, indeed, I've small chance of it after what I've gone through."

Christopher drove on, and tried not to think of Miss Mullen or of his mother or Pamela, while his too palpably discreet hostess elbowed her way through the crowd in the opposite direction.

Somerville and Ross *The Real Charlotte* (London 1894)

The Fish Market, Galway, seen from the west with the Spanish Arch in the background and the old Claddagh Footbridge. (Lawrence Collection, National Library of Ireland)

SUDDENLY A MELODIOUS STRAIN floated out over the sunlit water, and the music of a delicious female voice carolling a Celtic song was borne on the air.

It was a simple, artless song, a quaint old Irish ballad telling of the sorrowful loves of a certain fair MacDermott and a certain dark O'Rourke, and yet the enchantress Lurline, seated on her mossy rock beside the Rhine, could scarce have poured forth a more tender and bewitching melody than this, which seemed like the harmony of silver bells tinkled by music-loving fairies in some bosky dell beside the water.

The melody proceeded from beneath the shade of a magnificent sycamore that grew on the verge of the shore. There, on the trunk of a prostrate tree, were seated an old man and a maiden, and it was from the red lips of the latter that the stream of song was flowing.

The old man, who wore the high conical cap (or *fileadh*) and flowing robes of an Irish bard, was a venerable, white-haired patriarch, with a majesty akin to that of one of the giant trees of the primeval wood that stood at his back, robed with trailing ivy and hoary with moss. Manus O'Cuirnin had long followed the profession of seanachie — a combination of bard, story-teller, and historian — and his was long the place of honour at the feasts of the neighbouring Irish chieftains. But now his palsied fingers refused to touch the harp-strings as they had been wont, his shoulders were bowed with the weight of nigh a century, and he who had seen generation after generation pass away lived in daily and almost hourly expectation of the summons which was to open to him the the gates of another world. He had had two sons both of whom were gone before him to the grave: one perishing in the war in Flanders, the other dying at home. The latter had left two children, a son and a daughter, the daughter being the fair young songstress who now sat by her grandsire's side.

Despite the seanachie's great age his sight was almost unimpaired, and he was now poring over an old yellow manuscript. It was only when the maiden's song ceased that he raised his eyes from the black lines of Celtic characters.

"Gillamachree," he said, turning to his young companion, "I feel as if I were thirty years younger when I listen to your sweet voice, and the blood runs right warmly through my old veins. You remind me of the bird whose singing raised St. Fursey to the gate of heaven. What would I do at all without you avourneen?"

He laid his feeble hand caressingly on her head. A dainty, graceful little head it was — a head crowned

PATRICK G. SMYTH was born in Ballina in 1857 and became a teacher before emigrating to America and a life of journalism. His verse and novels are nineteenth-century romantic and like Lily MacManus and Grace Rhys he turned to earlier happier periods in Irish history for his plots. *King and Viking* (1889) was about the Norse invasions and his best-known novel, wildly popular at the time of publication, *The Wild Rose of Lough Gill* (1904) dealt with the brief bright glory of Owen Roe O'Neill. It is rather romantic and sentimental by modern tastes. Influenced by the newly formed Gaelic League and residual Connacht usage he incorporates many Irish words in his text.

with the natural "glory of woman," a wealth of hair that, bound by the simple ribbon of maidenhood, streamed down the owner's back in a mass of glossy brown tresses. She was barely sixteen, a brunette, and singularly handsome. Her beauty was of that sweet, piquant, peculiarly Celtic type that is so racy of the Irish soil. A perfect embodiment she looked of fresh young health, of gazelle-like grace and vigour — and the spirit of the seanachie's grandchild was pure as the wholesome air that breathed around her.

A shawl of dark woollen stuff was gracefully draped round her shoulders and fastened on one of them by a silver brooch representing a cluster of interwined serpents. Old Manus was dressed in his parti-coloured costume of Irish bard; and the pair made a quite picturesque little group — a group very suggestive of May and December.

"Now, grandfather mine," she replied, with a light laugh, "I fear you have too high an opinion of me. You praise my singing — you who taught me how to sing, ay, and to play your clairseach, too. You compare me to the bird of St. Fursey. Alas! 'tis not my poor voice can raise your mind to heaven."

"It can, asthore, and so can your face, for your bright eyes make me think of my poor dead Nuala, who is now with the saints — ay, brings her to my memory not as you saw her, ma colleen, a withered old vanithee, but a merry, handsome girl like yourself. Ah, wirrasthrue! wirrasthrue!" continued the old man, mournfully, "that was a long, long time ago. The old people are all gone, acushla, all gone; — but I'll soon follow them, and the gray worn heart shall have rest at last."

Patrick G. Smyth, *The Wild Rose of Lough Gill* (Dublin, 1883) pp2,3.

Killary Harbour Leenane (Lawrence Collection National Library of Ireland)

78 *Going to Hazelwood Races, Sligo* [*Kilgannon Collection, Sligo Museum*]

POLITICS

CONSTANCE GORE-BOOTH, later Countess Marciewicz, was the great heroine figure of the 1916 Rising. A very beautiful young woman, she fascinated the young Yeats and sorely disappointed the Anglo-Irish when she espoused the national cause. She was the first woman to be elected to the British House of Commons but did not take her seat. She was Minister for Labour in the Republican Government in 1919.

Constance, Countess Marciewicz, New York 1922 (Sligo Museum)

FLANAGHAN'S FLYING MACHINE

'Twas Flanagan found out the secret of flight,
And made such a perfect affair,
That Farman and Bleriot, Latham and White
Proclaimed him the King o' the air.
And, mind you, I think he deserved his success
For really he worked very hard;
Six days out of seven his private address
Was — the Hospital Accident Ward.
But soon he was safe and serene
And every day could be seen
By admiring crowds,
Leppin' over the clouds
In his marvellous flying machine.

Said the Kaiser — "On Britain I'm going to pounce
Like a terrier dog on a rat".
Said his officers — "Do, and you'll get the grand bounce,
For you're talking too much through your hat."
Said the Kaiser — "There's nothing on earth you'll allow
My army and fleet can defy."
Said his officers — "Nothin' on earth, sire, but how
About something up there in the sky?"
Said the Kaiser — "I know what you mean
Though faith! I'd forgotten it clean,
The war is postponed
While the atmosphere's owned
By Flanaghan's flying machine."

Percy French

One of the characteristic features of Percy French was his total acceptance of modern systems of transport for all their mechanical inefficiency. Such songs as 'Jim Wheelahan's Automobeel' (1903) and 'Maguire's Motor Bike' (1906) were popular with audiences who affected to disregard, envied and in time accepted the new-fangled. 'Flanagan's Flying Machine' written soon after Bleriot's successful English Channel flight, is typical of this happy opportunism.

Royal Flying Corps, Castlebar (*Wynne Collection, Castlebar*)
RFC contingent outside a hangar at Castlebar Aerodrome, c. 1918.
Though Baldonnel was the main Irish airfield there were several other bases

about the country.

THE VALUE OF PATSY

The old lady had asked to see the recruiting officer, and that functionary was now interviewing her.

"What can I do for you, mother? Want to enlist?" he inquired jocularly.

"Bedad no, sorr," said the visitor. "Oi wants to know whether me bhoy Patsy has 'listed."

"Patsy Roonan?" asked the officer.

"Yis, sorr."

"Then he joined the Connaught Rangers yesterday."

"Ochone! ochone! Phwat'll Oi do now widout him!" howled Mrs. Roonan.

"Buy him out, mother," suggested the officer.

"Bedad, Oi nivir thought av that!" cried the old lady, producing a purse.

"How much, now, Captain, will yez take for Patsy?"

"Ten pounds is the price," smiled the officer.

"Tin pounds?" shrieked Patsy's mother. "Tin pounds for Patsy! Sure Oi thought a matter av half-a-crown would square it. But tin pounds! Ye've made a bad bargain, Captain, if ye think Patsy's worth that, an' ye can kape him."

THE SOLDIER WHO TURNED

Some time ago I enlisted in a Cavalry Regiment, in which I remained twelve months, recounts a soldier.

Things not being to my liking, however, I managed to secure a suit of "civvies" from a recruit who was sleeping his first night in barracks, and deserted.

I got to Dublin by degrees, and having spent all my money, was on my beam ends. Work and food were not to be had, so for a second time I made my way to the recruiting depot. A sergeant spotted me, and this time I chose The Connaught Rangers.

I had passed the doctor, when I was sent before the Sergeant-Major. The latter asked me the usual questions, which I answered in a straightforward fashion. Then he said, "Turn round, young man," and, not thinking, I "about turned" in soldier fashion, and put both feet into it with regulation click.

After that I put both feet into the guard room.

THE RANGER The journal of the Connaught Rangers (July 1914, Vol.2 No.3) p12.

Renmore Barracks, Galway [Lawrence Collection, National Library of Ireland]

The Military Barracks, Castlebar (*Wynne Collection*)

County of _Galway ER_   District of _Loughrea_

NAME,   P. J Kelly

OCCUPATION.   Farmer

RESIDENCE,   Grangepark. Killenadeema. Loughrea

Regd No. 221

PHOTOGRAPH

The above is a good likeness

DATE OF DESCRIPTION,	12 Nov 94
HEIGHT,	5 Ft. 7 ¾ In.
AGE,	45 Years.
Make,	Medium
Hair,	Very dark turning grey
Eyes,	Dark grey
Eyebrows,	Dark
Nose,	Thick. Cocked
Mouth,	Broad, thick lips
Complexion,	Dark
Visage,	Round. high cheek bones
Whiskers,	Small side
Moustache,	None
Beard,	None
Native Place,	Killenadeema. Galway

REMARKS—(Here insert particulars of eccentric habits. peculiarities of gait, manner, &c., and marks on person).

Round shoulders + stoops forward when Walking

No. of File.   OBSERVATIONS.

History has been submitted

"IT IS THE MERIT of the force that its civil efficiency is as great as that of any body of police in the empire, and in emergencies it has shown military efficiency equal to that of the best regular troops. . . There are at present about 12,600 men in the force and 300 officers. The number of barracks or stations is about 1,575."

James Macaulay: *Ireland in 1872* (London, 1873)

With the complete disintegration of the RIC in early 1922 it became obvious to Michael Collins that a new police force was urgently necessary. A new force, the Civic Guard, was established in February 1922, with Michael Staines as first Commissioner. 97% of early entrants were recruited on the advice of local IRA commanders but the structure was almost identical to that of the older force with one vital exception , they were unarmed.

RIC, Turlough, Co. Mayo (*Wynne Collection*)

Part of the 'Boycott Expedition' 1880 (Wynne Collection)

MATTERS HAD BEEN GROWING WORSE and worse since the day of his brother's death. The storm of indignation which his denouncement of Hurrish had created, far from subsiding, was growing louder and louder every day. Even at the funeral — which, despite the elder Brady's unpopularity, had been largely attended — not a soul had spoken to him. He had been tabooed, sent to Coventry — "boy-cotted," in short. He had returned the following day to Miltown-Malbay, but his position there was, he soon discovered, if possible worse, in so far that it brought him more forcibly into contact with others. So intolerable was it, that a few days afterwards he gave notice to the master of the shop, and left hastily. The sudden revulsion from popularity to contempt and execration was horrible to him. The very men who had admired, followed, imitated him, were now the loudest in denouncing him. The whole of that anti-English, anti-legal machinery which he had so often gloried in, which he counted so fully on making use of for his own ends, was turned against him. He was in direct opposition to the whole popular sentiment of the country. An informer! What more was there to be said?

There was something bewildering to a man like Maurice Brady in the suddenness of this downfall. He had been sailing along so successfully; so buoyantly confident of the future; so absolutely secure of his own powers. And now! The rapidity of the fall made him fell literally sick. He could have torn his hair, gnashed his teeth, and rolled over and over on **86** the ground from sheer bitterness of rage and disappointment. He was

In 1873 Captain Boycott became agent for the Lough Mask estates of Lord Erne. He was unpopular from the beginning and relations between himself and the tenants worsened in 1880 when, instigated by the local branch of the newly formed Land League, they presented him with a schedule of what they considered fair rents. In spite of 10% and later a 20% reduction on the rents of the previous November they persisted and when he ordered evictions on September 22 the process-servers were attacked and had to retreat to Lough Mask House, Boycott's own place. The campaign, organised along the lines suggested by Parnell in his famous 'leper of old' speech at Ennis a few days previously, was very successful. Boycott was ostracised — 'boycotted', in fact and it was not until two thousand Orangemen on expedition from Monaghan, heavily protected by police and soldiers, arrived at Ballinrobe that his harvest could be saved.

The Woodford Evictions took place on the Clanricarde estate in 1887. They were notable for the presence of the English Radical reformer and poet, Wilfred Scawen Blunt, who had organised the resistance, and spent two months in Galway Gaol for his pains. He describes his experience in his poem 'In Vinculis'.

EMILY LAWLESS, the daughter of Lord Cloncurry, was born in Kildare in 1845 but was devoted to the west of Ireland. She was acquainted with and had written about the Aran Islands well before Synge had thought of going there. *Grania* (1892) is sentimental but the islanders are not portrayed as they might well have been as uncouth, uncivilised people. Her novel *Hurrish* (1886) treats the Land War from the landlord's point of view and her rendering of dialogue is of the Samuel Lover, export-only kind. She is most acceptable to modern taste in her books of quasi-mystical poems. Best of these is *With the Wild Geese* (1902) which includes the sequence 'In the Aran Isles'. She died in 1913.

done for! That was the long and short of it. Everything was at an end. His career wrecked, finished before it had fairly begun. Not in Clare alone, but from one end of Ireland to the other, his name was the signal, he knew, for contempt and execration. Never would any Irish constituency open its doors to receive him; never would his voice be heard in the halls of Westminster, or anywhere nearer home; never would a single one of those visions of success and triumph, upon which he had floated so securely, now come true!

Emily Lawless, *Hurrish* (London, 1886) pp242-244

Dr. Tully's House after eviction, Woodford (Lawrence Collection, National Library of Ireland)

A MONSTER DEMONSTRATION in favour of the Land League movement, which sought to reform the Irish land laws, was held at Straide, County Mayo, on the 1st February, 1880. Mr. Michael Davitt was amongst the speakers, and a peculiar interest was attached to the meeting from the fact that the platform from which he spoke was erected over the very ruins of the old homestead from which he, with his father and mother, had been evicted many years before. On that occasion Mr. Davitt delivered the following speech:-

While every nerve must be strained to stave off, if possible, the horrible fate which befell our famine-slaughtered kindred in 1847 and 1848, the attention of our people must not for a moment be withdrawn from the primary cause of these periodical calamities nor their exertions be relaxed in this great social struggle for the overthrow of the odious system responsible for them. Portions of the English press had recently declared that the charity of Englishmen would be more spontaneous and generous if this agitation did not stand in the way. Well, Ireland's answer to this should be that she asks no English alms, and she scorns charity which is offered her in lieu of the justice which is her right and her demand. Let landlordism be removed from our country and labour be allowed the wealth which it creates instead of being given to legalised idlers, and no more famine will darken our land or hold Ireland up to the gaze of the civilised world as a nation of paupers. England deprives us annually of some seven millions of money for Imperial taxation, and she allows an infamous land system to rob our country of fifteen or twenty millions more each year to support some nine or twelve thousand lazy landlords, and then, when famine extends its destroying wings over the land, and the dread spectre of death stands sentinel at our thresholds, an appeal to English charity - a begging-box outside the London Mansion House - is paraded before the world, and expected to atone for every wrong inflicted upon Ireland by a heartless and hated Government, and to blot out the records of the most monstrous land code that ever cursed a country or robbed humanity of its birth-right. The press of England may bring whatever charges its prejudices can prompt against this land movement, the Duchess of Marlborough may hurl her gracious wrath at the heads of "heartless agitators," but neither the venomed scurrility of Government organs nor the jealous tirades of politico-prompted charity can rob the much-abused land movement of the credit attached to the following acts. The cry of distress and national danger was first raised by the agitators, and all subsequent action, Government, Viceregal, landlord, and mansion House, to alleviate that distress, was precipitated by the action of the "heartless agitators." The destroying hand of rackrenting and eviction was stricken down for the moment by the influence of the agitation, and the farmers of Ireland were spared some two or three millions with which to meet the distress now looming on

Agrarian calamity threatened Mayo in 1879. After hearing in Claremorris of the plight of the Irishtown tenants, Davitt got local Fenians to organise the meeting on April 20, 1879 which was to be an important step on the road to Westport (June 8) where Parnell advised tenants to 'hold a firm grip on your homesteads and lands'. This led in turn to the founding of the Land League of Mayo (August 16) and to the Irish National Land League, with Parnell as president on October 21. This was the New Departure made flesh.

Right: *Land League Meeting at the Mall, Castlebar, c. 1880* (*Wynne collection*)

their families and country, while the rooftrees of thousands of homesteads were protected from the crowbar brigade; and the civilised world has been appealed to against the existence of a land monopoly which is responsible for a pauperised country, a starved and discontented population, and every social evil now afflicting a patient and industrious people, until a consensus of home and foreign opinion has been evoked in favour of a lasting and efficacious remedy. With these services rendered to Ireland, with a resolve to do the utmost possible to save our people from the danger immediately threatening them, the "heartless agitators" will not relax a single effort or swerve one iota from their original purposes — to haul down the ensign of land monopoly and plant the banner of the "land for the people" upon the dismantled battlements of Irish landlordism.

Michael Davitt, "The crimes of Irish landlordism", from *Irish Bits* (August 13, 1898)

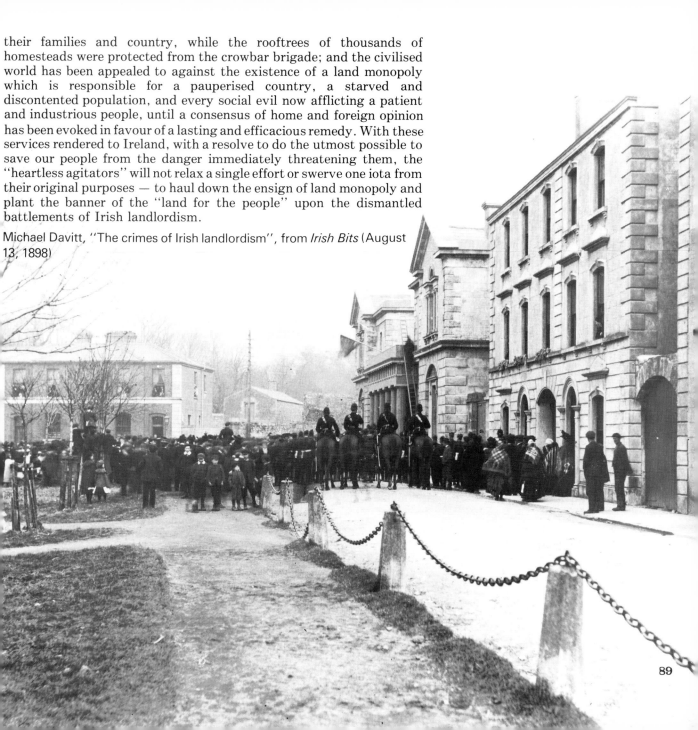

WE SOON SAW that the Republican Army was not going to do anything so desperate as attack. The men were gathering on the parade-ground for the much more agreeable purpose of listening to a speech. A motor-car drove up from the direction of Athlone, entered the camp by the east gate, and rolled across the grass to the parade-ground. There it stopped, and the orator, who was to provide the morning's entertainment, stood up on a seat. I noticed with some surprise that it was a woman.

The ancient Romans, according to Livy, always had speeches before battle, always long, always delivered in the most polished phrases. The Greeks — my recollections of Thucydides are a little vague — but I think the Greeks did the same thing. These classical orators were always generals, a fact which suggests that the course of study in the Staff Colleges of those days must have included elocution. Cromwell's Puritan soldiers liked sermons before and after battle, but the preachers were learned and more or less ordained clergymen, though very long-winded. The Irish system of listening to exhortations from women was new to me, and I felt interested in it. Genevieve and I passed the guardhouse, and made our way towards the parade-ground.

The speaker's back was turned to us and we could not hear what she was saying, but when we were within about fifty yards of her Genevieve suddenly clutched my arm.

"Aunt Josephine!" she said in a tense whisper.

Josephine — well named the Eloquent — was speaking with great force. I could see that she was waving her arms and flinging herself about in a way that imperilled her position on the seat of the car. We approached cautiously and were soon able to hear little bits of what she said, scraps of sentences which she shouted with particular emphasis. "Traitors to the memory of the dead" was a phrase which I heard three times in the course of ten minutes, and each time it sent a thrill down my spine. "The honour of Ireland," proclaimed with emotion which was unmistakably genuine, set my heart beating at far beyond its usual pace. Some one or other, I did not hear his name, had "sold the honour of Ireland." And

Josephine asked with austere dignity what profit man or nation could expect to find in gaining a whole world and losing its immortal soul. Her training as a Sunday-school teacher under Canon Sylvestre had not been entirely wasted. She still remembered several texts of Scripture. An unfortunate class of people whom she first described as "Lackeys of the English Crown," and later on as "Citizens of the

British Empire," were treated with ferocious derision.

"I wonder how long she'll go on," I whispered.

"Hours and hours and hours," said Genevieve. "She always does."

"Well," I replied, "we needn't stay for the whole of it. That's the advantage of not being in the front row. We can slip away whenever we like."

George A Birmingham, *Found Money*, (London, 1923)

GEORGE A BIRMINGHAM was the pen-name of Canon James Owen Hannay. He was born in Belfast in 1865 but served as rector in Westport, Co. Mayo from 1892 to 1913. Regarded as ascendancy by nationalist Ireland he had little sympathy with either the Anglo-Irish revival or the Gaelic League but wrote rather, as did Somerville and Ross, of an Ireland which is an acceptable personal construct. He died in 1950.

Free State Troops in Sligo (*Independent*! *Newspapers*)

Eviction Scene, Woodford (*Lawrence Collection, National Library of Ireland*)

BODY MIND & SOUL

Amateur concert party about 1895, Roscommon Town. (Gavin Collection, Roscommon)

SEÁIN MOR A BHÍ I GCEANNAS.

Shocruigh an Cléireach is fear na bhfatai an méid sin roimh-ré, mara dtagadh an Sagart. É fein a toghadh mar Rúnaidhe mar b' "é a b'fearr ceann is peann." Leig sé air nar shanntuigh se an obair sin chor ar bith, mar go raibh sé an-chruadhógach fé láthair, ag freagairt litreach bhíodh ag teacht chuige ó gach oifig in Ath-Cliath. Mar sin féin cuireadh iallach air glacadh leis an bpósta in aghaidh a thola. Toghadh Seáin Mór mar Uachtarán, agus mar Chathaoirleach, an Ministéara mar Chisteoir, mar be b'fhearr cleachta ag cómhaireamh na bpighinn. Toghadh an Cléireach mar thosuightheóir, agus fear na bhfatai mar bhreitheamh, mar bhí aithne aige ar gach duine san taobh sin tíre nach-mór. Gintí agus MacGiolla bhuidhe i gcóir an gheata, ionnus nach rachadh aon duine isteach gan airgead síos, agus bheadh faitchios rómpa seachas aon bheirt as an áit.

Toghadh Brian ar mhodh, ce gur ghráin le cuid aca é ach Fear na bhfataí amháin, go mbeadh sé ar aon Choiste leo. Ach ní raibh neart air. Bheadh se an-úsáideach ag cur suas fógraí agus ag bualadh an chluig. Thug bean ná lása cogar dón cléireach, ar abhfaca sé ariamh, gan ainm Bhriain bheith ar an gCoiste 'sna Fógraí. Gheall sé nach mbeadh aon bhaoghal.

Cainntigheadh ar an Dochtúir beag. Agus nuair nar thainig se níor chuir an Cléireach ar an gCoiste e.

Fiafruigheadh ar cuireadh fógra chuige, agus dubhairt an Cléireach — no an Rúnaidhe, gur cheap sé gur chuir sé a ainm le fógra dó, agus dubhairt fear na bhfataí gur cheap se féin, comh fada le-n-a bharramhail, gur sheol se leitir chuige.

D'fhiafruig Brian an bhfuair Tomás Pheadair cuireadh agus dubhairt an Rúnaidhe, gur cheap se nar ghádh e, agus nar mhaith leis bheith ag cur stampaí amugha.

"B'fearr liom stampaí chur amugha leis ná cuid de ghadharaibh Chamuis bhíos ag marbhú caorach i lár na h-oidhche, agus gan aon duine le cosg a chur leo."

"Sin e mo ghnó-sa," arsa an Sárgint go borb.

"Cé'n fáth nach ndéanann tú mar sin é?" arsa Brian.

Bhi Gintí agus MacGiolla bhuidhe ag druideadh leis chun an dorais a thabhairt.

Pádhraic Óg O Conaire, *Mian a Croidhe* (Baile Átha Cliath, 1922) ltn. 36-38.

94

PÁDHRAIC ÓG O CONAIRE (called 'Óg' to distinguish him from Sean -Phadraic who was born ten years earlier in 1883) is 'one of the few authors you may hear discussed lovingly by workingmen from the Gaeltacht here in Britain' (Donall Mac Amhlaigh). He was born in Connemara in 1893 and wrote of small town and Irish country life. *Mian a Chroidhe* a gently humourous novel was written in 1922. The excerpt describes in a gently satirical way the politics of electing a committee to run sports in a small western town.

Left: *A Mayo football team.* (*Wynne Collection*)

The start of the one mile race at Castlebar Sports which took place in the Mental Hospital grounds on 5 August 1896. (*Wynne Collection*)

Steve: Is that so? Yellow hair. (*Puts his hand uncertainly to his head*.)

Michelin: You wouldn't be tired listening to her telling out about him. As straight as in the line army! A true fowler with his gun! He never saw the snipe rising, but he'd knock it.

Julia: Stop your talk!

Michelin: The way she has him pictured out you'd say him to be the son of a King, by a Queen.

Steve: Where at all did she meet with such a one?

Julia: Stop your humbugging talk Michelin; You're entirely too supple with the tongue.

Michelin: And the riches he made out in England! There isn't hardly figures enough to count them in arithmetic.

Steve: I never heard of such a one at all.

Michelin: Steve, I believe, is the name he had. Steve Roland.

Steve: Roland! And she made him out so wealthy?

Michelin: A room full of gold in his house. Two labourers stripped of their clothes turning it over with forks.

Steve: She said him to have gold and means?

Michelin: She could have had square diamonds on her hands, and a lady's way of life. Starvation and misery with myself she chose, and he having full bags of coin.

Julia: You have too much chat!

Michelin: Let you go sing again, Julia. Draw down on them some of the old troubles of Ireland, that might make them turn to the cards or the dice.

(*Julia goes to the side again and looks through her sheaf of ballads*.)

Steve (*to Michelin*): Rich she said. To have gold she said? Well, she to have said so, it is so. I didn't tell you that I am a rich man myself!

(*He takes out his little bag, as Julia prepares to sing*.)

Michelin: Come on, so sir, take a turn at the board! (*Calls out*.) Sing out strong, Julia, we have the half of the day wasted! . . . Nominate your colour, sir, while the ball is rolling! Thank you, sir, and the black wins again. The lucky black—one down, two down, any more or any other! Off she goes again! (*They go on playing while Julia sings at the side with her back to them*).

Lady Gregory, *On the Racecourse* (London, 1926) pp.18-21.

LADY GREGORY, born Augusta Persse at Roxborough, Co Galway, 1859 is the mother-figure of the Irish Literary Revival. When her elderly husband Sir William Gregory died in 1892 she turned to writing and to a renewed interest in Irish (which had earned her the nickname of 'the little Fenian' in Gort). A wet day, the presence of Martyn and Yeats and a comfortable room at Dooras House all played their part in the generation of the Irish Literary Theatre. She contributed practically, artistically and politically and has only recently been given her due. *On the Racecourse* is a late reworking of the themes of benevolent deception that she used in *The Jackdaw* and *Twenty-five*. She died in 1932.

Bookies and touts at Castlebar Racetrack, c. 1900. (Wynne Collection)

NO MORE O' YER GOLFIN' FOR ME

Through life I have played all the games that one can,
At football I played on the good Gaelic plan,
You *may* miss the ball but you *must* kick the man,
Or else it won't count to your score.
At Cricket they never knew what I'd be at,
My very first welt laid the bowler out flat,
As they hadn't another I carried me bat,
While they carried him home on a door.

> Golf! Golf! Carry me off!
> Bury me down by the sea.
> The putters may put, still I won't stir a fut,
> No more of yer golfin' for me.

I'm an old fashioned dog to be larnin' new tricks,
But Murphy came round wid two bags full o' sticks,
At Hockey you've one club, but here you have six,
And that's a remarkable thing.
Then Murphy drove off the wee ball. Oh! Begor!
It rose through the air, till it looked like a star,
The head of my driver'd have gone just as far,
If it hadn't been tied with a string.

> Golf! Golf! Carry me off!
> Bury me down by the sea.
> The drivers may drive, but dead or alive,
> No more o' yer golfin' for me.

When I got to the bunker, of clubs I'd just two,
But one was a brass wan, sez I, "That'll do,
If the ball won't go over, I'll make it go through,"
So I slash'd and I hammer'd away.
Then Murphy came up, and sez he, "Ain't it grand,"
Says I, "It's a game I don't quite understand,
How much do they give here for shovellin' sand?
I'd like to get on by the day."

> Golf! Golf! Carry me off!
> Bury me down by the sea.
> The lofters may loft,
> Still my sleep shall be soft,
> No more o' yer golfin' for me.

(WILLIAM) PERCY FRENCH was born in Clooneyquin, Co Roscommon in 1854. He was educated among other places at Foyle College and graduated from Trinity with a BA in 1876 and B Eng 1881. Described in 1912 by D J O'Donoghue as a 'librettist and song writer of the present day.' Before becoming an author he was a civil engineer. The change from drains to strains made him the most famous comic song-writer in English ever and this includes W S Gilbert. He was also a skilled instrumentalist and painter. Known as the author of the 'traditional' American student song, 'Abdulla Bulbul Ameer'. Died 1920.

Percy French, (1906)

Castlebar tennis party (*Wynne Collection*)

Lawn Tennis became very popular in Ireland quite soon after the setting of the rules by the All England Club at Wimbledon. Dublin had the distinction of holding the first ever women's championship event in 1879. The earliest courts were hour-glass shaped but rectangular courts soon became standard. The rackets in the picture are at a kind of half-way stage in the evolution of the pre-1880 pear-shaped variety to the modern oval.

IN TENNIS COSTUME

Near the netting which encloses
  A delightful tennis-space,
Stands Miss Dollie, with the roses
  Blushing on her pretty face.
Come with me and I will show her
  To you as she lingers there;
You will really long to know her,
  She's so sweet and debonair!

Most reluctantly my pen is
  Forced to mention what is true:
Dolly doesn't play good tennis,
  And the points she wins are few.
But she's only just beginning—
  She'll do better, I've no doubt;
And, instead of points, she's winning
  Love from everyone about.

Watch the fellow in the blazer:
  Though he knows her play is tame,
Just to please her he will praise her,
  And lose nearly every game.
Yes, he dearly loves to flatter,
  Though 'tis plain she cannot play—
But to him this doesn't matter,
  Since she's won his heart away!

He would fain misunderstand her
  When she calls out "Thirty love!"
But she'd pose as reprimander
  If such things he murmured of!
That he fell in love, no wonder.
  When he felt those eyes of blue.
Can you tell me what in thunder
  Else a fellow has to do?

For so far is Mistress Dollie,
  As she stands beside the net,
That 'twould be the greatest folly
  To attempt her picture—yet
It is safe to say a sweeter
  Maiden seldom meets the glance;
Would you have the heart to beat her
  If you ever got the chance?

Anonymous, *In Tennis Costume* (Sligo Independent, 22 September, 1888)

Mo shlán-sa dhuit, a Mhuruisg, a bhí siamsamhail suairc,
Is dho na sléibhtibh breága mealadh bhi ar an taobh deas de'n Chruaich
Ba bhinne liom an roilleach is í 'siubhal suas ó'n tuinn
Ná ceólta na cruinne is bídís uilig cruinn.

Is nuair a eirighim féin ar maidin is feichim i bhfad uaim siar an Chruach
Bíonn mo cnroidhe istigh ar mire is m'aigneadh go buan;
Níl na daoine seo mar chleacht mise síodamhail ná suairc,
Acht mar déanfaidhe de'n ghlas-dair geárrtha amach le tuaigh.

Da bhféadainn-se féin seasamh go labhruigheadh an chuach
D'fhillfinn a bhaile is dhéanfainn mo chuairt.
Meireach an umhluigheacht a bhí agam ariamh do'n ord,
Ni thréigfinn choidhche Muruisg ná aoibhneas na gcuan.

MURUISG is a traditional song in praise of Murrisk, the village from which the ascent of Croagh Patrick is made each summer. (The 'Cruach' of the poem is of course the 'Reek' itself.)

Because of the language decline traditional singing had become much rarer than traditional instrumental music. The effort to keep it alive was made more difficult because the great collectors like Bunting and O'Neill were only interested in the music and many had not the competence to record the words. The new interest in the language inspired by the Gaelic League led to an eleventh hour attempt to rescue the vocal music tradition.

MICHEÁL AND TOMÁS O MÁILLE were born in Connemara in 1880 and 1883. The elder was a schoolteacher and journalist, a frequent contributor to *An Claidheamh Soluis*, the Gaelic League journal. He died in 1911. The younger brother became Professor of Irish at Galway University in 1909. *Amhráin Chlainne Gaedheal* was a collection of Connacht folksongs.

Irish piper (Lawrence Collection, National Library of Ireland)

Left: Scenes during the building and stormy collapse of Castlebar Catholic Church, 1900 (*Wynne Collection*)

Below: Presbyterian Church, Leenane (*Lawrence Collection National Library of Ireland*)

"I WAS JUST GOING, ELIZA. If I'd known that Oliver wanted to speak privately to you, I'd have gone sooner."

"No, no, I assure you, Mary."

Mary held out her hand to her brother, saying:

"I suppose I shall not see you again, unless, perhaps, you're stopping the night with Father Higgins. It would be nice if you could do that. You could say Mass for us in the morning."

Father Oliver shook his head.

"I'm afraid I must get back to-night."

"Well, then, good-bye." And Mary went out of the room regretfully, like one who knows that the moment her back is turned all her faults will become the subject of conversation.

"I hear from Mary that some French nuns are coming over, and want to open a school. I hope that won't interfere with yours, Eliza; you spent a great deal of money upon the new wing."

"It will interfere very much indeed; but I'm trying to get some of the nuns to come here, and I hope the Bishop will not permit a new foundation. It's very hard upon us Irish women if we are to be eaten out of house and home by pious foreigners. I'm in correspondence with the Bishop about it. As for Mary —"

"You surely don't think she's going to leave?"

"No, I don't suppose she'll leave; it would be easier for me if she did, but it would give rise to any amount of talk. And where would she go if she did leave, unless she lived with you?"

"My house is too small; besides, she didn't speak of leaving, only that she hadn't yet taken her final vows. I explained that no one will distinguish between the black veil and final vows. Am I not right?"

I think those vows will take a great weight off your mind Oliver. I wish I could say as much for myself."

The Reverend Mother opened a glass door, and brother and sister stood for some time admiring the flower vases that lined the terrace.

"I can't get her to water the geraniums."

"If you'll tell me where I can get a can—"

"You'll excuse me, Reverend Mother."

It was the Sister in charge of the laundry, and, seeing her crippled arm, Father Oliver remembered that her dress had become entangled in the machinery. He didn't know, however, that the fault lay with Mary, who was told off to watch the machinery and to stop it instantly in case of necessity.

"She can't keep her attention fixed on anything, not even on her prayers, and what she calls piety I should call idleness. It's terrible to have to do with stupid women, and the convent is so full of them that

Rev. Mother Arsenius, (Foxford Collection)

I wonder what is the good of having a convent at all."

"But, Eliza, you don't regret —"

"No, of course I don't regret. I should do just the same again. But don't let us waste our time talking about vocations. I hear enough of that here. I want you to tell me about the music-mistress; that's what interests me."

George Moore, *The Lake* (London, 1905) pp.64, 65 (1914 edition)

The Convent of the Divine Providence was established in Foxford by the Rev. Mother Arsenius (nee Agnes Morrogh-Bernard) in 1891. The district was extremely poor and a year after her school had been set-up she brought the first industry to a very congested district. In 1892, with expert help from J C Smith of Caledon and a grant from the Congested Districts Board and the blessing of Horace Plunkett's Co-operative movement, Providence Woollen Mills were born.

Teaser at work. (Foxford Collection)

"Won't you sit down, Father MacTurnan?" he said casually. "You've been writing to Rome, I see, advocating the revocation of the decree of celibacy. There's no doubt the emigration of Catholics is a very serious question. So far you have got the sympathy of Rome, and I may say of myself; but am I to understand that it was your fear of the religious safety of Ireland that prompted you to write this letter?"

"What other reason could there be?"

Nothing was said for a long while, and then the Bishop's meaning began to break in on his mind; his face flushed, and he grew confused.

"I hope your grace doesn't think for a moment that—"

"I only want to know if there is anyone — if your thoughts ever said, 'Well, if the decree were revoked —'"

"No, your Grace, no. Celibacy has been no burden to me — far from it. Sometimes I feared that it was celibacy that attracted me to the priesthood. Celibacy was a gratification rather than a sacrifice."

"I am glad," said the Bishop, and he spoke slowly and emphatically, "that this letter was prompted by such impersonal motives."

"Surely, your Grace, His Holiness didn't suspect — .."

The Bishop murmured an euphonious Italian name, and Father MacTurnan understood that he was speaking of one of the Pope's secretaries.

"More than once," said Father MacTurnan, "I feared if the decree were revoked, I shouldn't have had sufficient courage to comply with it."

And then he told the Bishop how he had met Norah Flynn on the road. An amused expression stole into the Bishop's face, and his voice changed.

"I presume you do not contemplate making marriage obligatory; you do not contemplate the suspension of the facilities of those who do not take wives?"

"It seems to me that exception should be made in favour of those in Orders, and of course in favour of those who have reached a certain age like your Grace."

The Bishop coughed, and pretended to look for some

Pilgrims at Knock 1892 (Wynne Collection, Castlebar)

paper which he had mislaid.

This was one of the many points that I discussed with Father Michael Meehan."

"Oh, so you consulted Father Meehan," the Bishop said, looking up.

"He came in the day I was reading over my Latin translation before posting it. I'm afraid the ideas that I submitted to the consideration of His Holiness have been degraded by my very poor Latin. I should have wished Father Meehan to overlook my Latin, but he refused. He begged of me not to send the letter."

"Father Meehan," said his Grace, "is a great friend of yours. Yet nothing he could say could shake your resolution to write to Rome?"

"Nothing," said Father MacTurnan. "The call I received was too distinct and too clear for me to hesitate."

"Tell me about this call."

Father MacTurnan told the Bishop that the poor man had come out of the workhouse because he wanted to be married, and that Mike Mulhare would not give him his daughter until he had earned the price of a pig. "And as I was talking to him I heard my conscience say, 'No one can afford to marry in Ireland but the clergy.' We all live better than our parishioners."

George Moore, *The Untilled Field*, (Dublin, 1902) pp. 114-115.

Left: *Corpus Christi Procession, Ballina (Lawrence Collection, The National Library of Ireland.)*

". . . I BEHELD ALL AT ONCE, standing out from the gable, and rather to the west of it, three figures which, on more attentive inspection, appeared to be that of the Blessed Virgin, St Joseph, and St John. That of the Blessed Virgin was life-size, the others apparently either not so big or not so high as her figure, they stood out a little distance from the gable wall, and, as well as I could judge, a foot and a half or two feet from the ground. The Virgin stood erect, with eyes raised to heaven, her hands elevated to the shoulders or a little higher, the palms inclined slightly towards the shoulders or the bosom; she wore a large cloak of a white colour, hanging in full folds and somewhat loosely around her shoulders, and fastened to the neck; she wore a crown on the head, rather a large crown, and it appeared to me somewhat yellower than the dress or robes worn by Our Blessed Lady. . ."

Testimony of Mary Beirne concerning the events of Thursday, August 21, 1879 at Knock, Co. Mayo.

"'THE HEDGE SCHOOLMASTER was not the sort of man whom Carleton and Lever have lampooned, no such thing; he was generally a well-informed stranger, the scion perhaps of some noble family who had been disinherited by Elizabeth, or by James the First, or by the inhuman Cromwell. The school boys carried with them to these masters Homer's *Iliad* and *Odyssey*, *Paradise Lost* and *Paradise Regained*, the *History of Greece and Rome*, the *Arabian Nights*, Thomas-a-Kempis, Dr. Gallagher and Keating, the *Old Testament*, Sallust in English, Ovid, Ward's *Cantos*, McGeoghegan's *History of Ireland*, and a hundred and one other books. Where they all came from is one of the things that now astonishes me, for these books were in every peasant's cottage on the little loft over the fireplace, along with the wool-cards, the balls of yarn, and the spindles; there the books rested, some without covers, and all of them stained with smoke. When a boy had his *Odyssey* read, he exchanged it with another chap for his *Iliad*, and so on. They spent seven or eight years at this kind of work, and got them off by heart, as we called it.

"'Each boy and girl had a favourite Grecian or Roman hero; some admired Socrates, some Leonidas, some Lycurgus, some Xenophon, and some Cincinnatus. The girls were taught to admire Susanna, Judith, the mother of the Machabees, Lucretia, and Virginia, while we all admired

Scholars at Roscommon, c. 1890, photographed by R W Simmons of Galway (Gavin Collection).

Hannibal. Often we had refined boxing matches, with each boy standing up for his favourite hero. This business was conducted according to the rules of the ring, for we had two seconds and a timekeeper, whose business it was to see that one boy didn't hit the other below the belt, or when he was down. "'The children were also taught how to sit at table, and how to handle a knife and fork. They were taught to salute and respect the aged, and to bow and draw their bob or forelock to all strangers; anyhow, the bob got its own share of pulling, for, alas, we had no cap to raise. When these ragged little boys, some wearing trousers, some wearing flannel petticoats, or dresses like females, left off going to school and began to handle their spades, their minds were made. In fact, they had the minds of fully-grown, noble men and women, for, to their credit, let it be said that some of the girls were the cleverest in the schools.

"'These little boys and girls when they left school were better informed than the fully grown men of the present day. One of them knew more about the world than all the National School boys in the parish if they were all melted down and cast into one huge National School boy of this day. It was in these hedge schools that the Irish peasantry learned to be steadfast, honourable and truthful, and to have fortitude, so that when the penal laws and the persecution set in, they thought of the woman and her seven sons in the Bible, of Daniel in the lion's den, and the fiery furnace, and they held to the faith of their fathers like grim death, and won. I wonder, if the penal laws and the persecution set in now in this frivolous age with its threepenny novels, novelettes, and penny horror tales, would we be able to give such a good account of ourselves. Indeed, I fear not.'"

James Berry; *Tales of the West of Ireland* (Dublin 1966)

JAMES BERRY was born at Bunowen near Louisburgh, Co. Mayo in 1842. His early education was at a hedge school, but when he moved to Carna, his uncle, a local clergyman, added to this perhaps inadequate beginning. His stories, originally published in the 'Mayo News' (1910-1013), are lively extravagant and implicitly hero-worshipping. The stories were edited and published in book form as *Tales of the West of Ireland* by Dolmen Press in 1966 and edited by Gertrude M Horgan. He died in 1914.

The National School system was established in 1831 in spite of known objections by the churches. The schools were intended to be multidenominational with a common curriculum of the three 'R's, geography, grammar, and book-keeping and needlework for girls. By 1861 they had become in fact denominational schools with clerical managers. School began at 9.30 and ended at 3 pm in winter and 5 pm in summer. Teachers were forbidden to live above licensed premises, could not take part in politics, were subservient to the managers and badly paid. **109**

Street Front, Castlebar, showing the extent of photographer Wynne's business interests as newsagent, auctioneer and furniture salesman (Wynne Collection)

112 *Grattan Street, Sligo*

Main Street, Killala, Co. Mayo

Harbour, Clare Island (*Lawrence Collection, National Library of Ireland*)

Book Three

Munster

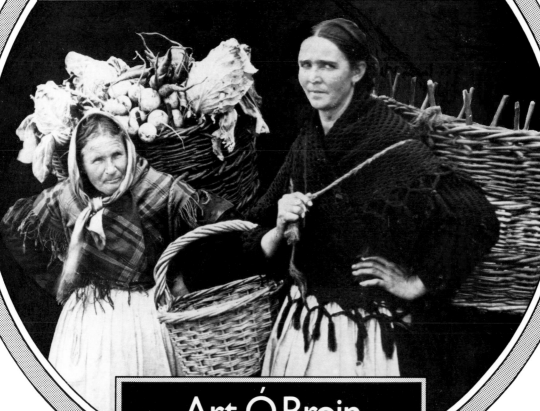

Art Ó Broin
& Seán McMahon

Preface

Our thanks are due to the director and staff of the National Library of Ireland, the staff of the Library of the Institute of Continuing Education (NUU) Magee College, Derry, especially Alan Roberts; the staff of the Belfast Central Library; Michael Coady of Carrick-on-Suir; Diarmuid O'Donavan of Cork; T. H. Murphy of Castleisland; James Clancy and Senan Rush of Kilrush; Liam Hogan of Ennis; John Galvin of the County Library, Tralee; Edmund Flaherty of Clontarf; Brud Slattery of Lahinch; Donnchadh O Suilleabhain, Secretary of the Oireachtas; Jim O'Neill Librarian, *Cork Examiner*; Frank D'Arcy of Derry.

Introduction

Comparisons, as a well-known, non-RIC constable once remarked, ate odorous; they are also inevitable. When one comes to contemplate the face of Munster after gazing with fascinated eyes at the West for a year or so one cannot but be struck at the differences. However arbitrary the division of the country into provinces may once have been, allowing for the ambivalence of a man from northwest Clare or east Waterford, they grew into self-conscious entities. Certainly the Munster of eighty years ago presents a different mien to the time-traveller than that of Ulster or Connacht; or perhaps one should say that the available materials with which an impression of that Munster may be built give a picture which is different.

This book follows the pattern of its predecessors and attempts to present a view of the southern province's past by the marriage—sometimes shot-gun wedding—of the distinct sources, the photographs and the literature of the period. One medium, by itself, might tend towards bias but the camera which had not yet learned to lie and the piece of imaginative literature as abstract and brief chroniclers of the time, set in opposition to each other, so to speak, may together hope to produce a more complete picture of the time.

The face of Munster as it appears in wet-plates and print is one of two great contrasts, richness and turbulence. The fields seem bigger, the roads wider and straighter, the mountains higher, the towns more populous, the people more comfortable than in the West. There is a city

Protest demonstration in Cork in the 1920s. (Photo: courtesy J. Cluskey)

5

*Pier at Coonanna, Cahirciveen
(Lawrence Collection, National
Library)*

at once sedate and rebellious, able to contain within its extension all kinds of dissonances. There is urban sophistication and a sense of rural plenty and the impression that the people had time to spare from the grind of survival—old men to see visions, young men to dream dreams. Fenianism and Republicanism run like green threads through the region's history. One becomes conscious of a country worth fighting for; and civil war seems more bitter here.

Unlike the western province there are no great writers here if one excludes the elusive George Fitzmaurice and the Munster half of Somerville and Ross. Yet there are many whose names to any generation but the present one were, as Parnell once said of Tom Kettle, household words. Charles Kickham, Canon Sheehan, An tAthair Peadar, the Sullivan brothers, William O'Brien used to fill our grandparents' bookshelves. They tended, on the whole, to reflect the rural scene rather than the urban. Cork's recurring golden ages have great gaps between them and there are few writers worth consideration between the time of Milliken and Mahoney and that of Daniel Corkery. For the full celebration of Cork's patchy urbanity you have to wait for Sean O'Faolain and Frank O'Connor. Contrariwise Youghal and Waterford have figured in better than average novels of the period by William Buckley and Katherine Cecil Thurston. Limerick had its own poetic child in Micheal Hogan, the Bard of Thomond, whose woodnotes wild tended at times to

Kissing the Blarney Stone, Blarney Castle, Co. Cork (Lawrence Collection, National Library)

7

grow sharp. There were none of the great originals like Yeats and Moore and Hyde; yet the Gaelic revival would have been rather different without An tAthair Peadar, Beirt Fhear and Ballingeary Teachers College, and the development of the theatre in Ireland would have suffered without such shapers as T. C. Murray and Lennox Robinson.

As for the pictures they are dominated by the work of Robert French whose elegant and unmistakeable photographs taken for his employer Lawrence have become one of the main resources of the social researcher of the period. We have also included some Lawrence photographs from a period earlier than when French was his main journeyman. These were originally stereograms, pairs of almost identical pictures to be viewed through Sir Charles Wheatstone's stereoscope to obtain a three-dimensional image. Most Victorian drawing-rooms had these and many a month of rainy Sundays was whiled away with them. The other great archive of Munster pictures of the period is the Cork Examiner Collection which consists of many boxes of mainly uncatalogued plates. One cannot help but be conscious of the daily disappearance of much excellent material through age, accident or spring-cleaning. One would recommend to UCC or the Cork Municipal Art Gallery or some such agency to follow the lead in this matter of the Public Records Office in Belfast and the Learning Resource Centre at Magee College, Derry. They have done what they can to encourage local people to search through their attics and albums so that precious and unique records of a past age may be copied and preserved. We have been conscious in this compilation that just as history was the story of the past as told by the winners, now it is built of what archives survive.

ART O BROIN & SEAN McMAHON

Work & Leisure

Verandah, Eccles Hotel, Glengariff, Co. Cork (Lawrence Collection, National Library)

They now reached a low swing-gate, painted white. A couple of men sprang, apparently, out of the ditch, to open and hold it. They passed through, and on to what was like another road, only narrower than that which they had left, and running through a field. After a minute or two they turned a corner, and a huge square white house, well lighted up, stood at the top of a wide field before them. A little white railing ran on each side of the grass as they approached, and marked off the sweep before the door.

As soon as the sound of the car was heard in the house, the hall door was thrown wide open, letting out a stream of light and noise, and mingled odors of all sorts, the basis of which was turf smoke; and a crowd rushed out to welcome the visitors. A half-dozen or more daughters, some grown up and others as yet in the chrysalis stage, seized on Dicky. Then they all bustled in; and in the hall, where was burning a huge fire of peats, Hogan was introduced to his hostess, a comely matron, with an amiable, good-humoured face,—a Kerry woman, as evidenced by her accent, and with the fine dark eyes and hair so often seen in that favoured district. Hogan and Dicky now followed a barefooted girl up to their rooms, which blazing turf fires made agreeable and homelike after the chilly journey.

May Laffan *Hogan M P* (London, 1896)

MAY HARTLEY (nee Laffan) though born in Dublin, really hailed from Cashel, Co. Tipperary. Best known as the author of slum sketches, *Flitters, Tatters and the Counsellor* she also wrote *Hogan MP* in 1876, a fairly scathing attack on the inadequacies of catholic education. It gives a rare and excellent account of the emerging native middle class.

Coole House, Millstreet, Co. Cork (Lawrence Collection, National Library)

. . . ní raibh an "Gioblachán" sásta fós. Thóg se anuas fidil bhí ar crocadh, de'n bhalla, agus chuir sé i gcóir í.

"An dtaithneann ceól leat?" ar seisean.

"Taithneann go maith," arsa mise, "Ta spéis mhór agam ann i gcómhnuidhe."

"Má's mar sin atá an sgéal," ar sé, "gheobhaidh tú ceól anois nó ríamh."

"Má tá sé mar an ceól do thug an mac alla uaidh ó cíanaibh ná bac leis."

"Éist," ar seisean, ag leigint gáire as, "agus tabhair do bhreith nuair táim críochnuighthe."

Tosnuigh sé ag seinm, agus dá mbéinn ag caint go ceann seachtmhaine ní fhéadfainn tuarasgbháil cheart do thabhairt ar an cóimhsheinm d'éirigh san uaimh. B'áluinn an bhleidhleadóir an "Gioblachán" agus bhí sé 'n-a chumas, "o neart na taithíghe," is dócha, ceól do bhaint as an mac alla chómh maith leis an bhfidil. Dá mbéadh gach éin-ghléas ceól i n-Éirinn bailighthe isteach i n-éan-halla amháin agus iad go léir ar siubhal i n-éinfheacht, ní fheadfadh síad céol níos binne ná níos áilne ná níos taithneamháighe do thabhairt uatha ná an ceól do thug an fhidil agus an mac alla dhúinn an óidhche úd. Thóg sé an cróidhe agus an t-anam asam. Níor mhothúigheas pían ná tuirse ná eagla ná éinnídh eile acht amháin aoibhneas agus sásamh aignidh an fhaid do bhí an "Gioblachán" ag seinm agus d'fhanfainn annsoin ag éisteacht leis ar feadh lae agus óidhche gan bheith tuirseach dhe.

Tomás Ó hAodha, *An Gioblachan* (Dublin, 1903)

TOMÁS Ó hAODHA was born in Milltown Malbay, Co. Clare in 1866, the son of a cooper. He became a teacher in 1886 in Dublin and was one of the early members of the Gaelic League. His greatest interest was in Irish music and in the teaching of Irish song in which he was an innovator. He wrote plays and short stories; the piece is from his novel *An Gioblachán.* He died in 1935.

An Gioblachán (Lawrence Collection, National Library)   11

Then, "He's away!" signalled from the lower end—a thundering charge of horses to the gateway, long ere there was time to get out of covert. Peter felt the reins almost wrenched from his grasp, Starlight tearing on, until his career was checked by bumping into a mass of horses jumbled into the narrow gateway, their paths barred by an enraged field master who had pulled his across the way. Hounds dashed out of covert, settling to the line; the field master fled with a clear lead, and the checked flood poured out, hustling and voluble. The pack were tearing down the hillside, and, judging by the yells which drifted across, the fox was making his way up the steep hill beyond the road. There were two ways to get down—one direct, embellished by a crop of jutting-out rocks, and so steep that horses slid on their tails; the other to the left, across a low bank, and down a more gradual slope. Fortunately for himself Peter chose the longer way, for, as he charged the bank, he felt very much as if the grey

had turned into a four-legged motor, with the brake out of order. His great Roman nose to the earth, Starlight thundered downwards, slid through a broken fence, and dashed at the wall fencing the road. Here Peter saw a fleeting vision of sound macadam, touched once, and another of an awkward stick of timber, vanishing, badly rapped, beneath him. This was mixed up with a third fleeting view of other horses, scuttling from his onslaught, and a faint peppering of comments, not precisely complimentary, echoing as he fled.

Hounds were slipping out of sight over a high green bank, flanking a whitewashed chapel and a churchyard. The men in front turned to the left; the grey, not Peter, turned after them over a thorny fence, half hedge, half wall, at which Starlight checked, and then took with a bucking lurch which set Peter's perfectly clad legs flapping widely, to find rest on his horse's neck. Also he thought he heard a chuckle somewhere behind him.

UHC Foxhounds at Fermoy Old Barracks on 17 March 1899 (Photo J Thompson, Fermoy: Crawford Municipal School of Art Collection, Cork)

12

Pink coats in front began to drop out of sight into a narrow lane, pausing cautiously as they slid down, but here fortunately, though he tore up to it, Starlight steadied himself, and just as Peter, his lips set grimly for the crash, was wondering whether his grave would be the well of a passing car, or the inside of an approaching governess cart, the grey propped, spun round, again laying Peter on his mane, sliding down the now broken bank with the steadiness of a trained hunter. Over fresh, a start downhill—it must be only that; so he rode on with the crowd, dubiously

Hounds had checked among the tombstones and were spread out, noses to earth, over the humping graves. "Twas a place for a sphortin' man to lie," observed a capped countryman by Peter's side. "With the fox crossin' in near ivery run from Doleen."

"See him across?" thundered the Master, peering down from the high fence above the graves.

A man with a spade hustled round from behind the chapel, waving the weapon of his gruesome toil, and indicating the line. "He wint over me very head," he cried, "ann' I diggin' Timsy Phelan's grave to be ready to-morry. Cleared it out, an' I seen him away goin' esht by Martin Hanlon's shlate house."

Dorothea Conyers, *Peter's Pedigree* (London 1904)

DOROTHEA CONYERS (born Miss Blood Smith in Limerick in 1871) was after Somerville and Ross the laureate of huntin' Ireland. Her stories are racy, funny and full of exterior characterisation of the 'types' associated with her material. She made no attempt to penentrate more deeply into character nor to examine closely the relationship between her Anglo-Irish protagonists and the 'peasantry'. *Peter's Pedigree* (1904) is one of the best of her stories and may be summed up as it was at the time of publication, 'Hunting, horse-dealing, and love-making in Co. Cork.'

DAN. Yeh, man, don't be talking like that a day like this! There isn't a mother's soul in this parish but yourself that wouldn't be out of his mind with delight this minute, and everyone to be praising his own flesh and blood! *(To Maura.)* I'm sorry in my soul you didn't see the match, Mrs. Morrissey. I nearly killed the little mare and killed myself hurrying back from the town to see if I could see even the end of it. An' 'twas a grand sight surely.

MAURA. Wisha, God help us, Dan, I'm a bit too old now to be going places like that.

DAN. Wisha indeed, and indeed you're not, ma'am. A person would think the way you talk you were drawing the pension. But sure whatever excuse there was for you there was none at all for himself here.

BAT. We'd look well, begor. Maura an' myself, going to yer tournament! *(laughs derisively).*

DAN. An' why not, Bat? Why not? The sight o' your son to-day would be giving you a kind of feeling, maybe, that your best cows and your heaviest pigs could never give you.

BAT *(shaking his head).* God help you, Dan Hegarty! An' you a young man just beginning to rear a little family!

DAN. If I am then, Bat Morrissey, I only wish to God one o' them would grow up something like your Hugh! So I would. *(To Maura.)* All the people, and the strangers even, were cheering like mad for him. Half a dozen times you's be seeing the ball it flying into the goal posts, an' your heart would be in your mouth, thinking the other side had the goal, when you'd see him sending it back again with a puck into the middle of the field. 'Twas like a miracle the way he used to save it every time!

MAURA. Well! well!

DAN. I galloped away when it was over as I wanted to clear away before the crowds, but I gave one look back, an' they were shouldering him, an' cheering mad, an' shouting for him as if it was a member of Parliament he was.

BAT. An' for what now?

14 DAN *(with a gasp).* For what?

BAT. Yes, for what, Dan Hegarty?

DAN. Didn't I tell you.

BAT. Is it because he hit a bit of a leather balleen with a twisted stick? Tch! tch! tch! *(standing up and going towards room).* 'Tis thinking I am that half the world is becoming a pack o' fools! *(goes into room).*

MAURA *(confidentially).* I'd know could you tell me was he hurt at all, Dan?

DAN, I don't know then—I don't think so . . . .I'm almost sure he wasn't, now that I think of it.

MAURA. Thanks be to the Almighty God an' his Blessed Mother for that!

T C Murray, *Birthright* (Dublin, 1911)

THOMAS CORNELIUS MURRAY was born in Macroom in 1873 and became a teacher in Dublin in 1893. From 1909 he contributed many plays to the Abbey, the best and most successful being *Autumn Fire* (1924) with a plot as old as *Phaedra*. The realism of his West Cork dialogue and the daring choice of some of his themes caused him some clerical opposition at home and he was glad to transfer to the Model Schools at Inchicore. *Birthright (1910) is typical of his mise-en-scene* and preoccupations. It tells of family rivalry between two brothers for the attention of their parents and the possession of the farm. Yeats called it as 'perfect as a Chopin Prelude'. Murray died in 1959.

Clonea (Co. Waterford) Senior Hurling Champions, 1902 (Willie Flynn/Carrick Society)

The game of hurling remained popular in rural areas of the south despite the anglicisation of much of Irish life by the end of the nineteenth century. The founding of the Gaelic Athletic Association by Michael Cusack (at Thurles in 1884) to organise and spread the game, was the natural outcome of the awakening sense of nationality of the period. In turn members of the GAA were to make an important contribution to the revolutionary movement. 15

KILKEE-THE-GRAND

Nor sea nor shore, by artist planned
No lauded scene, nor fairyland—
Not austral flood by coral strand,
Nor where the Sun doth Night command,
The purple tide by gods adored,
The climes Genoa's lord explored,
Nor region brighter—can afford,
Thy glory pale Kilkee-the-grand!

The Titan King, from pole to pole,
The sceptre sways without control.
His tide on countless strands doth roll,
Whose pride all times and tongues extol.
To Maghar from the Sacred Green
Being thine, come forth let boasted scene,
The vast Atlantic spread between,
Can equal thee Kilkee-the -grand!

Let scented gales their treasures bear
O'er plumed Ceylon and bright Cashmere;
Be Cheli's peaks without compare;
To Como from Calabria fair.
No brilliant by Hesperian sea,
Nor Orient pearl, jewelled Italy,
Can dim the glow that lustres thee,
Ierna's gem, Kilkee-the-grand!

What time was wrecked that halcyon isle
Whose fall th' Egyptian told erstwhile,
(Whose vision still doth men beguile,
When Eve reflects that amaranth smile)
'Twas then was cleft thy sculptured coast,
Our Edward's empire's proudest boast,
Of thrilling plaudits worthy toast,
Atlanta's bride, Kilkee-the-grand!

M. A, MacNamara, *Kilkee-the-Grand,* (Galway, 1904)

The celebration of the beauty of the Edwardian watering-place caused many a poetaster to burst into lyrical praise but few went the lengths of Miss Mac Namara who composed anthem music to go with this celebration of the only bourgeois seaside resort on the West Coast

The sea-bathing craze which, highly recommended by medical men 'for reasons of health', had swept England during the 1860's had an equal effect upon Irish resorts. The custom of wearing bathing costumes was a later and undesirable development as were such soft notions as Ladies bathing places. In Kilkee the ladies won hands down as one English visitor records: 'Wishing to bathe I ask a woman on the sand the regulations of the place. She said ladies might bathe from the machines, or boxes rather, at any time of the day they pleased but gentlemen only within particular hours, which had long passed. 'What', said I, 'not from a box?' 'No', she replied, 'not nohow.' This seems rather one-sided; however, nothing remains to be done but to walk over the hills to the north and to have an uncomfortable bathe from a recess under the rocks, for the sea was beating in strongly.'

An Englishman, *A Walking Tour Round Ireland in 1865* (London, 1867)

Below: *Kilkee Amphitheatre (Lawrence Collection, National Library)*

"Don't be comparing grandmother with lumps of children, like Patsy," said Jane Katy sharply. " 'Tis different altogether, and that's why I want to explain to you. Have you your copy-book below?"

"Yes, an' my pin-an'-ink," said Tommy eagerly. Jane Katy was a "good scholar," who had gone triumphantly through the Fourth Book and the double rule of three and wrote a beautiful "copperplate" roundhand. To get a copy set by Jane Katy, would be something, indeed.

"Very well," his cousin said. Bring 'em up with you in the morning. Are you out of the words with one syllable yet?"

"Yerrah, one syllable!" he said indignantly. "I could spell the longest of 'em as fast as I'd walk — b-l-a-s-t, blast; t-r-i-b-e, thribe; s-p-e-a-k, speak; — an' plenty more like that."

"Yes. Well, I'll give you a copy in your own book, and the same copy to grandmother in hers—a nice half-hard and half-easy one—'Strike the iron while 'tis hot,' or, maybe, 'Praise a fair day at night.' "

"Oh! wait till you'll see the way I'll write it," Tommy interrupted excitedly, "an' as fast as the wind—"

"But that's what I don't want you to do at all," said Jane Katy. "You must take plenty of time with it, for grandmother is always terrible careful and slow with her copies,—like any good scholar. You ought to understand, yourself, that good writing is better than—fast writing."

"I suppose it is," admitted Tommy, not wholeheartedly. "Well, I'll take time with it so!"

"And here's a Spelling Book Superseded, with some grand words of two syllables—"

"Oh, show 'em to me! Ut! Ut! I can spell an' pronounce everyone of 'em," cried Tommy. "Although, it may be I couldn't write 'em all right," he added conscientiously.

Julia Crottie, *Neighbours* (London, 1900)

Baltimore School, Co. Cork (Lawrence Collection, National Library)

JULIA CROTTIE was born in Lismore, Co. Waterford in 1853 but lived most of her life in the Isle of Man. Her best work is a series of realistic sketches of small town Irish life, which were published under the general title of *Neighbours*.

The *'Technical School of Fisheries'* was opened in Baltimore in 1848 with help from the Baroness Burdett Coutts. The founder was Fr. Davis to whom a memorial was erected in the grounds. Baltimore was an ideal situation for such an institute. Later under the agency of the Congested Districts Board a vessel called the *Saturn* was established as a floating laboratory. The mackerel fishery was protected by the *Helen.* The boom years before 1900 saw much shipping of cured mackerel to the US from this area.

Net-making at Baltimore School (Lawrence Collection National Library)

THIS EVENING A CIRCUS was advertised in Dingle, for one night only; so I made my way there towards the end of the afternoon, although the weather was windy and threatening. I reached the town an hour too soon, so I spent some time watching the wild-looking fishermen and fishwomen who stand about the quays. Then I wandered up and saw the evening train coming in with the usual number of gaily-dressed young women and half-drunken jobbers and merchants; and at last, about eight o'clock, I went to the circus field, just above the town, in a heavy splash of rain. The tent was set up in the middle of the field, and a little to the side of it a large crowd was struggling for tickets at one of the wheeled houses in which the acrobats live. I went round the tent in the hope of getting in by some easier means, and found a door in the canvas, where a man was calling out: 'Tickets, or money, this way,' and I passed in through a long winding passage.

The performance was begun by the usual dirty white horse, that was brought out and set to gallop round, with a gaudy horse-woman on his back, who jumped through a hoop and did the ordinary feats, the horse's hoofs splashing and possing all the time in the green slush of the ring. An old door-mat was laid down near the entrance for the performers, and as they came out in turn they wiped the mud from their feet before they got up on their horses. A little later the clown came out, to the great delight of the people. He was followed by some gymnasts, and then the horse-people came out again in different dress and make-up, and went through their old turns once more. After that there was prolonged fooling between the clown and the chief horseman, who made many mediaeval jokes, that reminded me of little circuses on the outer boulevards of Paris, and at last the horseman sang a song which won great applause:

Here's to the man who kisses his wife,
And kisses his wife alone;
For there's many a man kissed another man's wife
When he thought he kissed his own.

Here's to the man who rocks his child,
And rocks his child alone;
For there's many a man rocked another man's child
When he thought he rocked his own.

J. M. Synge, *In Wicklow and West Kerry* (Dublin, 1910)

The most obvious characteristic of
Synge's work is his pleasure in wildness, of character, of imagination, of
language and of life. As he wrote in
the foreword to *The Playboy*: . . . 'the
wildest sayings and ideas in this play
are tame indeed, compared with the
fancies one may hear in any little hillside cabin in Geesala, Carraroe, or
Dingle Bay.' He sought this wildness in
Wicklow, Kerry and Connemara. This
description of a Dingle circus is typical
of the passion and colour that he
loved, in spite of a fastidiousness that
he never lost. The faint embarrassment
at the horesman's mildy bawdy song is
one of several indications that the
evangelicalism of the Co. Antrim
Traills, inherited from his mother, was
never totally exorcised.

*Johnnie Patterson, well-known clown,
and partner at circus at Deerpark, Co.
Tipperary, 1890. (Mae Stallard/Carrick
Society)*

Chevalier O'Dowlam Thomas O'Brile, and Roland Glenpower remained loyal in their allegiance to Mr. Fireframe, and were, therefore, most abnoxious to the clerical party. The minds of the laity were confused. The Land Acts had failed to realise the sanguine expectations of the farmers, and the labourers were still struggling for new cottages. Legislation, it had been found, could not supply the want of regular industry in the community. Irish produce had lost its place in the British markets, where the Dane, the Norman, and the Colonial now carried off the lion's share of the profits. The people were in a remorseful frame of mind, suffering from a reaction after the undue excitement of the agitation, and were, therefore, plastic material for the religious experts to operate upon.

Under these circumstances the priests redoubled their efforts to concentrate upon themselves the attention of the uneducated masses; and ceremonial succeeded ceremonial, mission followed mission, in quick succession all over the diocese. Constant appeals for money were sent forth from the altars. Gallowglass new church, erected in Bullrush Street and now dominating the town, was dedicated with an amount of pomp and ritual which dazzled the barony of Killafastare.

There were present and officiating at the function the Cardinal himself, the Archbishop of Tara and Lough Neagh, and six bishops. The brass bands, which used to turn out for Mr. Fireframe and his political friends, now serenaded the Irish-Roman ecclesiastics in whose honour torchlight processions were arranged and public holidays were decreed. A religious pageant, in which the Host was carried under a canopy of cloth of gold by the Cardinal, marched through the Main Street. The "Prince of the Church," as the newspapers styled him, resplendent in his red hat and robes; the archbishop; the six bishops; the hundreds of priests of all ranks; the confraternities of surplices boys and little girls in white; the thousands of grown men, mostly labourers, with red

Convent of Mercy, Skibbereen, Co. Cork (Lawrence Collection, National Library)

22

ribbons and medals suspended round their necks; all constituted a display of supernatural power by which those who beheld it felt overawed.

Father Lawnavawla rushed out of the procession and knocked Mr. McCameron's hat off his head, because the unimaginative Scotchman did not remove it when the Cardinal, bearing the Host, was passing the Distillery Road. The luxuries supplied from Canon O'Darrell's larder at the evening banquet eclipsed all the previous records of hospitality achieved at the Parochial House.

In fine, religion was rampant in Gallowglass, and, of all the townsfolk, the O'Dowlas and the O'Briles seemed to be the only people uninfected by the contagion of delirium. Both families stood aloof from the proceedings, and when they surveyed all the superstition and ritualism by which they were surrounded, the feeling uppermost in their minds was a thrill of disgust at such a debasement of Christianity to the level of fetichism. Even Mrs. O'Dowla, though she attended the devotions, has "lost the faith" so far as to abstain from spending any money on masses "for special intentions," or on the other religious indulgences in which there was such a colossal bosom.

It was when this fervour was at its height, shortly after the solemn dedication of Gallowglass new church, that the election of medical officer for the infirmary took place, and Ignatius O'Dowla was ignominiously defeated by the incompetent Doctor O'Grauver.

Michael J. F. MaCarthy, *Gallowglass* (London, 1904)

MICHAEL J. F. McCARTHY was educated at Midleton College, Co. Cork and TCD and had a colourful career as anti-cleric. His book *Five Years in Ireland* (1901) is a list of crimes committed by church and clergy against the people. *Gallowglass* still in the same vein was a fictional satire which at times rises to heights of uproarious invective.

Monk outside Mt Melleray (Lawrence Stereoscopic Collection, National Library)

IN A FIELD, surrounded by a hedge, sat an old man. He appeared to be long past middle age, but still seemed hale and strong. His habiliments were extensively patched, said patches not always agreeing in colour. Around, under the hedge, were seated about fifty or sixty boys. Some of these had seats built of turf, constructed by themselves for their own special use and accommodation, and their exclusive right to which was never invaded by their schoolmates. The schoolmaster's seat—for such was the avocation of the individual we have already mentioned, and whose external adornment was completed by a leathern cap and a huge pair of horn spectacles—was, in its way, quite a pretentious affair, and was built of sods of turf welded by clay into a solid mass, and then overlaid with grass. There were also some attempts at decoration, which gave additional dignity and importance to the structure, both in the eyes of the builders themselves, who were some of the elder boys, and their friends.

The pupils, as we have said, were seated around the field under the hedge. The greater numbers were barefooted, some had no coats, and many were without coat or vest; but we question whether among the students of a fashionable academy there was more light-hearted, innocent gaiety or more genuine racy wit.

The schoolmaster, at the period of which we write, was seated in his chair of state hearing the lesson of a little boy, whose head did not indicate any very recent acquaintanceship with either comb or brush. In his right hand he grasped a cane symbol alike of his authority and power to compel obedience. The lesson he was engaged in hearing was grammar, and the pupil acquitted himself most creditably, and to the entire satisfaction of the master, as was evidenced by the expression of approval visible in the latter's countenance.

E R McAuliffe *Grace O'Donnell* (Dublin 1891)

The Industrial Schools were established under the *Habitual Criminals Act* of 1869 which incorporated the main provisions of the English *Industrial Schools Act* of 1861. The schools were meant to relieve 'the little sufferer and the community, without waiting until vice and crime shall have effaced all innocence and moral goodness.' In other words children could be sent there by a JP on such non-charges as begging, vagrancy, destitution and consorting with low company.

E R McAULIFFE was born in Cork in the early 19th-century and died in 1916. Her only recorded work is *Grace O'Donnell* (1891) an historical novel of Irish life in Penal Ireland with excellent period detail of the sufferings of catholics, and graphic accounts of hedge-schools, tithe-collectors and other horrors of subjugation.

Industrial School, Cashel (Lawrence Collection National Libary)

JOHN. He must so. But he'd be more knowledgable still if he had a wife to teach him.

MALACHI. And more shame to you, John Fitzgibbon, to be saying the like and you knowing dam well the promise I made me mother.

T.J. And what was that, Malachi?

MALACHI. That I'd marry no gerril without herself consenting. Sure 'twas in terror she always was I'd take up with some common cauboge of a creature from the village, for I was always a soft man with the women, and so I promised her. And now God rest her, she's dead, and I'll go a single man to me grave.

JOHN. And is it spoiling the living you'll be, Malachi Phelan, for the sake of the dead?

MALACHI. 'Twas a great feeling I had for her, John, and sure I wouldn't go agen her for the world. 'Twould draw bad luck on me.

T.J. 'Twas the pity of God she went so sudden.

MALACHI. Aye so. Mixing food for the pigs she was, and she gave one screech, and after that the speech was whipped from her the way she never spoke after—

T.J. *(crossing himself)*. Holy Virgin, but that was no Christian way to die.

JOHN. And do you mean to tell me you're going to live a puckered man on the hillside, because an old woman fell into her grave without speech?

MALACHI *(with a wink)*. If I'm puckered I'm safe, John. Sure the promise is a great fence round the alatar, and God knows if I broke it maybe herself would come back to haunt me.

JOHN. If she came back to teach you sense, 'twould be the good work for her.

MALACHI. Maybe so. Women have great knowledge in affairs of love.

JOHN. They have so, there's Mary now. Begannies, meself would be glad of a word of advice about her. 'Tis time she settled down, but 'tisn't every man would please her.

MALACHI. Why wouldn't she take Timothy James there?

JOHN. Yerra, Mary wouldn't consort herself with the likes of him. It's a strong farmer with good land and an odd sheep or two she'll be looking for.

T.J. *(ruffled by John's contempt)*. There's no fear she'll look at Malachi anyway. Sure she says he'd frighten maggots from a corpse.

JOHN. What the devil do you mean by saying that? It isn't likely she'd tell you what she thought of Malachi Phelan.

T.J. She tolt Katie Downey, anyway.

JOHN. Tcah. Katie Downey, that would give the skin off her feet to marry him herself.

MALACHI. I passed her now and I coming down the road. She's an on-coming woman is Katie. She has me that haunted, the flutter of a petticoat puts me in a palpitation.

JOHN. You'll have no peace till you marry. Be said by me now, choose a sensible wife and settle down with her on the hill above.

MALACHI. A sensible woman? And where do you suppose I'd find one?

JOHN. Maybe ye mightn't have to travel as far as you think.

MALACHI. If I travelled from here to the Equator I couldn't be matched with one of them. My cripes! but the female sex is hard to unravel.

T.J. You have no opinion of them at all, I'm thinking, Malachi.

MALACHI. I have not, and may the Saints themselves protect me from falling into their clutches.

(A plateful of wet tea leaves skilfully thrown through the doorway falls on Malachi, spattering and wetting him. He springs to his feet shaking himself.)

JOHN. Mary! Mary! What in the name of God are you doing?

MARY *(thrusting an innocent face round the door)*. What ails ye, John?

G D Cummins & S Day, *Fox and Geese* (Dublin, 1917)

GERALDINE DOROTHY CUMMINS & SUZANNE DAY both born in Cork in 1890 collaborated on several Abbey plays including *Broken Faith* (1912) and *Fox and Geese* (1917). In later life Miss Cummins published a novel, *The Fires of Beltane* (1936) but is better known as the best Irish biographer of Edith Somerville. *Fox and Geese* has as theme the perennial tragi-comic situation of the ageing oedipal Irish bachelor considering the possibility of marriage.

Mountain Stage Cabin, Glenbeigh Co. Kerry (Lawrence Collection, National Library)

A 'stage' cabin was one in use during the summer months for 'booleying'—the practice traditional in Irish husbandry of moving with the cattle to mountain pastures.

Meadowvale Creamery, Charleville, Co. Cork (Lawrence Collection, National Library)

There was a loud call for the 'sets' from an impatient young man seated on the end of the table nearest the room-door. Thereupon a chair was placed in a convenient position for the concertina player, who, having fixed himself in it, commenced at playing the usual tune, his countenance assuming that half-comical, half-diabolical expression which seems inseparable from the endeavour of trying to knock sweet sounds out of the now very common, cheap German instruments.

The selection of partners was now about to take place, when all of a sudden frantic cries of joy and loud shouts of laughter arose in all directions. This was caused by a very unlooked-for movement on the part of Mr. Reilly, who, having bounded on to the middle of the floor, signified his intention to take part in the dance. Then, amidst much disconcerting applause, he advanced, with somewhat faltering footsteps to procure a partner. But when he got to where Katie Dolan and Johanna Ruane were chatting together, it would be easy for anybody who knew anything of his secret to observe that he was then in a state of intense nervousness. He stood before them for a second, his heart palpitating widly.

At last said he—"Will you dance with me, miss, if you plaze?'

Katie Dolan's soft orbs were raised for an instant, then fell with precipitation.

A shade of perplexity was visible on Johanna Ruane's broad-shining countenance.

In truth Philip's courage had pitfully vamoosed at the critical moment; he was staring at an imaginary point in the wall parallel with Katie's pole. No wonder both the girls were in a dilemma!

The short but painful pause was broken by Johanna Ruane.

'Yerra, Phil's, she cried with· a loud titter, Is it me or Katie you want?'

He withdrew his gaze from the wall in a twikling. At that moment the poor fellow felt overwhelmed with shame and a helpless kind of vexation.

"Sure amn't I after axin' ye, Johanna?' he said half-fiercely, but with such well-feigned astonishment at her doubting it, as it were, that that young damsel's mind became so confused as to baffle description. So Philip heroically carried her through the 'sets', whilst poor Katie Dolan sat strangely silent on the stool. But never did Phil Reilly go through the several parts of the dance so mechanically before—his body in motion but the dead weight almost of coma on his mind. No wonder that once or twice his partner found herself comparing him quite unfavourably with many of the other boys! and this in spite of the fact that he danced in his old graceful manner—that manner that had become a part of him almost. Indeed, when they had reached the sixth set—where everybody changes partners for each revolution till in the finish he winds up with his own—Johanna felt an obvious relief, for with Phil in his present incomprehensible mood she could by no means give herself up to that unbounded hilarity and abandon which usually ensues in the last part of the 'sets' in the Kingdom of Kerry.

George Fitzmaurice, *The Crows of Mephistopheles* (Dublin, 1970)

GEORGE FITZMAURICE was born in Listowel in 1877 and spent most of his deliberately obscured life as a minor civil servant in Dublin. He was one of the first playwrights to make his name in the early days of the Abbey and had a remarkable success with *The Country Dressmaker* in 1908. In all he wrote sixteen plays which were published after his death in three volumes representing the three main categories of his work, Folk, Fantasy and Realistic. Though he had claim to property and position in his native Kerry he preferred the anonymous life of the city clerk. *The Crows of Mephistopheles* is a collection of his short stories edited by Professor Robert Hogan. The excerpt is from 'The Bashfulness of Philip Reilly' which first appeared in *The Weekly Freeman* on 19 March 1904. He died in 1963.

32 *At Waterville, Co. Kerry (Lawrence Collection, National Library)*

City
Town
Country

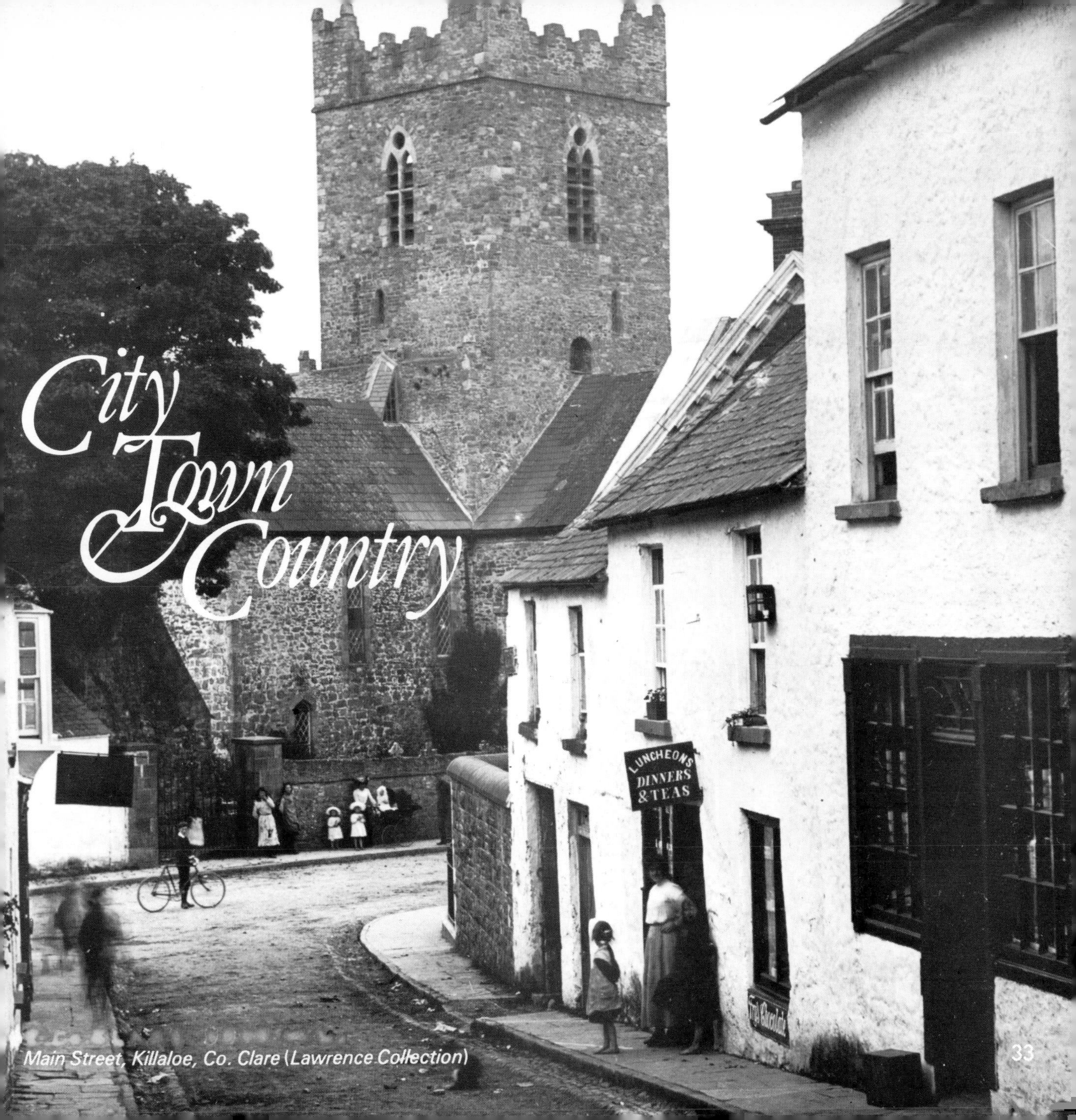

Main Street, Killaloe, Co. Clare (Lawrence Collection)

33

For the purpose of getting into touch with my fellow-passengers I always carry with me newspapers of various kinds, and it is seldom that one of them does not give a starting point for a conversation. This afternoon I had *The Irish Times*, *The Leader* and *Grania*—the latter being an obscure little paper of very extreme views, which only lived for a year or two. I tried the young man first with *The Irish Times*.

He took his eyes from the fields and came back to current affairs with an obvious effort, and I had to repeat my offer. He thanked me, but said he had already read the paper.

He had a southern accent but not in any marked degree. In my mind I registered him as a gentleman by birth, and, probably a Protestant. To make sure I pressed the other two papers on him.

He looked at *Grania* first. I think he can never have seen the paper before (its circulation, indeed, was infinitesimal), it evidently puzzled him very much, but as soon as he caught the drift of it he allowed his mouth to smile a little—in faint pity, I suppose—and laid the paper gently on the seat. His father is a Unionist, I said to myself.

I knew that no young man of that age in Ireland coming up from the country for the first time (as I somehow guessed this young man was coming) has any political or religious views except those which he has inherited from his parents. I knew that in his native place Catholicism or Protestantism, Unionist or Home Ruler, cling to certain families like scent to flowers: a change in either is a thing monstrous and abnormal. But to make quite certain I watched his face as he read *The Leader*.

Really it was rather violent that week. I confess I felt a little ashamed of myself as I saw him reading it, a little ashamed of my fellow-Catholics who can support and enjoy such a paper, a little disgusted by its vulgarity.

Lennox Robinson, A Young Man from the South (Dublin, 1917)

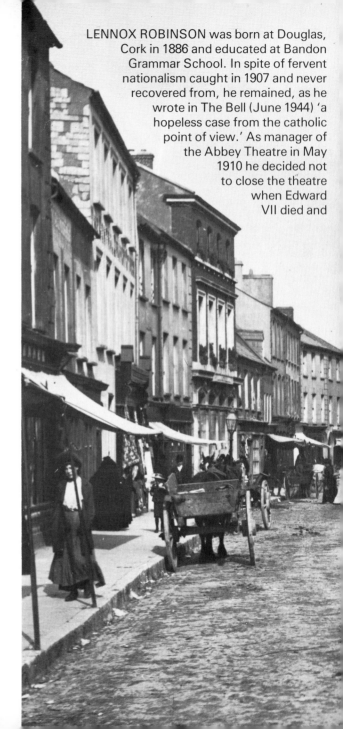

LENNOX ROBINSON was born at Douglas, Cork in 1886 and educated at Bandon Grammar School. In spite of fervent nationalism caught in 1907 and never recovered from, he remained, as he wrote in The Bell (June 1944) 'a hopeless case from the catholic point of view.' As manager of the Abbey Theatre in May 1910 he decided not to close the theatre when Edward VII died and

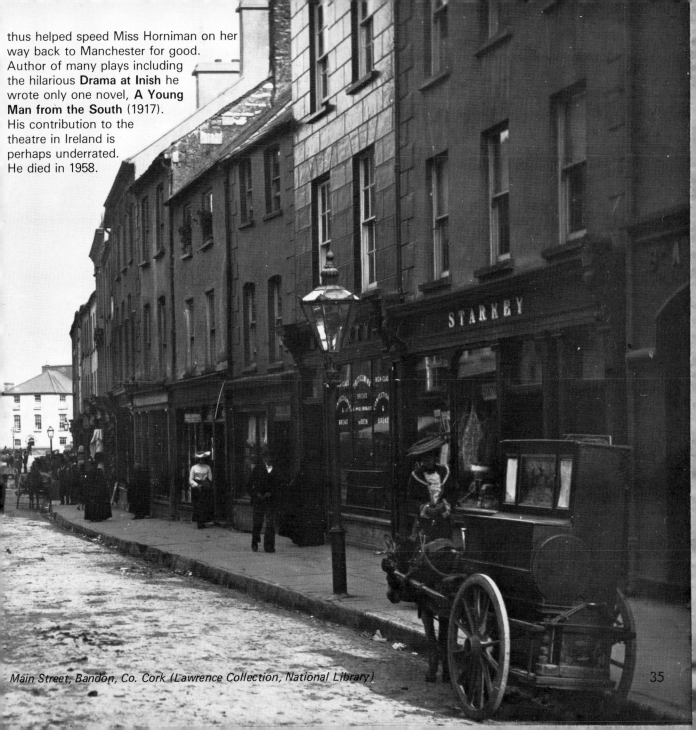

thus helped speed Miss Horniman on her way back to Manchester for good. Author of many plays including the hilarious **Drama at Inish** he wrote only one novel, **A Young Man from the South** (1917). His contribution to the theatre in Ireland is perhaps underrated. He died in 1958.

Main Street, Bandon, Co. Cork (Lawrence Collection, National Library)

35

When Mr. Neville came to discuss the evidence for the footprints of his glacier in more detail, he found his lively companion less communicative; but a man once put in good humour with his own knowledge seldom objects to imparting more than he receives. Jack Harold know enough about geology, as about many other things, to be able to throw a certain lambent brightness over what he could not understand; and Mr. Neville informed Miss Westropp that they had had a most interesting chat, and that he found Gougaun Barra charming; upon which Mabel shot a glance of gratitude to our young geologist.

'But what on earth has become of our American Captain? I thought he was with you,' exclaimed Miss Westropp, in some alarm.

The Rector put his finger to his lips, and pointed to a figure half concealed by the ruined wall that overhung the Holy Well. They stole over on tiptoe and looled in. Captain Mike was on his knees bareheaded under the wild ash tree which shaded the Holy Well, and whose branches were drooping under the poor tags of coloured cloth which were hung there by grateful pilgrims. There was something in the spectacle of the bronzed soldier, kneeling there under the open sky, his hands clasped, and his great chest shaken with strong emotion, which caused the lookers-on to hold their breath, and the men unconsciously to doff their hats. The soldier rose, his bosom still heaving. He pulled out a large blue silk handkerchief, and drew it across his eyes; and then, as if a sudden thought had struck him, knotted the handkerchief to one of the boughs of the ash tree among the peasants' humble tributes of their faith. He knelt down again at the foot of the ash tree and pulled out his clasp-knife. The lookers-on watched him with painful intentness. He scooped out carefully with his knife a tiny green sod at the root of the wild ash, placed it tenderly in his hat, which he put on his head, and then rose to go. As he did so, and before they could retreat, his eye caught the guilty faces of the eaves-droppers. He was not in the least disconcerted.

'So, I guess you people seen the whole show?' he said, good humouredly. 'Wal, it does a man good to make a real stark blithering moon-calf of hisself once in a life or so, anyway. There is nothin' in our Re-publican Constitooshun agen it. No, sir! 'Tis three-and-twenty year last Lady Day in Harvest since I paid my rounds before at St.

36

Fin Barr's Well. There were them with me then that are not here now—that never'll be here again. God rest you, little Mauryeen, an' the poor ould father, Jack!'

'Amen,' said Father Phil reverently. 'He was a decent man!'

'I guess a petrified old Grand Army man's got things to sink Artesian wells in him when he looks back to his boyhood a few, and I just struck water there a moment ago, that's all. Don't you be skeered, Rector, at my hangin' up the han'kecher on that ould bush. When a man sheds a tear or two on bottom principles, over all that's past an' gone, I kind o' think an honest Irish saint will be as glad to get 'em as if they was di'monds the size of a Wall Street speculator's.'

Miss Westropp looked as if she could have kissed Captain Mike's gunpowder-stained yellow cheek.

'An the green sod you cut?' she whispered softly.

'Oh!' laughed Captain Mike, taking off his hat, and

surveying its verdant contents complacently. 'Wal, you see, Missie, I couldn't get the saint's autograph lyin' around nohow, so I thought the next best thing would be a sprig of shamrock that was wathered with his blessin'. I've got an ould mother out yonder in East Thirty-second Street, Worcester, Mass, corner Kalabash Avenue, and won't her ould eyes jest skip when she sees that or'nery lookin' sod of Irish airth! Guess she'll go prayin' around a darn'd sight holier than if 'twar a block of real estate willed to the family—'twill fit where the real estate won't, in her coffin. An' you go Nap! she'll bring it along where she's goin'; and if I don't see them shamrocks shinin' in Heaven yet—wal, 'twill be because even the ould mother's prayers can't smuggle a perditioned old grizzly from the Ninth Massachusetts inside the line.'

William O'Brien, *When We Were Boys* (London, 1890)

WILLIAM O'BRIEN was born in Mallow in 1852. He became editor of Parnell's paper, *United Ireland* in 1881. His 'pepper-pot' style and flamboyant politics caused him to spend some time in jail, serving in all nine terms. Indeed he blamed the length of his famous book, *When We Were Boys* (1890) upon the length of his sentence, saying that if it had been shorter he could have been more economical in his verbal effects. The book is about the sentimental education of a Fenian and portrays with little disguise such real characters as Archbiship Croke and the author's brother, Jim. He died in 1928.

'In the middle of a scrubby grove, a little way from the enclosure, is a wishing-stone, which had evidently been much used, I hope to good purpose, for the stone itself was covered with trinkets and the bushes around were hung thickly with rags and hairpins and rosaries and other tokens. I picked up somewhere, perhaps from the jargon of the guide, that this wishing-stone is the altar of Fin Barre's old chapel, but I haven't been able to veryify this, and it may not be so; but the game is to put up a prayer to the saint, and make your wish, and leave some token to show that you are in earnest, and the wish will surely come true. Of course we made a wish and added some half-pennies to the collection on the altar. In turning over the trinkets already deposited there, we were amused to find two bright Lincoln cents.'
Burton E Stevenson, *The Charm of Ireland* (London, 1915)

St Finnbar's Oratory, Gougane Barra, Co. Cork (Lawrence Collection, National Library)

37

IT WAS AN APRIL morning in the Irish town of Waterford; beyond the suburbs, the grass lay thick and green upon the country-side in the virgin freshness of the spring, and the chestnuts glinted with the delicate sheen of bursting leaves; but in the streets, the dust of March was whirling to the April breeze, powdering the narrow by ways with a cloak of grey, eddying in a mad dance along the open spaces.

Portion of this dusty, characteristic, sparsely-populated town is dedicated to business—the business of the shops; a second and more important portion of it is given over to the quays, from whence a constant traffic is carried on with the hereditary enemy, England; while a third part, that holds itself aloof from commerce, is to be reckoned as half residential, half professional. It is to this third quarter that the eye of the story-seeker must turn on this April morning; for it is here, Lady Lane,—a thoroughfare as long and narrow as a Continental street, composed of tall old houses with square-paned windows and mysterious hall doors giving entry to vast and rambling interiors,—that the story, comedy or tragedy, is to find its stage; here, in the dining-room of one of the flat-fronted houses, that the student of human nature is to take his first glance at Stephen Carey—hero, so far as middle-class Irish life produces heroes, of the anticipated romance.

A man's room, one would have said at half a glance,—moreover, the room of a man self-made! There was no art, no beauty suggested or displayed; but there was comfort of a solid kind in the fire that burned ruddily in the grate, and in the breakfast-table that stood awaiting occupation. A man's room, although a closed work-basket stood on the sideboard, and the china on the table indicated breakfast for two.

And this first impression would have proved correct; for if the title of man be won by work, by patience, by a spirit that holds firm in face of great odds, then Carey's room was unquestionably the property of a man; for he had carved his own path to worldly success, hewing it from the rough material by days of toil and nights of thought.

Carey was a type,—a type of that middle class which by right of strength has formed its huge republic, and spread like a net over civilisation—invincible, indispensable as the vast machines from which it has sucked its power. It is as parent of this new republic that the nineteenth century will go down to futurity; and it is from the core of this new republic, virile in its ambition, tyrannical in its moral code, jealous of its hard-won supremacy, that we have garnered such men as Carey—the men of steel, drawn from the great workshops, tempered, filed, polished to fit the appointed place; helping to move the mighty engine of which they are the atoms, useless if cast out from its mechanism.

Katherine C. Thurston, *The Fly on the Wheel* (London, 1908)

KATHERINE CECIL THURSTON, nee Madden in Cork in 1875, was a firmly friend of Parnell and a nationalist. She married the 'anti-catholic' writer, E. Temple Thurston, in 1901 and published her first novel, *John Chilcote MP* in 1904. She divorced her husband in 1910 and committed suicide a year later. *The Fly on the Wheel* (1908) set in middle-class Waterford describes an unhappy love affair between a married man and a young girl who takes her own life.

Barron Strand Street, Waterford, 1901 (Lawrence Collection, National Library)

ROBERT DWYER JOYCE born in Glenosheen, Co. Limerick in 1830 was the younger brother of P. D. Joyce the Irish antiquarian and linguistic scholar whose *Old Celtic Romances* had such an effect upon Yeats and the other writers of the Anglo-Irish Renaissance. He lived in America for seventeen years where he had a successful and exclusive medical practice; it was there that he published most of his work: Prose, *Legends of the Wars in Ireland* (1868) and *Irish Fireside Tales* (1871) and verse, *Ballads of Irish Chivalry* (1872). To these should be added a collection published in Ireland in 1861., *Ballads, Romances and Songs.* The poem, *The Ballad of Dark Gilliemore,* is set in the Suir Valley, near the town of Carrick.

John Wogan of Castle Street, Carrick-on-Suir, solicitor and last seneschal of the Butlers. (Photograph taken April 1865 by McGrath of Carrick.) (Hugh Ryan/Carrick Society Collection)

A seneschal was the official in the house of a sovereign or great noble to whom the administration of justice and the entire control of domestic arrangements was entrusted.

I PLEDGE ye, comrades, in this cup
Of usquebaugh, bright brimming up;
And now while winds are blowing rude
Around our camp fire in the wood,
I'll tell my tale, yet sooth to say
It will be but a mournful lay.

Glenanner is a lovely sight,
Oun-Tarra's dells are fair and bright,
Sweet are the flowers of Lisnamar,
And gay the glynns 'neath huge Benn Gar;
But still, where'er our banner leads,
'Mid tall brown hills or lowland meads,
By storied dale or mossy down,
My heart goes back to Carrick town.

By Carrick town a castle brave
Towers high above its river wave,
Well belted round by wall and fosse
That foot of foe ne'er strode across.

Well belted round by wall and fosse
That foot of foe ne'er strode across.
Look on me now—a man am I
    Of mournful thoughts and bearing sad;
Yet once my hopes flowed fair and high,
    And once a merry heart I had;
For I was squire to Ormond then,
    First in his train each jovial morn
He flew his hawks by moor and fen,
Or chased the stag by rock and glen
    With music sweet of hound and horn.
Young Ormond was a goodly lord
As ever sat at head of board.
If Europe's kings, some festal day,
Sat round the board in revel gay,
And he were there, and I in hall,
The seneschal to place them all,
I'd place him without pause or fault
Among their best above the salt.
You need not smile, Sir Hugh le Poer,
    Nor you, young Donal of Killare;
I'prove my words, ay, o'er and o'er,
    With skian   in hand and bosom bare,
Or sword to sword and jack to jack,
For sake of Thomas Oge the Black!

R. D. Joyce, 'The Ballad of Dark Gilliemore' from *Ballads of Irish Chivalry* (Boston, 1872)

Bridge Street, Skibbereen, Co. Cork (Lawrence Collection, National Library)

MY PRISON CHAMBER

My prison chamber now is iron lined,
An iron closet and an iron blind.
But bars, and bolts, and chains can never bind
To tyrant's will the freedom-loving mind.

Beneath the tyrant's heel we may be trod,
We may be scourged beneath the tyrant's rod,
But tyranny can never ride rough-shod
O'er the immortal spirit-work of God.

And England's Bible tyrants are, O Lord!
Of any tyrants out the cruelest horde,
Who'll chain their Scriptures to a fixture board
Before a victim starved, and lashed, and gored. . .

Without a bed or board on which to lie,
Without a drink of water if I'm dry,
Without a ray of light to strike the eye,
But all one vacant, dreary, dismal sky.

The bolts are drawn, the drowsy hinges creak,
The doors are groaning, and the side walls shake,
The light darts in, the day begins to break,
Ho, prisoner! from your dungeon dreams awake. . .

"Rossa, salute the Governor," cries one,
The Governor cries out—"Come on, come on,"
My tomb is closed, I'm happy they are gone,
Well—as happy as I ever feel alone.

J. O'Donovan Rossa, 'My Prison Chamber' in *Irish Literature VIII* (Philadelphia, 1904)

JEREMIAH O'DONOVAN *(ROSSA)* was born in Rosscarbery, Co. Cork in 1831. He first attracted the attention of the authorities when as a grocer in the town of Skibbereen he founded the literary and political group, the *Phoenix Society.* This was swept into the Fenian movement and O'Donovan remained a relentless Fenian for the rest of his life. His inevitable privations in English jails were described in *Prison Life* (1874). Exiled on amnesty in 1874 he went to America where he died in 1915. The arrival of his remains in Dublin were the occasion of one of Pearse's more emotional speeches: 'Life springs from death and from the graves of patriot men and women spring living nations' and the demonstration became the prototype of 44 many such in subsequent years.

Main Street, Lismore, Co. Waterford (Lawrence Collection, National Library)

The meeting of the waters between
Long Range and the middle lake,
Killarney, looking up towards Dinis
Cottage. (Lawrence Stereoscopic
Collection, National Library)

Nuair do bhúail an bheirt Cill Áirne b'eigean doibh deoch bheith aca i dtigh Shéamuis Ui Bhruighin 'sa Sráid Nuaidn, agus níor bh'fhada dhoibh go raibh braon eile aca i Sráid na gCearc nuair casadh orra nuair bhí an gabha súgach go leor.

Ní raibh Neilli i bhfad ar a' sráid gur chonnaic sí a hathair agus é ar leath-mheisge. Is gairid do bhí sí féin agus an cailín eile ag déanamh a ngnótha. Nuair do bhíodar ullamh chun teacht abhaile do dhein Neilli a dícheall a hathair do mhealladh leí, acht na raibh maitheas dí bheith a tathant air; d'fhan sé fein agus Séamuis ar an sráid go dti tuitim na hoídhche agus go rabhadar araon ar meisge nó i ngiorracht dó.

Bhí capaillín beag cneasta ag Séamus Táilliura. Bhí an bóthar reidh agus an oídhche geal, agus dá mbéadh an beirt sásta leis an méid do bhí ólta aca nuair fhágadar sráid Cill Áirne bhéadh an sgéal go maith aca, acht ní rabhadar. Nuair thángadar go Droichead na Leamhna bhi deoch le bheith aca, agus nuair bhí an gabha ag teacht amach as an dtrucaill thuit se ar fhleasg a dhroma ar an mbóthar, agus 'san am cheadna do chuir rud eigin an capall ar siubhal. Chuaidh an roth treasna láimhe Thaidhg. Do sgread an fear bocht cómh géar sin gur rith na daoine amach chuige, agus nuair chonnacadar e sínte ar an mbóthar shaoileadar go raibh a lámh briste, acht ni raibh.

Ba mhór an ní go raibh an dochtúir 'n-a chomhnaidhe ar thaoibh an bhóthair ag Droichidín na Spiodóige; bhí sé ag baile. Tar éis féachaint ar láimh an ghabha 'sé dubhairt an dochtúir, "Ní'l aon chnámh briste, acht beidh sé tamall go mbeidh greidhm agat ar chasúr, a Thaidhg."

Séamus Ó Dúbhghaill, *Tadhg Gabha* (Dublin, 1900)

SÉAMUS Ó DÚBHGHAILL was born in Tuogh, Co. Kerry in 1855. An excise officer he had postings all over the British Isles and was stationed in Derry at the height of his literary fame, which coincided with the years of greatest success of the Gaelic League (from 1898 to 1904). His first public appearance as a writer was at the second Oireachtas (1898) when he won a prize for three humorous stories in Irish. He was a regular prizewinner after this writing not only stories but phrase-books, grammars and general text-books. These last gave him a great if impish delight since he was not a teacher. Known in later life by the pseudonym *Beirt Fhear* from his book *Beirt Fhear o'n dTuaith* his best known work *Tadhg Gabha* became an examination textbook for those who wished to be travelling teachers. The piece describes an occupational hazard of the smith's life, aggravated by the plenitude of public houses in Killarney.

'The town of Killarney is next in importance to Tralee, the capital of the county, and it has a population of 5,204. It is situated about a mile to the eastward of the largest of the lakes, and consists of four streets of which the Main Street is the principal. There are many small streets and lanes inhabited by poor people, and the whole town looks miserably decayed, presenting a melancholy contrast to the rich landscapes that surround it. The demesnes of the gentry take up all the ground up to the town, not leaving room even for small gardens, where the people might cultivate some vegetables, and they complain much of the want of a supply of milk.'

J. Godkin & J. Walker, *Handbook of Ireland* (Dublin, c.1870)

College Street, Killarney (Lawrence Collection, National Library)

Picnic at Killarney (Lawrence Collection, National Library)

Puck Fair, Killorglin, Co. Kerry (Lawrence Collection, National Library

"Oh, glory be to goodness, Father, 'tis a yaller Munster top!" he croaked.

He became silent, put his head upon one side, with a look almost of antique coquetry, and regarded Father Egan with imperative beseeching.

"Oh, it's to whip it, is it?" Father Egan said. "And what'll I do for the whip!"

An eager snuffle sounding close at hand, Father Egan turned, to behold young Feeney sprung up in silent magic at his side, flicking his pinafore with a rag fastened to a stick, while he clenched the fingers of the other hand on some pet jewel of his play. The Priest took the stick with the rag-lash from the child; he chose the smoothest flagstone before the door of the house, gave a sharp twist of his two hands, and round the Munster top went spinning, so fast, you could not see it move.

The old man shut his eyes in rapture, and his mind went back to the scenes from which the Munster top had hailed.

"Oh, 'tis the third day of the Munster Fair!" he said, "the day the horses do be coming with the long tails floating to the town . . . and the little donkeys goin', and the littles asseens trottin' under them, and the foxy-haired Tinkers drivin' 'em in the dreepin' rain!" . . .

He opened his eyes to see Father Egan encouraging the Munster top.

"Would you ketch it in the hand!" he cried.

By this time a shawled group of women had gathered round the gate. For all the world as if they had never set their eyes upon a top before, they clapped their hands with glittering eyes, and spurred its whirling movements with cries of approbation, as though it were a greyhound at a coursing match. " 'Tis down!" cried one. " 'Tis goin' still!" cried another. "You could ate your dinner while 'twas dancin'!" cried a third.

Drawn to her own gate from a neighbour's house by cries, Sara Feeney now ran forth and joined the group.

"Glory be!" she cried, "if the darlin' man hasn't sent to Munster for the top!"

Rosamond Langbridge, *The Green Banks of Shannon* (London, 1929)

ROSAMOND LANGBRIDGE was born in Glenalla, Co. Donegal in 1880 but was brought up and educated in Limerick where her father was Rector of St. John's. An unspecific and quasi-mystical nationalist she regarded Ireland as 'the child-soul among nations' which put the 'Traffic of the Heart before the Traffic of the Mart'. The characters of her novels though pretty mild by our standards were regarded as a trifle 'fast' by the readers of her heyday. Her last book, *The Green Banks of Shannon* (1929) is a collection of pleasantly sentimental sketches of life as she remembered it in her adopted county.

Puck Fair—Aonach an Phuic ('the fair of the he-goat) is held each year on the three days August 10–12 in the town of Killorglin, between Tralee and Cahirciveen. The origins of the ritual are shrouded in mystery but the anthropological aspects of the goat and the revelry seems fairly obvious. The goat is hoisted on top of a platform in the market square on the evening of the first day (the 'gathering') and presides over the trafficking in cattle sheep and horses until the evening of the third day (the 'scattering'). The photograph shows the 'gathering' day; the *puc* not yet in position and a general air of restraint and respectability that tends to disappear as the fair gets in its stride. The streamer bearing in Irish the slogan, 'Victory and Strength to the united Gaelic League' places the scene as around 1898.

The Lough, Cork, 1924. (Cork Examiner)

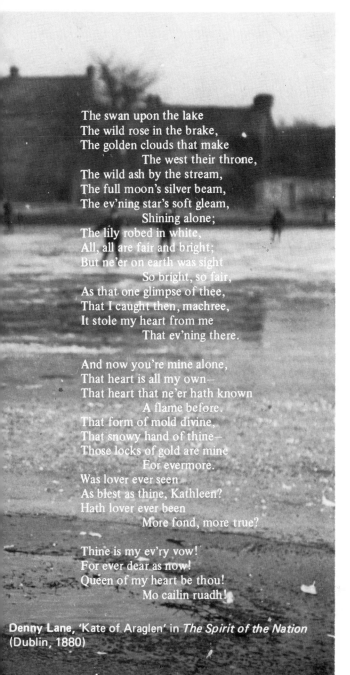

The swan upon the lake
The wild rose in the brake,
The golden clouds that make
       The west their throne,
The wild ash by the stream,
The full moon's silver beam,
The ev'ning star's soft gleam,
       Shining alone;
The lily robed in white,
All, all are fair and bright;
But ne'er on earth was sight
       So bright, so fair,
As that one glimpse of thee,
That I caught then, machree,
It stole my heart from me
       That ev'ning there.

And now you're mine alone,
That heart is all my own—
That heart that ne'er hath known
       A flame before.
That form of mold divine,
That snowy hand of thine—
Those locks of gold are mine
       For evermore.
Was lover ever seen
As blest as thine, Kathleen?
Hath lover ever been
       More fond, more true?

Thine is my ev'ry vow!
For ever dear as now!
Queen of my heart be thou!
       Mo cailin ruadh!

Denny Lane, 'Kate of Araglen' in *The Spirit of the Nation*
(Dublin, 1880)

DENNY LANE was born in Cork in 1818, the only child of Maurice Lane, a distillery owner. He is remembered for two poems 'Kate of Araglen' and 'An Irish Maiden's Lament' both of which appeared in *The Nation.* He was an ardent but sensible Young Irelander and warned the gorgeous peacocks of the Eighty-Two Club not to attempt to introduce their club uniform (like Robert Emmet's only more splendid in gold, green and white) into Cork because of the hatred of those citizens for uniform. 'This' he wrote in *The Nation,* 'I think, arises from the morbidly keen sense of the ludicrous that Cork men generally possess.' He died in 1899 having in his time been President of the Institute of Gas Engineers of Gt. Britain.

As they crossed the Norgate five times over,
  "The devil," says Padna, "Such light!"
Dinny Lucy clung on like a lover
  To Padna, "Begob 'tis a fright."

And they paused where the lamps on the water
  Danced up in reflections of red;
"Be the holy," says Din, "There's been
  slaughter—
Such blood!" "Yerra, God help your head!"

Padna pulled at his arm, reassuring,
  "Them lights are the lights on the port
Of grand ships with the cargoes maturing:
  'Tis bagging that lot 'll be sport."

But my Padna all through, and he straying,
  Watched out, "Oh we've passed Mallow
  Lane!"
"Yerra whisht," says Din Lucy, surveying,
  "We're down at the Jetties again."

So they clutched for a stanchion to steady
  The street that spun round like a midge,
An' Din dreaming cried, "Heave away, ready!"
  Till Padna said "Look! Vincent's Bridge!"

"Where the h—?" at that instant, such clatter
  And, rushing up, oh, I declare,
Katie Drew, (Padna's "flame"), an' no hat or
  Coat on her, and she "in a tear!"

An' "Come on!" and "Have sense!" and
  "Ye foolahs!"
Half coaxing—a woman knows how,—
"Christmas times," Padna whispered as cool as
  You please, Dinny dumb as a cow!

D. L. Kelleher, *Cork's Own Town* (Dublin, 1920)

DANIEL LAWRENCE KELLEHER was born in Cork
in 1893 and set most of his poems in that city. *Cork's Own
Town* is a ballad sequence in which the colour and vitality
of 'the highly individualistic Southern City' is conveyed in
the adventures and opinions of Padna Dee, the Cork
'cockney' born within the sound of Shandon Bells.

*P.S. Albert on her regular service run to Queenstown,
Crosshaven, Ringaskiddy and other wharfs on Cork
Harbour. 1912. (Cork Examiner Collection)
The Albert, a 54-tonner plied, the Lee and Cork Harbour
right up until 1925 when the steamers were withdrawn.*

Excursion Crowd on Cork Quay with P. S. Albert dressed over all for excursion 1897 (Cork Examiner Collection)

Hospital Flag Day, Cork. c.1900 (Cork Examiner Collection)

"JURRY Jurry! Yerra, look, man alive!"

"What! Where? Yerra, what ails yi at all?"

"Look hether at Oul' Dan, th' oul' dickens! Look at what he's carryin' home to dround the Shamrock wid!"

It was at the Cork Terminus of the Muskerry Line on St. Patrick's Eve, and crowds of homeward-bound passengers were eagerly endeavouring to collect the parcels sent to meet them from the various shops.

As usual, pandemonium reigned supreme. A babel of messengers shouted at the tip top of their discordant voices the names of the firms they represented—"Cash-ays," "Bay-less," "Queen's Oul' Castle," "D'Arcade," &c., &c.— while the anxious passengers strained their ears to catch the name of the firm they were awaiting.

You thought you heard "D'Arcade" half way up the platform, and you elbowed through a packed crowd of equally anxious inquirers towards your goal, but when you reached it, as you thought, "D'Arcade" was being called "away back" where you started from! No messenger was ever known to remain in the same spot for five seconds; they dodge about up and down while the perplexed passengers follow the voices, as elusive as a score of corncrakes, hither and thither, and after endless elbowing catch the object of their hunt.

"Hallo, boy! are ye Bailey's?"

"Yes, Mistero!" finger touches cap politely.

Your name may be Buckley, Bung, or Blennerhassett, but it's "alldesame" to the messenger, the familiar "Mr. O" embraces the lot. He addresses you with the ease and intimacy of an old acquaintance.

"What name, Mistero?" he promptly inquires. You tell him, and he searches through his basket, and lifts up your parcel with much unnecessary exertion, and hands it over, looking anxiously into your eyes, canvassing the chances of a tip. If you are oblivious to his suggestive glances, several gentle hints are thrown out.

"Put it in di van for yi, Mistero?"

And he does so if you permit him, then comes back again, touching his cap profusely, assuring you—"Dass all right now, Mistero." And if you are still slow to respond he lingers on till his magnetic eyes draw coppers from even the most miserly!

"Oul' Dan" had come in to Cork to get the necessaries to celebrate St. Patrick's Day according to his own idea. The receipt of an unexpected twelve dollars from his daughter in New York helped him to prepare, and so he was well laden when Jack Fitz and Jurry Hegarty, two neighbouring lads, saw him at the station.

"A jar of whishkey, no less! Glory be to oul' Cork!" cried Jurry in surprise.

"Yes, man alive! and a basket of full aitables besides!" added Fitz.

"Ha, then," said Jurry reflectively. " 'tis he ought be sick wid the whiskhey—'twas it losht the farm for him!"

"True for yi! All the same," added Fitz, "he's the dacint oul' Dan if he's fond o' the dhrop inself."

"Come over and we'll give him a hand," said Jurry.

The messenger boy was palavering oul" Dan for a tip.

"Dass all now, Mistero; de're all in," but Dan was dense.

"Ah, Mistero," persuasively urged the lad, "don't forget me Patrick's Pot, alldesame!"

At last oul' Dan was softened. After much cogitation he dug his hand deep down into his trousers something to the eagerly watchful boy, with a "Run away now and don't be botherin' me."

"Tanks! Tanks, Mistero!" Then finding his tip was only a single solitary copper, he wheeled round to a group of his colleagues, and holding the penny aloft between his fingers, remarked solemnly—"A box at di Palace Monday night!"

"Sound man, Dan!" said Fitz, patting the old fellow patronisingly on the back.

Oul' Dan looked around suspiciously and clutched his jar tightly.

"Oh, Jackey! is that you, a vic o? It's the dickens own own job gettin' the parcels"—he was out of breath.

"Yer well loaded, Dan," said Fitz, smiling.

"Fairly. The little girl didn't forget me, God bless her! She sint me three poun'."

"Begor we'll be all callin' to see you to-night," said Fitz.

"An' welcome," said Dan, cheerfully.

William Cronin ('Liam), *A Hamper of Humour* (Dublin, 1913).

'LIAM' (WILLIAM CRONIN) was the author of a collection of sketches called *A Hamper of Humour* (1913) showing two interests that are almost obsessions, the Cork accent and trains.

Tram at Father Mathew Statue, Cork (1900) (Lawrence Collection, National Library)

A photograph taken almost certainly in Adare about 1898. It is very obviously posed, the girl if 'colleen' she be is wearing her Sunday best and perched precariously and temporarily upon a wooden cask.

GLAUCE

I love you, pretty maid, for you are younger:
I love you, pretty maid, for you are fair:
I love you, pretty maid, for you love me.

They tell me that, a babe, smiling you gazed
Upon the stars, with open, asking eyes,
And tremulous lips apart. Everlong, self-taught,
You found for every star and every flower
Legends and names and fables sweet and new.
I, since I loved you, am grown half immortal.

O that when far away I still might see thee!
How oft when wearied with the din of life
On thee mine eyes would rest, thy Latmian heavens
Brightening that orbed brow and those white shoulders!
Hesper should shine upon thee—lamp of Love,

Beneath whose radiance thou wert born.—O Hesper!
Thee will I love and reverence evermore.—
Bind up that shining hair into a knot,
and let me see that polished neck of thine
Uprising from the bed snow-soft snow-white
In which it rests so gracefully! What God
Hath drawn upon thy forehead's ivory plane
Those two clear streaks of sweet and glistening black
Lifted in earnest mirth or lovely awe?
Open those Peiad eyes, liquid and tender,
And let me lose myself among their depths!
Caress me with thine infant hands, and tell me
Old tales divine that love makes ever new
Of Gods and men entoiled in flowery nets,
Of heroes sighing all their youth away,
And which the fairest flower of Venus' isle.
Come forth, dear maid, the day is calm and cool,

58

And bright though sunless. Like a long green scarf,
The tall Pines crowning yon gray promontory
In distant ether hang, and cut the sea.
But lovers better love the dell, for there
Each is the other's world—How indolently
The tops of those pale poplars bending sway
Over the violet-braided river brim!
Whence comes their motion, for no wind is heard,
And the long grasses move not, nor the reeds?
Here we will sit, and watch the rushes lean
Like locks, along the leaden-coloured stream
Far off; and thou, O child, shalt talk to me
Of Naiads and their loves. A blissful life
They lead, who live beneath the flowing waters:
They cherish calm, and think the sea-weeds fair;
They love to sleek their tresses in the sun;
They love each other's beauty; love to stand
Among the lillies, holding back their tresses
And listening, with their gentle cheek reclined
Upon the flood, to some sweet melody
Of Pan or shepherd piping in lone woods,
Until the unconscious tears run down their face.
Mild are their loves, nor burdensome their thoughts—
And would that such a life were mine and thine!

Aubrey de Vere, 'Glauce' from *Irish Odes and Other Poems* (New York, 1869)

AUBREY DE VERE, was born in 1814 in Curragh Chase, the ancestral home of the de Vere family, situated six miles south east of Adare, Co. Limerick. The son of Sir Aubrey de Vere (himself a poet) he was a romantic unionist. Educated at Trinity he became a catholic in 1851 and an obvious choice for the faculty of Newman's Catholic University (though as Professor of Political and Social Science) when that unique venture was established after 1852. Though his poetic works run as with most 19th-century versifiers into many volumes his most successful, and to modern taste most readable, work was *Inishfail, A Lyrical Chronicle of Ireland* (1863). 'Glauce' is typical of his bland and, considering his experience of women, naive style. There is no suggestion in this mild ode that the mythological Glauce was the woman that Jason rejected for Medea or that she died horribly at the hands of that resourceful sorceress. He died unmarried in 1902.

Adare, Co Limerick was the invention of the 3rd Earl of Dunraven who had become a catholic at the time of the Oxford Movement. Its exotic appearance, like a Costwold village, was due to his interest in architecture and landscaping.

Broad Street, Adare, Co. Limerick (Lawrence Collection, National Library)

Scríobhas go mionchruinn ar a lán dár gcúrsaí d'fhonn go mbéadh cuimhne i bpoll éigin orthu agus thugas íarracht ar mheon na ndaoine a bhí i mo thimpeall a chur síos chun go mbeadh a dtuairisc inár ndiaidh, mar ná beidh ar leithéidi arís ann.

Táim críonna anois. Is dócha gur iomdha rud eile a tháinig trasna orm i rith mo mharthan go dtí seo dá mbéadh slí sa cheann doibh. Tháinig daoine ar an saol le mo linn i mo thimpeall, agus d'imíodar. Níl ach cuigear is sine ná mé beo ar an oileán. Táid sin ar an mbunchíos; níl uaimse ach cupla mí, leis chun an dáit chéanna, dát nach rogha liom. Is ag bagairt chun báis a bhíonn sé, dar liom cé go bhfuil morchuid daoine arbh fhearr leó a bheith críonna agus an pinsean acu ná a bheith óg á éagmais, lucht na sainte agus an scanraidh.

Is cuimhin liom a bheith ar bhrollach mo mháthar. Thugadh sí suas ar an gcnoc mé i gclíabh a bhíodh ag tarraingt mhóna aici. Nuair a bhíodh an chlíabh lán den mhóin is faoina hascaill a bhínn ag teacht aici. Is cuimhin liom a bheith i mo gharsún; i m'fhear óg; i mbláth mo mhaitheasa agus mo nirt. Thainig gorta agus flúirse, ráth agus miráth le mo mharthain go dtí seo. Is mór an fhoghlaim a thugaid sin ar an nduine a thugann faoi ndeara íad.

Beidh an Blascaed lá gan aoinne den dream atá luaite agam sa leabhar seo—ná aoinne a mbeidh cuimhne aige orainn. Tugaim buíochas le Dia thug caoi dom gan an méid den saol a chonac féin agus a raghas ag broic leis a dhul amú, agus go mbeidh a fhios i mo dhiaidh conas mar a bhí an saol le mo linn agus na comharsain a bhí suas le mo linn agus an méid ata fós beo acu, gan focal searbh idir mé agus íad ríamh.

Rud eile, níl tír ná dúthaigh ná náisiún ná go dtugann duine an chraobh leis thar chách eile. Ó lasadh an chéad tine san oileán seo níor scríobh aoinne a bheatha ná a shaol ann. Fágann sin an chraobh ag an té a dhein é. 'Neosfaidh an scríbhinn seo conas mar a bhí na hoileánaigh ag déanamh sa tseanaimsir. Bhí mo mháthair ag tarraingt na móna agus mise ocht mbliana déag d'aois ar scoil aici. Tá súil le Dia agam go bhfaighidh sí féin agus m'athair an Ríocht Bheannaithe agus go mbuailfeadsa agus gach n-aon a léifidh an leabhar seo leó in Oileán Párthais.

Tomás Ó Criomhthain, *An tOileanach* (Ath Cliath, 1929)

TOMÁS Ó CRIOMHTHAIN (1856-1937) was born, lived and died on the Great Blasket Island off the coast of Co. Kerry, the greatest of the Irish writers who came from that area so incredibly fertile of writers. *An tOileánach* is his life-story, written in a style so spare and muscular as almost to defy the skill of the translator and to deprive Europe of one of its finest pieces of primitive writing. Ó Criomhthain writes consciously of a vanishing way of life; as he notes with a kind of desperate pride: *mar beidh ár leithéidí aris ann.*

Tomás Ó Criomhthain at the door of his house, Great Blasket Island, Co. Kerry, 1932. (MacMonagle Collection)

At half-past one the town was silent,
Except a row raised in the Island,
Where Thady,—foe to sober thinking,—
With comrade lads, sat gaily drinking.
A table and a pack of cards
Stood in the midst of four blackguards,
Who, with the bumper-draught elated,
Dash'd down their trumps, and swore, and cheated.
Four pints, the fruits of their last game,
White-foaming, to the table came;
They drank, and dealt the cards about,
And Thady brought *fifteen wheel out.*
Again, the deal was Jack Fitzsimon's,
He turned them up, and trumps were diamonds;
The ace was laid, by Billy Mara,
And beat with five, by Tom O'Hara;
The queen was quickly laid, by Thady,
Jack threw the king, and douced the lady.
Bill jink'd the game, and cried out, "Waiter,
Bring in the round, before 'tis later!"
The draughts came foaming from the barrel;
The sport soon ended in a quarrel;—
Jack flung a pint at Tom O'Hara,
And Thady levell'd Billy Mara;
The cards flew round in every quarter,
The earthen floor was drunk with porter;
The landlord ran to call the Watch,
With oaths half English, and half Scotch.
The Watch came to the scene of battle,
Proclaiming peace, with sounding wattle;
The combatants were soon arrested,
But Thady got off unmolested.

Michael Hogan, 'Drunken Thady' from *Lays and Legends of Thomond* (Limerick, 1865)

O'Connell Street, looking towards Patrick Street, Limerick c.1870 (Lawrence Stereoscopic Collection, National Library).

MICHAEL HOGAN, known to many loyal hearts as 'The Bard of Thomond', was born in Limerick in 1832 and as a wheelwright, lampooner, broadsheet poet and nightwatchman lived a life more appropriate to 18th-century Grub Street than 19th-century Limerick. His main work, *Lays and Legends of Thomond,* is rather decorous compared with some of his satirical squibs. His invention, 'Drunken Thady' is fit to take his place beside Burn's 'Tam-o'—Shanter' in the hall of inebriate fame. The bard died in 1899.

Troubles

Cork Fire 1900 (Cork Examiner) 63

He pulled strongly, and woke to life a venerable old seaman, who was sleeping calmly in the shelter of the boats. He rose lazily, lazily drew himself together, and stared at the intruders.

"Hello, old salt," said Ashley, "we disturbed you! Is there any place in this Sleepy Hollow where we could get a bite, or a drink for our nags?"

James Carroll resented this familiarity for two reasons. First, because "old salt" was an irreverent expression to a man who had spent half his life before the mast in Her Majesty's Navy, and had several medals hanging up near the altar of the Blessed Virgin in his little bedroom at home. And second, because "Sleepy Hollow" was an untoward epithet for the cleanest, tidiest, healthiest little fishing hamlet in Ireland. He took up in silence the tar-brush with which he was coating the little fishing smacks that, with their broad, black blacks were now glistening in the hot sun, and, after a few moments' reflection, during which he was gathering his thoughts and concentrating them in a deadly form, he sent forth the missile.

"I'd give you one advice, young man, and maybe you'd thank me for it when you have grey hairs. There are two things that carry a man safe through life — the Grace of God, an' a civil tongue."

He bent down to his work again; but after a moment he thought he could improve on the aphorism.

"An' a civil tongue is no load," he said.

Ashley looked at his companion and laughed.

"Stranded, by Jove!" said he.

Hugh Ireton, more diplomatic, because more kind, said nothing; but running his horse's bridle under his arm, he took out his tobacco pouch and filled his pipe. Then, without offering it to Ashley, he said to the old mariner:—

"You have got your cutty about you?"

The old man hesitated for a moment between wounded pride and the temptation. But it was only for a moment. The flesh conquered the spirit; and, like most mortals, he yielded. He put his pride in his pocket and took out his pipe. He filled it well from the proffered pouch, and taking a light from the young man, he sat and smoked leisurely. When his anger, excited by the young man's ir-

64

reverence, had calmed down, he said apologetically:—

"Ye'll pardon me, young gintlemin, for the liberty; but we, old navy men, were always addressed respectful-like by our officers. And they had to mind their P's and Q's themselves, I tell ye. If the Lieutenant on watch had only to tell the Cap'n that the cook was drunk, he had to tech his cap and say:— 'I've the 'anner to report the cook is drunk, Sir!' and if the Cap'n replied:—'You may go to the devil, Sir!' the lieutenant had to tech his cap again, 'and say, respectful-like:—'Ay, ay, Sir!' That was manners for you. But this is rare tobacco!"

"May I be permitted, Sir, to join the pow-wow, Sir, with this?" said Ashley, holding out a capacious flask.

"Ay, ay, Sir," said Ireton. "But that's new whiskey, Ashley. Is there any fresh water around here?" he asked, addressing the old man.

"Ay, ay, Sir" said the latter, entering into the fun with twinkling eyes, and the expectation of better things.

He took them up to his little cottage; and a very neat, clean, well-kept cottage it was. For its tutelar deity was Anstie, James Carroll's only daughter, "the light of his life and the pulse of his heart.'. It was her pretty presence threw sunshine wherever she cast a shadow; and it was her swift, deft fingers that made the whole place a "moral" of neatness and beauty. Of course it was only a sailor's cabin; but the sailor's lass kept it as sweet as the stateroom in a British man-of-war.

Canon Sheehan, *Miriam Lucas,* (London, 1912)

PATRICK AUGUSTINE SHEEHAN was born in Mallow in 1852 and became parish priest of Doneraile in 1895. His tastes were scholarly and he was rather better read than most of his compeers—facts which influenced his literary style. His works have always been officially approved reading for the young and this has led to an unjust disregard and underrating. His portraits of priests, horn beads and all, have rarely been equalled; only in the work of Gerald O'Donovan is there comparable portraiture. Known to many who have never read the book as the author of *My New Curate* (1899) he wrote in all eleven novels of which *Luke Delmege* (1901) is probably the best. He became a DD in 1903 and died ten years later still pastor of Doneraile.

British Warship, 'Dreadnought' Class, Bantry Bay, 1907. (Lawrence Collection National Library)

The first of the class, HMS *Dreadnought* was launched in 1906, of 17900 tons and with a main armament of ten 12-in guns in five turrets and a speed of 22 knots. The gun turret may be seen centre picture with tompions covering the barrels. Bantry Bay was a good deep anchorage but somewhat unsheltered.

65

"A select combination of the circus and music-hall. I hope our 'umble endeavours will be acceptable to you—in fact, I—"

"No, sir, a penny is no good; fetch another one."

"In fact, I make no doubt you will be pleased that not only will you come back again to-morrow night, but that you will also bring those among you who have not come."

"One penny—half-price for the child, madam; our invariable rule."

"The performance will now open with the good old Punch and Judy Show, after which there will be variety entertainment, concluding with the wonderful magicograph, depicting scenes, sentimental and comic, and also the grim tragedies of the Boer war."

Great applause from the audience.

During the performance; the eloquent Theodore made five other speeches, pointing out how interrupters would be dealt with in Ginnett's and Sanger's circus.

"Not only would the hinterrupter be ejected from the theatyer, but the 'ole performance would be abandoned. I, 'owever, am not going to allow the audience who have paid for an entertainment to suffer from the conduct of any hindividual or hindividuals, and, therefore, the programme shall be given in full."

More applause, and then the wonderful magicograph.

"Now ladies and gentlemen," said the irrepressible Theodore, "I am about to show you something that has never yet been exhibited by a travelling company. In one of the pictures you will catch a glimpse of the Boers on the brow of a hill firing on the British in the plains below. This, ladies and gentlemen, is the honly photograph which has ever been taken of the Boers in action."

"Begob, but I believe that's thrue for him," said Jerry to the sapper. "There's a captain home, invaleded from South Afrikey, staying back on a visit at Master George's at present. Murra, but he has wondherful tales o' the front. I heerd him tell how wan day himself an' the docther an' a gineral was ridin' out from the camp, ridin' along the themselves, it appears, on a tower of pleasure. Well, they was ridin' along when they hears two shots; the reports was so far away that they took no notice, but rode

66

on continuing their tower o'pleasure, in the direction they was going. They was hardly gone a hundred yards when shlap goes another shot, an' down falls the gineral from between the two o' thim. Murra, the docthor jumped off his horse, an' there he was dead, with a bullet in his heart. The captain wheeled round an' galloped back as hard as he could to the camp, an', hanom-an-deoul, but he was three weeks in bed with the fright av it. After that he got up and did some manoeuvres agin, but he caught that faver an' aguy, an' shure I suppose he let on to be worse than he was, too, for they sint him home on sick lave, and the divil a wan o' him, he says, 'll ever go out agin."

Now, during all this recital the sapper was becoming more and more uneasy and indignant. To add to his ill-humour, something kept pushing itself under the

tent between his feet. Taking it to be a dog, he pushed it away time after time, and finally gave it a very smart kick back wards. There was a savage growl and some whispering outside, and just as Flanagan's story was finished a sod of turf hopped off the tail of the sapper's coat, setting alight a box of matches he carried therein.

The sapper gave a bound in the air; of course there was nobody to be seen.

"Jest loike yer bloomin' Boers," he said to Jerry; "they foires an' they runs away."

"An' be the same token," said Jerry, "I see that ye have yer wounds in the rere."

"What do ye mean?"

"Och, ne'er a ha' porth but jest what I say."

"Now, gentlemen," said the showman, "this can't be allowed; if ye want to fight, why go outside."

After a preliminary tussle and terrible threats on both sides, they went out. Awaiting them was the local sergeant, who ordered them home from the village. As they were rather disinclined to follow his directions, he helped them with a stout blackthorn stick, with such good effect that the argument has never since been resumed.

Joseph K. O'Connor ('Heblon') *Studies in Blue* (Dublin, 1905)

JOSEPH O'CONNOR was a barrister in Dublin whose literary fancy it was to contribute humorous essays to the Dublin Evening Mail. Born in Ashford, Co. Limerick in 1878 most of his essays are about the City.

Military Barracks, Clonmel, Co. Tipperary (Lawrence Collection, National Library)

Killarney Pipe Band, 1912 (MacMonagle Collection Killarney)

TIMOTHY DANIEL SULLIVAN was born in Bantry, Co. Cork in 1827. He had the same kind of journalistic and political career as his brother A. M, representing Westmeath, Donegal and Dublin at Westminster. He was the editor of that nineteeth-century staple of Irish bookshelves, *Speeches from the Dock* and his name will be forever famous as the author, in response to the treatment of the Manchester Martyrs, of 'God Save Ireland', a rather ironical twist this when one considers his conservative-nationalist career. He died in Dublin in 1914.

THOMAS ASHE was the outstanding guerrilla leader who gave the Volunteers their only victory outside Dublin in 1916. He captured four RIC barracks in the Ashbourne district of Co. Dublin and held out until Pearse ordered the general surrender. He died in Mountjoy Jail during forcible-feeding on 15 September 1917. At his funeral three volleys were fired over his grave and Michael Collins uttered just two sentences: 'Nothing additional remains to be said. The volley which we have just heard is the only speech which it is proper to make above the grave of a dead Fenian.'

GOD SAVE IRELAND

High upon the gallows tree
Swung the noble-hearted Three,
By the vengeful tyrant stricken in their bloom;
But they met him face to face,
With the courage of their race,
And they went with souls undaunted to their doom.
"God save Ireland!" said the heroes;
"God save Ireland!" said they all:
"Whether on the scaffold high
"Or the battle-field we die,
"Oh, what matter, when for Erin dear we fall!"

Climbed they up the rugged stair,
Rang their voices out in prayer,
Then with England's fatal cord around them cast,
Close beneath the gallows tree,
Kissed like brothers lovingly,
True to home and faith and freedom to the last.
"God save Ireland!" said they all:
"Whether on the scaffold high
"Or the battle-field we die,
"Oh, what matter, when for Erin dear we fall!"

Never till the latest day
Shall the memory pass away
Of the gallant lives thus given for our land;
But on the cause must go,
Admidst joy, or weal, or woe,
Till we've made our isle a nation free and grand.
"God save Ireland!" say we proudly;
"God save Ireland!" say we all:
"Whether on the scaffold high
"Or the battle-field we die,
"Oh, what matter, when for Erin dear we fall!"

T. D. Sullivan, 'God Save Ireland' from *Songs and Poems*
(Dublin, 1899)

Thomas Ashe (Keogh Collection, National Library) 69

TOMAS MacCURTAIN was Lord Mayor of Cork in 1920 when the centre of the city was burned and looted by British troops. He had been O/C of the Cork Brigade of the Irish Volunteers in 1916 and was known to be the head of disaffection in Munster. On the early morning of March 20, 1920, plain-clothes men and uniformed police and military isolated the area around his house and at 1.30 am a group of men with blackened faces burst in and shot him at the door of his bedroom. The coroner's verdict was one of wilful murder against Lloyd George, Lord French, Chief Secretary MacPherson and certain officers in the RIC. The body lay in state at the City Hall, Cork from Saturday 21 to Sunday 22, March.

Lying-in-state of Tomás MacCurtain, Lord Mayor of Cork, March 21, 1920
(Cork Examiner Collection.)

'I envied him because the society—the Young Italy—that I belong to——'

'Yes?'

'Intrusted him with a work that I had hoped—would be given to me, that I had thought myself—specially adapted for'.

'What work?'

'The taking in of books—political books—from the steamers that bring them—and finding a hiding place for them—in the town——'

'And this work was given by the party to your rival?'

'To Bolla—and I envied him.'

'And he gave you no cause for this feeling? You do not accuse him of having neglected the mission intrusted to him?'

'No, father; he has worked bravely and devotedly; he is a true patriot and has deserved nothing but love and respect from me.'

Father Cardi pondered.

'My son, if there is within you a new light, a dream of some great work to be accomplished for your fellow-men, a hope that shall lighten the burdens of the weary and oppressed, take heed how you deal with the most precious blessing of God. All good things are of His giving; and of His giving is the new birth. If you have found the way of sacrifice, the way that leads to peace; if you have joined with loving comrades to bring deliverance to them that weep and mourn in secret; then see to it that your soul be free from envy and passion and your heart as an altar where the sacred fire burns eternally. Remember that this a high and holy thing, and that the heart which would receive it must be purified from every selfish thought. This vocation is as the vocation of a priest; it is not for the love of a woman, nor for the moment of a fleeting passion; it is *for God and the people; it is now and for ever.*'

'Ah!' Arthur started and clasped his hands; he had almost burst out sobbing at the motto. 'Father, you give us the sanction of the Church! Christ is on our side——'

'My son,' the priest answered solemnly, 'Christ drove the money-changers out of the Temple, for His House shall be called a House of Prayer, and they had made it a den of thieves.'

After a long silence, Arthur whispered tremulously:

'And Italy shall be His Temple when they are driven out——'

He stopped; and the soft answer came back:

' "The earth and the fulness thereof are mine, saith the Lord." '

E. L. Voynich, *The Gadfly* (New York, 1897)

ETHEL LILIAN VOYNICH was born in 1864 in Cork, the daughter of Prof. George Boole whose work in Mathematical Logic led to the development of Set Theory and the Mathematics of Circuity. She married Count Voynich, a Polish emigre, in 1890 and through him was introduced to the Italy about which she had had so many romantic dreams. Mazzini had been the great hero of her girlhood and *The Gadfly* (1897) her greatest novel was set in the time of the *risorgimento.* She died in 1960 at the age of 96 having spent the last forty years of her life in New York.

TERENCE MacSWINEY was born in Cork in 1879. He trained as an accountant and afterwards took a degree in philosophy from the Royal University. He was an enthusiastic supporter of the Gaelic League but was deflected from linguistic concerns when the League went political in 1913. Interned at Frongoch in 1916 he returned to full-time Volunteer activity in 1917. He became Lord Mayor of Cork on the death of Tomas MacCurtain in 1920 but was arrested in the August of that year. His death after seventy days of hunger strike aroused a great deal of emotion. The remains lay in state for a day in Southwark Cathedral. The intention to bring them to Dublin was foiled by the authorities who commandeered them at Holyhead and had them brought to Cork. He was buried in the Republican Plot, Cork after an immense funeral on Sunday, 1 November, 1920.

The Revolutionist was written in 1909 but was not produced until after his death (at the Abbey in 1921). The play in its political philosophy and in its sense of the need for personal, supreme sacrifice is clearly autobiographical.

72

FOLEY. Yes. Dead.

CON. This hand is warm.

FOLEY. The breath has only just left him.

CON. But there's colour in his face.

FOLEY. It sometimes happens—he died in great pain.

CON. And no one near him.

FATHER O'CONNOR. God never left him.

CON. I can't realize 'tis death. Look at his face.

FOLEY. He's composed now.

FATHER O'CONNOR' He's very beautiful.

> *(Hugh's look is strangely beautiful. The last struggle forced the blood to his face; it has not entirely receded and leaves a colour behind with an effect strangely natural. The lines of pain are smoothed out; his expression is quiet and happy with the trace of a smile. The others stand looking at him in silence. His look acts on them for a moment like a spell. Foley's reference to Nora breaks the spell.)*

FOLEY. She will be coming.

CON. My God, what shall we do?

FOLEY. There may be a delay. She missed me and ran for others.

CON *(to Father O'Connor).* Could you keep her out?

FATHER O'CONNOR. I'll try

FOLEY. There's some one coming.

CON. Quick.

FATHER O'CONNOR. She has courage, thank God. *(Going.)*

CON *(looking on Hugh).* Thank God, he's so beautiful. *(Father O'Connor goes out quickly. Immediately an altercation is heard outside.)*

Terence MacSwiney, *The Revolutionist* (Dublin, 1914)

Funeral of Terence MacSwiney (MacMonagle Collection, Killarney)

'Eighteen Pounder' pictured in the old barrack yard, New Street, Carrick-on-Suir. The officers are Colonel Heslip and Joyce (rank unknown) of the National Army. (Mrs Pike, Carrick Society).

Shaun Foddha was posted, with half-a-dozen others, behind the pile of rocks near Elsie Dhuv's cabin, to at least delay the artillery, in case they should come that way, by rolling large stones down to the narrow roads, and discharging their firearms, such as they were. Of course the tall blacksmith had his blunderbuss—in the efficacy of which he had such perfect faith, that the fully expected to see the King's troops—not to mention the hated but despised yeomanry—recoil in terror and consternation before the first discharge. He contemptuously rejected Chris Carmody's advice to take an old musket, which though rust-eaten outside, and a very shaky weapon, either to handle or to look at, Chris assured him was sound at the breech, and but slightly honeycombed on the inside of the barrel. But Shaun Foddha would not have exchanged his stumpy blunderbuss for the best and newest musket in Europe, or the surest and deadliest rifle that every rang in an American forest. One 'bellus' at the enemy was all Shaun wanted with the blunderbuss, loaded as it was for a week with slugs to the very muzzle.

The chances, however, were but slight that the military would come by the narrow road that crossed Glounsoggarth. Hubert Butler saw this, and collected as many men as he could, and posted them in a grove a mile or two from the bridge in the glen which commanded the wider and more level road at a point where he thought an attack could be successfully made upon the guns, and the carriages broken, so as to enable him to raise the siege of O'Carroll's house by an attack upon the yeomen before they could be reinforced by the regulars, who would require some time to recover from the shock of an unexpected sortie from the grove.

Both Fergus O'Carroll and Captain Branton saw a horseman ride to the crest of the hill opposite the house two or three times, within a couple of hours, and after apparently surveying the ground below, wheel round and disappear down the other side of the hill, but neither the captain nor the rebel chief whom he had entrapped, as he believed, beyond all hope of escape, could form the remotest guess who the inquisitive horseman might be, or whether he was friend or foe, or merely an indifferent looker-on.

That he was not an idle spectator, at all events, was soon apparent, both to the besieged and besieger. The report of an irregular discharge of musketry was borne over the hill, and almost immediately after the horseman appeared again. But instead of retiring, as he had so often done before, on he came, followed by a small but compact body of men who, to his infinite delight, Fergus O'Carroll, looking from the small window in the gable of his barricaded house, saw plainly enough were not regular soldiers. And, seeing that nearly the whole of the Garryroe Corps were posted round the house, he concluded neither could they be yeomanry. The only other possible conclusion was that they were friends. His heart beat quick; for he had really made up his mind to die. In the hurry of the moment he had let Dick Maher down from the window, desiring him to collect as many of the boys as he could, and make some demonstration that might give him a chance of making a rush through the yeomen, who surrounded the house on every side. But when he had time for reflection, he saw the hopelessness of this project.

Charles Kickham *Elsie Dhuv* (Dublin, 1886)

This was the gun used by General Prout of the Free State forces to soften Republican resistance in Waterford from Ferrybank on 19 July 1922. A similar gun had been used to take Limerick earlier in July. Even before Limerick had fallen the Republican general Liam Lynch had drawn back to the mountainous region of South Tipperary around Clonmel and Carrick. Carrick became a Republican headquarters and at one stage De Valera, Childers and Markiewicz operated the government of the Provisional Republic from there. Dinny Lacy and Dan Breen established HQ at the Workhouse with around 500 men. McCarthy, Ryan and Byrne (under Gen. Prout) took Carrick with the 18-pounder on 2 August 1922. As the Republicans withdrew they burnt the local RIC barracks and the courthouse. In the movement up the Suir valley by Prout the gun was used continually to push the Republicans back to Clonmel and thence to the mountains of North Cork.

CHARLES JOSEPH KICKHAM was born in Mullinahone, Co. Tipperary, in 1828. Nationalist journalism which was carried on in spite of congenitally poor hearing and eyesight damaged in a youthful accident led to involvement in Young Ireland and Fenianism. He was on the staff of *The Irish People* when he and John O'Leary were arrested and sentenced to fourteen years imprisonment for involvement in the Fenian Conspiracy. He received the harsh treatment that prison staffs reserved for Fenians but he was less able to withstand it than O'Donovan Rossa and the others. After four years he was released, broken in health and almost totally blind. He died in Blackrock in 1882, three years after the publication of his book, *Knocknagow*, surely the most famous of all 19th-century Irish books.

TO GOD AND IRELAND TRUE.

I sit beside my darling's grave,
   Who in the prison died,
And tho' my tears fall thick and fast,
   I think of him with pride:
Ay, softly fall my tears like dew,
For one to God and Ireland true.

"I love my God o'er all," he said,
   "And then I love my land,
And next I love my Lily sweet,
   Who pledged me her white hand:
To each—to all—I'm ever true;
To God—to Ireland—and to you."

No tender nurse his hard bed smoothed
   Or softly raised his head;
He fell asleep and woke in heaven
   Ere I knew he was dead;
Yet why should I my darling rue?
He was to God and Ireland true.

Oh! 't is a glorious memory;
   I'm prouder than a queen
To sit beside my hero's grave,
   And think on what has been:
And, oh, my darling, I am true
To God—to Ireland—and to you.

> **Ellen O'Leary,** 'To God and Ireland
> True' in *Lays of Country, Home and
> Friends* (Dublin 1891)

ELLEN O'LEARY was born in Tipperary in 1831. She was an ardent Fenian as befitted the sister of John O'Leary the great philosopher-king of Yeats's 'Romantic Ireland'. She had helped Stephens escape in 1866 but for the fifteen years of her brother's imprisonment and exile she lived quietly at home in Tipperary writing occasional poems for periodicals.
In 1887 she moved to Dublin to keep house for her repatriated brother and it was here that she met Yeats, T W Rolleston, 'Eva of the Nation', and the other members of the nationalist-literary salon who gathered round the old patriot. After her death in Cork in 1889 (sixteen years before her brother) her verse was published as *Lays of Country, Home and Friends*— a just description.

Dinny Sadlier, 1920 (Mrs Pike/Carrick Society)

DINNY SADLIER was commandant of 7th Battalion, 3rd Tipperary Brigade, IRA, during the War of Independence. He was accidentally shot dead while on active service in 1921. He was buried secretly in Grangemockler but during the truce he was re-interred in his native place, Drangan. His brother, Michael, was killed in the Civil War.

All Ireland south of the Boyne seemed to be suddenly converted into the training-ground of a rebellious organisation. The young men of the towns and of the more populous country places were openly drilled of nights for armed insurrection. Funds were raised everywhere for the purchase of rifles from Birmingham factories; and the weapons were imported at first without let or hindrance on the part of the constituted authorities, who were too much puzzled and bewildered to take any serious purpose in it. Clubs and associations were formed everywhere for the open teaching and propagation of armed rebellion. Then, when the constituted authorities had time to breathe and to recognise the fact that rebellion was in the air, there set in a season of hurried repressive legislation; and arrests and imprisonments became the common events of every day. As might well be expected in such a season of alarm and of panic, the action of the constituted authorities was often widely indiscriminate; and some of the men, elder and younger, who could best have been relied upon to keep the national movement within reasonable bounds, were among the first to be arrested and put on trial, or sent to prison without any form of serious judicial investigation.

All this was to be expected at such a time of commotion and is common enough in the history of very passionate popular agitation, or at least was common in the history of such agitations during those somewhat distant days; but the immediate result of the course taken by the constituted authorities was to convert from ardent nationalists into avowed rebels many of those who had up to the latest moment, still believed that the misgovernment of Ireland could be remedied by argument and appeal addressed to the intelligence of the ruling classes and to the Imperial Parliament.

Justin McCarthy, *Mononia,* (London, 1901)

Michael Collins, C-in-C National Army, inspecting troops at the Square Newcastle West, Co Limerick, on 11 August 1922. (Photo: W F Knight, Newcastle)

JUSTIN McCARTHY was born in Cork in 1830 but spent the last fifty years of his life in London. His career had the recurring nineteenth-century pattern of journalism, editorship and politics. He led the Nationalist Party after the fall of Parnell until 1896, when he retired from active participation in politics. After his resignation he continued an awesome output of writing, including biography and history. He was editor-in-chief of a ten-volume anthology of Irish Literature produced in Philadelphia in 1904. *Mononia* (1901) is set in Munster during the Smith O'Brien rising of 1848. He died in 1912.

The fall of Newcastle West to the National Army under Brig. James Slattery on 5 August 1922 marked the end of Irregular resistance in W Limerick — N Kerry. It was the culmination of General Patrick Daly's clever strategy which involved sea-borne operations at Fenit and Ballylongford, with a third prong of the attack moving westwards from Adare.

On 9 August Collins set out from Dublin to make a tour of the Limerick command. By the 12 August he had reached Tralee where he received word of Arthur Griffith's death and returned to Dublin immediately. On the 22nd he died in an ambush.

IRA officers, Ennistimon, Co Clare, 1919. (Photo: J Arthur)

Incident during a boycott at Kilshanny Church, Co. Clare
(Photo: Joseph Arthur) •

80

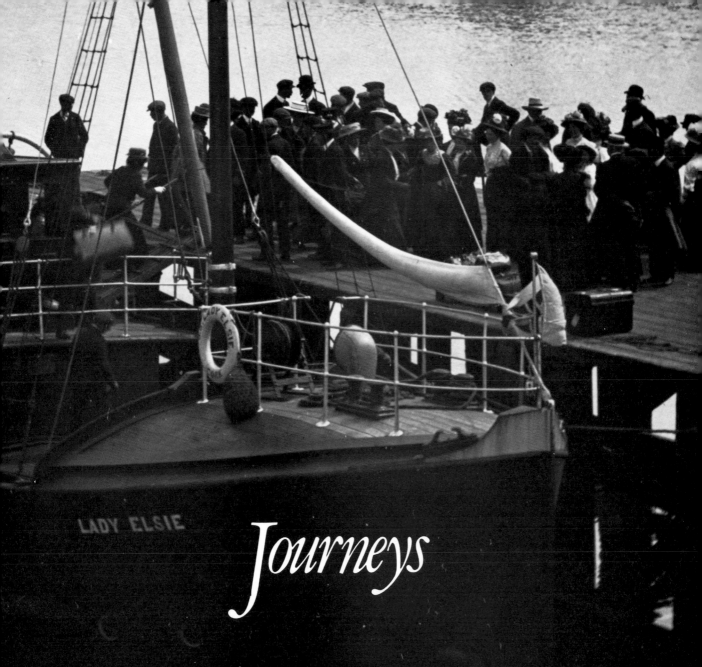

LADY ELSIE

Journeys

'St. Senanus knew well what he was about, Masther Willie, whin he turned in there to pray an' do pinnance for his sins,' observed the skipper. 'I'll go bail, if he searched all over Ireland ground, he couldn't find a betther place for makin' his sowl than that very sport. He built eleven fine churches there, to the glory of God an' the honour ov the saints; an' why he stopped at the odd number, an' didn't make it the full dozen, I never could rightly make out, but I suppose he did it for good luck. But though the saint build eleven churches, there are only seven, or what's left ov the seven, to the fore to-day. Ov coorse you know that, sir?'

'Of course I do—sure, I often saw them.'

'Well, sir, there they are, sure enough; the ould ancient ruins ov 'em I mane, for it's only the bare walls that' there now, an' more's the pity, for they say that them churches wor great churches entirely wanst upon a time. Sure, 'tis well known that powers ov people used to come from forrin parts in the ould ancient times to get the larnin in Ireland that they hadn't at home in their own country, an' to be taught the light ov the thrue religion. An' that's why Ireland is called the Island ov Saints an' will be called by the same name as long as her fields are green, an' sure that will be to the ind ov the world. But maybe, Masther Willie, you don't b'lieve what I'm tellin' you?'

'Why should not I believe you? It is an historical fact that many holy and learned men lived in Ireland in old times, when the rest of Europe was sunk in the greatest ignorance and barbarism. Of course I believe you.'

'See that now!' exclaimed Lanty, quite delighted to find that his auditor agreed with him. ''Tis a fine thing, sir, to be talking' wid a knowledgable person, like yourself, instead ov the ignorant galloots that's goin' now a days;

KILRUSH on the lower Shannon estuary had an old maritime tradition. There was a regular trade up the estuary from the outport of Cappa to Limerick. The better-off citizens of Limerick travelled on summer holidays to the seaside resort of Kilkee via Cappa. (At first they completed the journey by side-car but after 1892 they used the newly built South Clare Railway.) Cappa also had a coast-guard station, while Scattery Island, a short distance offshore, was the centre from which ships navigating the Shannon took on pilots.

Below: Cappa Pier, Kilrush c.1910 (Lawrence Collection, National Library) The naval gentleman is Michael Pryle the coastguard.

82

an' if you'll b'lieve me, sir, I'd as lieve be breakin' stones for a pavior as holdin' discourse wid wan ov 'em.'

'But the story, Lanty! you forget that I'm waiting for the story of all this time.'

'Sure enough, sir, but plase the piper you won't have to wait for it long. Did you ever hear ov how St. Senanus or S. Sinan, as we call him for shortness, was converted, an' why it was that he came all the ways to Scatthery Island to do great pinnance for his sins, an' to prove to all the world how greatly he hated women?'

'No, Lanty, I never heard it, but would be very glad to hear it now from you.'

'Arrah, sir! sure a Protestan' like you wouldn't give in at all to such ould shanahus.'

'I don't see what religion has to do with it, one way or other. I hope a Protestant may be allowed to hear a good story, and to enjoy it too, as well as the people who differ from him in creed. So begin at once, Lanty; I am sure you will do the story justice.'

Margaret W Brew, *The Burtons of Dunroe* (London, 1880)

MARGARET BREW lived in Co. Clare, probably near Kilrush and is known mainly as the author of two very popular books, *Chronicles of Castle Cloyne* (1886) and *The Burtons of Dunroe* (1880). Her phonetic rendering of West Clare speech looks odd but her writings have an authenticity which makes them well worth reading even today.

Below: Scattery Island, Kilrush c.1890 (Lawrence Collection, National Library)

The coach of the Cork and Bally-gotton Motor Service Co. Ltd, South Mall, Cork, proprietor J.R. Cross. In inclement weather passengers could keep dry by means of a hood on rails which ran the entire length of the coach. Price of a return trip - four shillings and ninepence.
(Photo; courtesy J Cluskey)

A Clare currach is a boat of almost the lightest construction, but it will carry twenty people. In build it is clumsy and shapeless-looking. It has neither keel nor keelson. Like a Dutch galliot, its stem and stern are round; like the craft they call a prong or prom in the south and west of Ireland, its bow and stem rise out of the water, and when under way it skims over the waves rather than cuts through them. On the Shannon and other rivers, the prong is chiefly used for shooting rapids. It has a flat bottom and flat bow, and by this bow being raised out of the water there is less danger of the craft swamping when it rushes headlong into the white foam.

The long heavy swells of the Atlantic on this coast are so many rapids to be climbed and shot, and the light tarred canvas currach, with its round blunt bows and its unresisting keelless bottom, enabling it to be spun swiftly this way or that to meet the eddying sweep, is found to be the safest and most serviceable model. Two men can carry it with ease, but not more than one man in all Killard could by himself lift it and carry it, arms up, and this one man was Edward Martin. All the villagers had seen him do it.

Two years before this morning a bet was made. A number of fishermen subscribed twenty shillings, and laid the money against him. He, the best of fishermen in Killard, put down his pound, raised the currach in his huge arms, and carried it aloft five hundred yards amid the cheers of all, of even those who had lost.

When he lowered the currach, he sat down on it to rest and wipe his flushed, steaming face. Pat Casey, who had arranged the bets and held the money, came to him, and, stretching out his hand, said cordially:

The Harbour, Liscannor, Co. Clare (Lawrence Collection, National Library)

Flagstones were exported from Liscannor to many British cities where they were used for paving. (The Royal Mint in London was floored with Moher flag.) Nine companies in all worked four quarries, at Doonagore, Caherbarna, Luogh and Moher. The largest was at Doonagore around which a sizable village grew and the stone was taken the four miles from that quarry by good metalled road to Liscannor. The wagons were drawn by the steam engine to the berth of the 'County Clare', the company's ship. The first world war, political change and concrete put an end to the trade.

86

The Beach Liscannor, Co. Clare (Lawrence Collection, National Library)

'Well done, Edward Martin! You won fairly, and deserve the money. Take it, for no other man in this parish, or the next one to it, could do the like of that.'

Martin did not reach out his hand, but continued to wipe his face and neck.

'Take your money, man!' cried Casey, in a tone of expostulation. Casey knew Martin did not like the idea of the bet.

Martin turned to his wife, who stood beside him. She was weeping for joy at the triumph of her husband.

'You would not think,' she was saying to her heart, 'that he had the strength to raise an oar when he takes our little Mary in his arms; and look at what he has done to-day! But strong as his arms are, his love is stronger, and his goodness as strong as ever was goodness in man. My husband!'

At the crowning thought that he was hers, she gave a sob of gratitude, and, sitting down beside him, put her arm on his great shoulder, just as he turned to speak to her.

'Mary,' he said, 'take the money, you. Take the money from Pat Casey, and I'll tell you what to do with it by-and-by.'

Richard Dowling *The Mystery of Killard* (London, 1879)

RICHARD DOWLING was born in Clonmel in 1846. After work as a shipping-clerk in Waterford which gave him an interest in the sea and a taste for nautical yarns that he never lost, he took to journalism. He edited the comic journals *Ireland's Eye* and *Zozimus*. In 1874 he went to London and lived by freelancing for the many magazines which were published in that golden age of popular journalism. He died in 1898. *The Mystery of Killard* is pure Irish Gothic with an anti-hero who is a deaf-mute and who hates his own normally equipped child. The setting is the sea-coast of Clare, near Bishop's Island.

If Jack Creedon did not get to where the road from Carrignadoura crosses the road to Acharas in time to catch up the mail car — well, he would have to walk the whole long ten miles into Raheen, to walk them every step instead of sitting, neighbour-like, on the car chatting to Larry O'the driver. With him Jack Creedon loved to chat — that is when Larry could be got to speak at all. For the most part he spoke only to his horse.

Above an edge of the hill he presently saw the tail-board of Larry's car; the car was not moving, a thing that made him wonder. And soon he saw Larry himself, a little away from his horse, stamping about on the watery road. His hands were deep in his pockets, his whip was gripped under his elbow, and his face was looking more crusty than ever. There he was stamping about on the mountain-top, impatience itself. A twikle came into Jack Creedon's eye. He could make no guess at what was causing Larry to delay in so windy a spot after driving through miles of rain; he did not try to guess; the vision before him was sufficient, he enjoyed it, and he knew he would treasure it up in his memory. He raised his voice:

"Eh." he cried, "is it taking the air ye are?"

Old Larry turned.

"The air!" he snarled.

"Ye might be civil — Is it anyone ye're waiting for?"

"Him!" Without taking his hands from his pockets Larry twisted himself until his whip pointed towards a series of striplike rocks that rose to a fine view-point. There Jack Creedon saw a well-dressed stranger staring intently over the streaming valley into the sunset. Its glare had caused him to put his hand above his eyes.

"Who is he?" whispered Jack.

"One of them tourists — leave me alone!"

Then Jack made a motion towards the car; would he mount? Larry surlily nodded; and without causing the crazy old thing to creak in a joint or spring, Jack Creedon got up on it and bided his time. Meanwhile old Larry stamped on the wet rocks.

The sunset soon parted with its glory; the sky grew cold and livid, the clouds became the colour and shape of dusky wings. Turning from it, the American silently made for his seat in the car. He took in the new passenger with a soft glance amd slow nod.

Dusk thickened; night fell as they swung along the slopes of the interminable hills. They would climb slowly up a long rise, the stroke of every hoof echoing from the rocks above their heads. Then, a quick change, they swung down the descent at a reckless pace, the car swaying from side to side.   **Daniel Corkery**, *A Munster Twilight* (Dublin, 1916)

DANIEL CORKERY was born in Cork in 1878 and as teacher, critic and author helped to confirm the respectable existence of an Anglo-Irish literature which he professionally decried. His novels and stories are provincial in the deepest and best sense of that word. An able pamphleteer for the Gaelic League, his general criticism suffered from an understandable but debilitating anti-Englishness. He died in 1964.

'In the twenty-one miles between Glengarriff and Kenmare one does not see a score of dwellings. How do the inhabitants of these wretched huts make a living? During the season they live on the mendicity of their children. You cannot go half a mile without an escort of both sexes and all ages, indescribably ragged, trotting barefoot in the wind around the vehicle, and offering you bouquets of heather, bunches of moss and sprays of bog-myrtle. This goes on the whole way. For a quarter of an hour there may be a respite, then a new band emerges from some ditch, and you are thus handed over from brigade to brigade until you reach your destination.'
Madame de Bovet, *Three months in Ireland* (London, 1891)

Gap Cottage, Killarney
(Lawrence Collection, National Library)

88

"Talkin' about railways," said my friend Pat Hurley to me one July evening, as he sat in the little garden in front of his cottage, "I could tell you a quare wan." Now we were not talking about railways, though we could have found plenty to say about this particular line, which runs from Cork "to the back of God-speed"; we were watching the train go out from a little country station in the South of Ireland. My friend was a porter on the same line, but just at present was on sick-leave for a few days. His tongue was as the pen of a ready writer; and, conscious of his powers as a story-teller, he kept his eyes and ears open for everything which added to his fund of entertainment.

"If ye'll give me lave to light me pipe, sir, I can tell ye something that'll divart ye."

I graciously granted his request, and as he filled a very decent-looking briar he began:

"Och, if Jim Walsh only heard what I'm talkin' about he'd murther me, for the same matther made a hullabaloo in the town, and the laugh that was riz agin the two of us ye never heard the like; not but many of thim that was laughing didn't know betther theirselves. Wan evenin' when we was clanin' out the carriages afther the thrain was in, we come on the quarest-lookin' tin box; the like of it we never sot an eye on before. There was nathar mark nor token on it to tell a body who ownded it.

" 'Bedad, that's the onhandiest-looking' luggage I iver see,' sez Jim.

" ' 'Tis so,' says I, 'an' powerful heavy,' takin' a grip of it an' haulin' it out on the platform.

"There was only three ladies in that carriage, an' in coorse it had to belong to wan o' thim. We argued it somethin' mighty particular from the quare shape of it, let alone belongin' to wan o' the quality, so I conthrived to persuade Jim that 'twas the dacint thing to take it home to the craythur, an' lave it wid her that night before she'd be feelin' the want of it. Poor Jim is a very soft-hearted kind of bhoy, an' being younger and smarter than me, he shouldhered the conthrapshin and sthreeled off. Troth, he was back in an hour's time, an' the box wid him.

" 'Be jabers,' sez he, 'me back's bruk; ye might as well offer to carry the pyramids of Agypt.' He sot down wake like and wiped the seat off his face an' round his neck wid his cap.

" 'Why didn't ye get shut of it?' sez I.

" 'Sure,' sez he, 'ye must be thinkin' it's for an ornament I'm wearing it; divil a wan o' thim would own up to it at all. I took it first to Miss Mary Murphy, an' she was at her tay, but she sent me out word that she had all her thraps right. I wint on thin to Mrs. Barry, an' afther her Mrs. Kelly. I was mistook wid thim too, bedad, for they was only in Cork for the day, an' they had no luggage that you might call luggage. I was bate entirely carryin' what might be a quarry o' stones for the weight, an' leppin' wid rage for havin' to do it. I thraced my steps back to Miss Mary Murphy, she being' the likeliest of the three faymales, an' toult the girl for God's sake to ax her misthress to have a look at the box, if it wouldn't be throublin' her honor, for I was heart-scalded wid dhraggin' it over land an' say. Miss Mary couldn't talk to me at wanst, be rayson o' company in the parlor, but she sint ordhers that I was to

come in an' rest meself, the Lord bless her kind heart. She's a raal lady, is Miss Mary Murphy; there's not her aqual in the town. She sint me out a dhrink o' porter; bedad I was glad to get a hoult of it, an' whin I had me fingers on the glass I was ready to face the ould bhoy. After a bit Miss Mary come out, an' took wan look at me weight o' calamity, an' thin she laughed fit to shplit her stays.

" 'Och, Jim,' sez she, 'but ye're the omadhaun.'

" 'For the love o' the Blessed Vargin, Miss,' sez I, 'say ye own this misfortunit thrunk.'

" 'I don't,' sez she, 'but I know who does.'

" 'Thin tell me,' sez i, very polite, 'where the blazes am I to take it to?'

" 'I'd advise ye,' sez she, 'to take it to the Lost Property Office in Cork,' an' wid that she roared out laughin' agin an' ran away. I could hear 'em all inside screechin' at the fun, whatever it was. So I shouldhered the moniment wanst more, an' here I am.

Sophie MacIntosh, 'Jim Walsh's Tin Box' in *Irish Literature VI* (Philadelphia, 1904)

SOPHIE MacINTOSH was born in Kinsale as Sophie Donaclift. She married H F MacIntosh who became headmaster of Methodist College, Belfast. Her school stories were published in 1902 as *The Last Forward*. *Jim Walsh's Tin Box* is typical of her uncomplicated approach to her fellow Cork people.

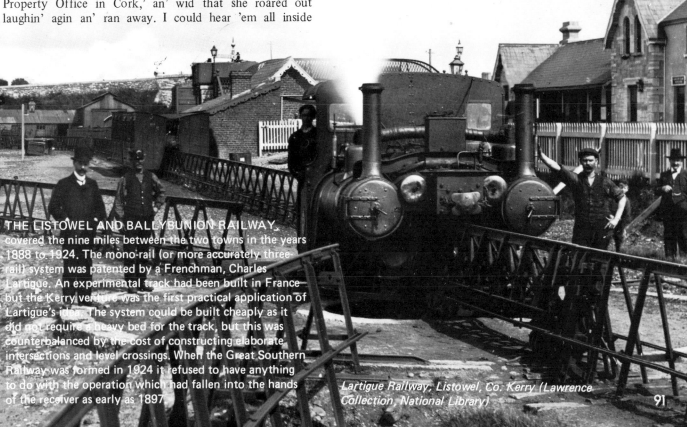

THE LISTOWEL AND BALLYBUNION RAILWAY covered the nine miles between the two towns in the years 1888 to 1924. The mono-rail (or more accurately three-rail) system was patented by a Frenchman, Charles Lartigue. An experimental track had been built in France but the Kerry venture was the first practical application of Lartigue's idea. The system could be built cheaply as it did not require a heavy bed for the track, but this was counterbalanced by the cost of constructing elaborate intersections and level crossings. When the Great Southern Railway was formed in 1924 it refused to have anything to do with the operation which had fallen into the hands of the receiver as early as 1897

Lartigue Railway, Listowel, Co. Kerry (Lawrence Collection, National Library)

91

The French ship *Leon XIII* went aground off Quilty in a great storm on 2 October 1907. Twelve local men in currachs made an heroic attempt to rescue the crew. The local church was built in 1909 to commemorate the deed.

Wreck of the *Leon XIII* at Quilty, Co. Clare with the crew still on board (Photograph; Joseph Arthur/M J Glynn Collection)

The ship was, or had been, a three-masted barque; two of her masts were gone, and her bows stood high out of water on the reef that forms one of the shark-like jaws of the bay. The long strand was crowded with black groups of people, from the bank of heavy shingle that had been hurled over on to the road, down to the slope where the waves pitched themselves and climbed and fought and tore the gravel back with them, as though they had dug their fingers in. The people were nearly all men dressed solemnly and hideously in their Sunday clothes; most of them had come straight from Mass without any dinner, true to that Irish instinct that places its fun before its food. That the wreck was regarded as a spree of the largest kind was sufficiently obvious. Our car pulled up at a public-house that stood askew between the road and the shingle; it was humming with those whom Irish publicans are pleased to call "Bona feeds", and sundry of the same class were clustered round the door. Under the wall of the lee-side was seated a bagpiper, droning out "The Irish Washerwoman" with nodding head and tapping heel, and a very young man was cutting a few steps of a jig for the delectation of a group of girls.

So far Murray's constabulary had done nothing but exhibit their imposing chest measurement and spotless uniforms to the Atlantic, and Bosanquet's coastguards had only salvaged some spars, the debris of a boat, and a dead sheep, but their time was coming. As we stumbled down over the shingle, battered by the wind and pelted by clots of foam, someone beside me shouted, "She's gone!" A hill of water had smothered the wreck, and when it fell from her again nothing was left but the bows, with the bowsprit hanging from them in a tangle of rigging. The clouds, bronzed by an unseen sunset , hung low over her; in that greedy pack of waves, with the remorseless rocks above and below her, she seemed the most lonely and tormented of creatures.

About half an hour afterwards the cargo began to come ashore on the top of the rising tide. Barrels were plunging and diving in the trough of the waves, like a school of porpoises; they were pitched up the beach in waist-deep rushes of foam; they rolled down again, and were swung up and shouldered by the next wave, playing a kind of Tom Tiddler's ground with the coastguards. Some of the barrels were big and dangerous, some were small and nimble like young pigs, and the bluejackets were up to their middles as their prey dodged and ducked, and the police lined out along the beach to keep back the people. Ten men of the R.I.C. can do a great deal, but they cannot be in more than twenty or thirty places at the same instant; therefore they could hardly cope with a scattered and extremely active mob of four or five hundred, many of whom had taken advantage of their privileges as "bona-fide travellers", and all of whom were determined on getting at the rum.

As the dusk fell the things got more and more out of hand; the people had found out that the big puncheons held the rum, and had succeeded in capturing one. In the twinkling of an eye it was broached, and fifty backs were shoving round it like a football scrummage. I have heard many rows in my time: I have seen two Irish regiments—one of them Militia—at each other's throats in Fermoy barracks; I have heard Philippa's water spaniel and two fox-terriers hunting a strange cat around the dairy; but never have I known such untrammelled bedlam as that which yelled round the rum-casks on Tralagough strand. For it was soon not a question of one broached cask, or even of two. The barrels were coming in fast, so that it was impossible for the representatives of law and order to keep on any sort of terms with them. The people, shouting with laughter, stove in the casks, and drank rum at 34 degrees proof, out of hands, out of their hats, out of their book. Women came fluttering over the hillsides through the twilight, carrying jugs, milk-pails, anything that would hold the liquor; I saw one of them, roaring with laughter, tilt a filthy zinc bucket to an old man's lips.

Somerville & Ross, *Some Experiences of an Irish R.M.* (London, 1899)

EDITH OENONE SOMERVILLE and Violet Martin, though both grand-daughters of Charles Kendal Bushe, the Chief Justice who strenuously opposed the Act of Union did not meet until 1886 when Edith was 28 and Violet 24. From this time they became inseparable friends and formed a literary patnership as fecund and rather more easy than that of Gilbert and Sullivan. The more gifted of the two (and the more consciously Irish) was Violet as may be discerned from Edith's solo attempts after her partner's death of cerebral cancer in 1915. To her are due the regular elements of 'Gothic' atmosphere which can bring a chill to even the most light-hearted sketch. The *R M Stories*, originally begun as hunting sketches for the Badminton Magazine in 1899, became and still are minor classics whose combination of the hilarious, the macabre and acute social observation has eased the sting of their snobbery and disregard of the native Irish. Edith lived on until 1949 in apparent amity with the new state.

FAREWELL

Sail bravely on, thou gallant bark,
    Across the Western sea;
And safely guard the precious freight
    Thou bear'st away from me.
Sail on, nor heed the frowning skies,
    Nor angry wave nor wind;
Nor reck the grief of aching hearts
    Thou leavest here behind.

Great God! Protector of the world,
    Guard Thou both wife and child.

Like miser watching from the shore
    The argosy that bears
O'er ocean paths to distant lands
    The treasures prized of years,
I sit and graze, through streaming eyes,
    Across the darkening main,
And fain would have the good ship turn
    And bring back again.

Sail on, brave ship; a priceless stake
    Is on thy fate for me!
May angels waft thee on thy course,
    And calm each threatening sea!
Sancta Maria! to thy care
    Are child and mother given,
Whether we meet again on earth,
    Or meet our next in heavn!

A. M. Sullivan 'Farewell' in *Irish Literature* (Philadelphia, 1904)

ALEXANDER MARTIN SULLIVAN was born in Castletownberehaven, Co. Cork in 1830 and broke into literature, so to speak, when he bought *The Nation* from the severely disenchanted Charles Gavan Duffy in 1858. Mingled careers of politics and journalism made his name and that of his brother TD well-known throughout England and Ireland. His *Story of Ireland,* a colourful, romantic history written in 1870 became very popular and was admired, among others, by Winston Churchill. His poems and songs were published mainly in *The Nation.* He died in Dublin in 1884.

Lusitania (Cork Examiner)

COBH, one of the great victims of the Gaelic Revival, was known decently enough as the Cove of Cork until 2 August 1849 when the visit of Victoria, Albert and their four young children caused the city fathers to change the name to Queenstown. Complaints about facilities encouraged by the royal visit led to the building of the Victoria Quay. It remained unsalubrious as at least one sensitive traveller noted:

'Should it ever be my happy lot to revisit the city and haven of Cork, I shall most certainly decline to land at Queenstown. The gentleman who took a census of the smells of Cologne might perhaps be interested in this locality and would find an ample field for his nasal arithmetic. The heat was intense, the tide low; and though I have no doubt that, farther from the sea, the place is sweet and healthy enough, I never remember to have inhaled so offensive an atmosphere as that which prevailed . . . in the front street of Queenstown.' S Reynolds Hole, *A Little Tour of Ireland* (London, 1896)

Golf Hotel, Harbour View, Bandon (Lawrence Collection, National Library)

Book Four

Leinster

Art Ó Broin
& Seán McMahon

Preface

Our thanks are due to the late Billy English of Athlone; the director and staff of the National Library of Ireland; the staff of the library of the Institute of Continuing Education (NUU), Magee College, Derry, especially Alan Roberts; the staff of the Belfast Central Library; Kevin Etchingham of Dundalk; Cathal O'Shannon; Mike Byrne of Tullamore and the Offaly Research Library; Don Roberts and James Delehanty of Kilkenny; Arnold Crawford of Mountmellick; Séamas de Vál S.P.; John Hayes of Wexford; Harry Fairtlough of Drogheda; Mgr L Ryan of Carlow; Paddy Laird of Dublin; James O'Donnell of Mullingar; and Frank D'Arcy of Derry.

Introduction

With *Faces of Old Leinster* the quartet of Irish faces is complete. The double vision of Ireland on the brink of the modern world has been extended to cover the eastern province. This double vision, originally devised by the compiler of the first volume in the series, Brian Walker, is obtained by the juxtaposition of contemporary pictures and literary excerpts. Such a procedure is both objective and subjective — objective in that the photographs and associated pieces are proper relics of the period, subjective because it is the *surviving* evidence that paints the picture of the past for the present and because the book is made from a personal (and perhaps idiosyncratic) choice of the compilers from these survivals. The result would seem to show that Leinster is a separate part of Ireland, as distinct in its nature and in its appearance as Munster or Connaught or the North.

The most obvious element of distinctiveness of this part of Ireland is, of course, the City *-the great wen -* at once the pride and the despair of the patriot, the invader and the moralist. Because of its separate history, its diverse elements, its place at the centre of land and sea routes, it never seemed to fit the accepted nineteenth-century image of Ireland; and yet for all its complexity and its exoticism it was as Irish

Tram on the summit of the Hill of Howth, Co. Dublin c. 1913 (Lawrence Collection, National Library).

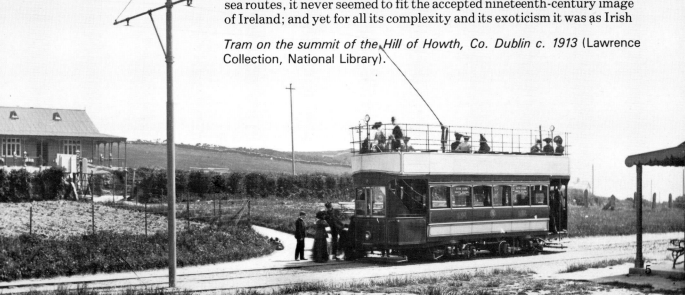

5

Bull Alley, Dublin (Lawrence Collection, National Library).

as the Bog of Allen or the Mountains of Mourne. To say it dominated Leinster is to put it too strongly but politically, morally, culturally and topographically its presence was and is felt. On the great distorted dart-board that a road map presents (a spider's web, if your imagination is darker) all tracks lead to and all forces pull towards the urban centre. At Dundalk, Longford, Carlow or New Ross the power of the magnet is felt.

It is probably fanciful, a kind of self-fulfilling prophecy, but one cannot avoid the impression that by comparison the ancillary counties seem shadowy and their towns however prosperous and their people however busy give the impression of perpetually looking east. The region too, was *English* Ireland. Pale faces were as prevalent as native Irish ones. Gaelic as a spoken language had disappeared, drained from all parts but the wilder north of Co Louth. Fenianism, Land Agitation, 'troubles' played a less dramatic part in Wicklow and Kilkenny, Meath and Carlow than in the west and south; '98 was the last time that Leinster was actively in arms. And yet all ideological movements, whether political, industrial or revolutionary had to have their nerve centres in Dublin. So had the government and the forces of the Crown. If at times travellers got the impression of dehydration or anaemia about these 'home counties' it was not that the people 'down the country' lacked vitality but that the City's needs seemed to drain them.

As for the Dublin Irish they grew up with typical urban suspicion of the rural mind and fear of the empty silences, finding within a few miles of their birthplaces their total universe. Many who sang in pubs and street corners of Killarney's lakes and Bantry Bay were unlikely to have seen either and had no strong wish to; and they viewed with cynical satisfaction and some jealousy the steadily increasing flow of culchies into *their* metropolis. The middle class Catholics and Protestants were beginning to find accomodation each with the other, while the working class obstinately refused to fulfil Engels' prophecies. Matt Talbot was no more untypical of the scene than Jim Larkin. Besides, the City was its own theatre with a ruritanian panoply of public events. The universities, the Castle, the imperial presence, the race meetings, the levees and garden parties provided a rich atmosphere even for the non-participants. The meanest and the grandest almost rubbed shoulders with each other. The finest dwellings cohabited with some of the worst slums in Europe: a short step from the Green brought you to the Cathedral hovels. The Church and State, only officially at odds, dominated the place and when the military presence became too obviously a reminder of a palliated subjection there was always the relief of the civilian police force, the D M P as jolly as a light opera chorus line till the batons came out in 1913.

The writers of Leinster show the same lurch towards the City.

Some of the greatest names in Irish literature are here: O'Casey, Joyce and Synge. Mixed with these are less luminous beings who nevertheless have their own brightness: Padraic Colum, Katherine Tynan, Bram Stoker, Oliver Gogarty, Brinsley MacNamara, James Stephens, Francis Ledwidge. Most were born in Dublin or gravitated towards it in the course of their careers. A matter of little surprise; for, sociological truism or not, the tremors of change begin and end in the centre of greatest population. The literary revival may have been conceived in the remote west but it was born and lived in the city.

The pictures come from several rich archives — French, of Lawrence, Keogh and the careful gleanings of the growing number of local historical and antiquarian societies who have at last succeeded in prodding the people into a sense of the riches of their past. Respect grows with knowledge; impatience turns to sympathy. As we look upon the faces and listen to the voices of these 'faithful departed' we begin to understand ourselves through them, to evaluate more precisely their bequests to us. And we begin to understand that those who do not learn from history are punished by having to experience it themselves.

Scouts on Killiney Hill

Down The Country

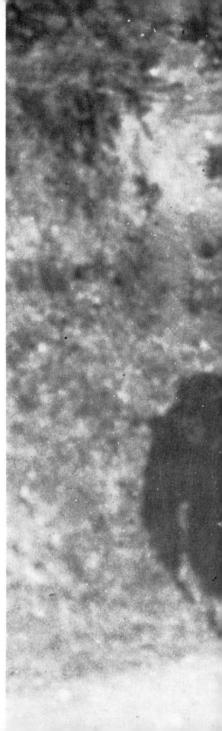

SOME features of County Wicklow, such as the position of the principal workhouses and holiday places on either side of the coach road from Arklow to Bray, have made this district a favourite with the vagrants of Ireland. A few of these people have been on the roads for generations; but fairly often they seem to have merely drifted out from the ordinary people of the villages, and do not differ greatly from the class they come from. Their abundance has often been regretted; yet in one sense it is an interesting sign, for wherever the labourer of a country has preserved his vitality, and begets an occasional temperament of distinction, a certain number of vagrants are to be looked for. In the middle classes the gifted son of a family is always the poorest - usually a writer or artist with no sense for speculation - and in a family of peasants, where the average comfort is just over penury, the gifted son sinks also, and is soon a tramp on the roadside.

In this life, however, there are many privileges. The tramp in Ireland is little troubled by the laws, and lives in out-of-door conditions that keep him in good-humour and fine bodily health. This is so apparent, in Wicklow at least, that these men rarely seek for charity on any plea of ill-health, but ask simply, when they beg: 'Would you help a poor fellow along the road?' or, 'Would you give me the price of a night's lodging, for I'm after walking a great way since the sun rose?'

John M Synge *In Wicklow and West Kerry* (Dublin, 1912).

Wicklow Tramp 1906 (Synge Collection, Trinity College).

SYNGE'S characteristic amalgam of romanticism and wildness is most clearly seen in his attitude to vagrants. The tramp in *The Shadow of the Glen* (1903) is the most complete character, holding some of the quality of Christy Mahon. He loved the travelling-men he met on his many journeys on foot in Wicklow and Kerry and he had almost total empathy with them. He often signed his letters to Molly Allgood 'your old tramp' and he believed that 'in a family of peasants . . .the gifted son sinks . . .and is soon a tramp on the roadside.'

11

Fair Day Longford c. 1908 (Lawrence Collection, National Library).

12

A DROVER

To Meath of the pastures,
From wet hills by the sea,
Through Leitrim and Longford
Go my cattle and me.

I hear in the darkness
Their slipping and breathing.
I name them the bye-ways
They're to pass without heeding.

Then the wet, winding roads,
Brown bogs with black water;
And my thoughts on white ships
And the King o' Spain's daughter.

O! farmer, strong farmer!
You can spend at the fair
But your face you must turn
To your crops and your care.

And soldiers - red soldiers!
You've seen many lands;
But you walk two by two,
And by captain's commands.

O! the smell of the beasts,
The wet wind in the morn;
And the proud and hard earth
Never broken for corn;

I will bring you, my kine,
Where there's grass to the knee;
But you'll think of scant croppings
Harsh with salt of the sea.

Padraic Colum *Wild Earth* (Dublin, 1907).

PADRAIC COLUM (Patrick McCormac Colm) was born in Longford in 1881,
the son of the workhouse master of that town. As novelist, playwright and
author of many poems he was a considerable figure in the Irish Literary
Renaissance. An early Abbey dramatist his naturalistic plays such as *Land*
(1905) helped turn the Abbey away from Yeats's earlier vision of its purpose.
A friend of Synge and Thomas MacDonagh, the 1916 Proclamation
signatory, he died in Enfield, Connecticut in 1972.

IT WAS a cold sunny day early in April; there is a saying that April borrowed twelve days from March, and that is what skins the old cow. On one of these days Marting Macevoy was fencing his barley field, as soon as it got a bit green the cattle would be breaking in over the dry earthen bank. Ever since he came there he had been thinking of planting a right quick set hedge, but like a great many greater and smaller things in the country, it was thought of a long time without being done, put on the long finger as we say. He had gathered a lot of bushes and briars from round the other fields, and that was a good job, too, to get them out of the way of pulling the wool off the sheep. He was laying them along the top of the bank in a thick beard, keeping them in place with stones and scraughs cut off the grass field. It was tedious work and hard on hands and clothes, but he could keep an eye on the servant boy, who was ploughing the next field for turnips. When he looked round he could see, too, though it was near a mile away, the big field at Drummond, and make out his own five acres to a sod, there was a bush at one side and a white stone on the wall at the other. He said to himself:

'For all the harsh wind it's beginnin' to look green, God bless it, but it would take with a dash of rain if it was the will of God. If it turns out well it will pay all, and we'll have a great plenty of straw. My blessin' on him that thought of it, only for him we were broke, horse and fut. Sure we never can ask a day's delay in the rint again or a shillin' abatement. I don't know how I'll ever face Mr. Humphreys. Mary must take the rint to him, 'twas none of her side gave the annoyance. And if it would be hard on me what would it be on that poor angashore of a brother of mine? Mag must go, she has the face of the worl - spake of the divil!''

Here he was struck dumb at the sight of his sister-in-law opening his eyes but it was indeed she coming straight towards him. He turned his back and worked diligently, not seeming to hear her step, but the voice that said, ''Good evenin', Marting,'' was so low and quiet that he had to turn round to see if it was indeed Mag, then he said:

''I wonder, Margaret, to see you here.''

''You don't wonder more than I do to see myself, after the way you treated me the last time.''

M A Rathkyle, *Farewell to Garrymore* (Dublin, 1912).

M A RATHKYLE' (Miss Marianne Younger) lived in Rathdowney and contributed many stories and sketches to an American magazine called *Ireland*. Her novel, *Farewell to Garrymore* (1917) was reckoned at the time to be among the most realistic books about Irish peasant life. She died in 1917.

Ploughing at Skerries c. 1903 (Lawrence Collection, National Library).

The Foys in their motor-car at Church Street, Athlone. (Phot. Simmons/Old Athlone Society Coll.).

Sir Thomas [*to O'Reilly*]. There's sense in what he says.

Fogarty. So, I see it's all a plot, a Yankee plot and swindle. But I'm too wide awake for all of you. And I've backers in the parish priest and all the well-off people. O dear, ay! I could raise a thousand pound to-morrow if I wanted it.

O'Reilly. You'll want it, Mr. Fogarty.

Fogarty. Oh, yes! So will you to take you out of this. I'm off to rouse the country, me and Mr. Casey. O Lord, ay! You'll smoke me out. You'll cut off sun and wind from me. Ho, ho! It's me will smoke you out and cut off water from you. Wait a bit, my boy! Good day to you, Sir Thomas. Poor old Ned Mulroy! (Goes out.)

Sir Thomas. We daren't move an inch if he can raise the money.

O'Reilly. You keep your word, Sir Thomas. Press the bank claim on him. Leave the rest to me. Do you think a skunk like that is going to stop my progress?

Mrs. Walton. There's fight still left in Stephen J., believe me.

O'Reilly. If you stand by me, Mrs. Walton, I defy creation.

Mrs. Walton. Oh, I'll stand by you, never fear, my friend.

Sir Thomas. But really, Mr. O'Reilly, I don't see my way.

Patrick. The country will be on us if we treat him harshly.

Ned. In Ireland a man's land is as sacred as his wife. I wonder if I offered Kitty to him now! Kitty and two hundred of a fortune -?

Mrs. Walton. The very thing. A suitable match for both of them. [*Pulls Ned aside.*]

O'Reilly. My friends, I'm into this. My automobile is starting for a run. If a child or lady [*Bows to Mrs. Walton*] wanders in my way, I'll stop and move them gently. But if a grown-up man plumps down on my track deliberately and plugs his ears, I'll just advance the speed a twist, and rip!! The car may jolt. I'm staring, staring straight ahead. I've got no time to look around for accidents.

Mrs. Walton. Stephen J., I hope I'll be allowed a seat in that same car.

O'Reilly. The engineer is honoured. [*Bows.*]

Ned. The Lord in heaven save us. This man wouldn't stop at anything.

O'Reilly. Not if stopping meant destruction to my passengers. [*Takes Sir Thomas aside.*]

Mrs. Walton [*aside to Ned*]. You and I, Mulroy, will see about this. You think your daughter is willing?

Ned. She'll do it to save her family.

(Curtain.)

William Boyle *The Mineral Workers* (Dublin, 1910).

THE MINERAL WORKERS was the most seriously intended of Boyle's plays but the large cast of characters proved too much for his limited dramatic talent. The story is of a returned American engineer and of his struggles with the conservative small-holders whose lands he hopes to mine. A possible Ibsenesque theme was not developed and Boyle settled for comedy - or indeed, farce - as in his two earlier plays.

Mrs. Dempsey. Well, Jerry, what side are you on now?

Dempsey. The right side, to be sure, my dear.

Mrs. Dempsey. There can't be two of them in the same quarrel. Can there?

Dempsey. God help your wits, woman. When a man's in public life there's as many sides as there's people to discuss them with.

Mrs. Dempsey. Double-dealing, Jerry. Double-dealing never thrives.

Dempsey. There's no more double-dealing in this than selling one man porter and another ginger-beer. You don't argue downstairs with your customers about their tastes in liquor.

Mrs. Dempsey. I'm not talking about customers, but about yourself, Jerry.

Dempsey. Well, what about me?

Mrs. Dempsey. You're like Lanna Macree's dog - a piece of the road with everybody. One minute you're all for Cloghermore and the sky over it, and the next you're all for moderation and the Government. It's the same way with you in everything. You're a publican by trade and a member of the Anti-Treating League for recreation. You denounce

Blackrock Bazaar Dundalk 1900's (Lawrence Collection, National Library).

Emigration on the platform, and behind the counter you sell tickets for the shipping companies. You'll go anywhere and subscribe to anything if they'll only let you make a speech about it. [*Dempsey protests by a gesture.*] Jerry, you're a rag on every bush, fluttering to every wind that blows; and [*tenderly*] if you weren't the best husband and the best father that ever broke the bread of life, I'd say you were the biggest rascal in the whole of Ireland.

Dempsey. Sure, every one's a rascal in the eyes of somebody.

Mrs. Dempsey. And if you don't mind, you'll be a rascal in the eyes of everybody. "Never mix your drinks," my father used to say, and never mix your principles is my advice to you, Jerry.

Dempsey. Faith, Catherine, the best of drink is often made by blending.

Mrs. Dempsey. Oh, I see!

Dempsey. Yes; and the curse of this unfortunate country is that people can't be got to blend their views at all. We all want to run our own spirit into other people raw.

William Boyle *The Eloquent Dempsey* (Dublin, 1909).

WILLIAM BOYLE was born in Dromiskin, Co Louth in 1853. He is best known as the author of three early Abbey plays of small town life: *The Building Fund* (1905) *The Eloquent Dempsey* (1907) and *The Mineral Workers* (1907). They were very popular comedies though Yeats admitted to Synge that he and Lady Gregory found *The Eloquent Dempsey* 'impossibly vulgar'. Boyle withdrew his plays after the Playboy row in 1907. The description of Dempsey, the time-pleasing publican, by his wife, 'You're like Lanna Machree's dog - a bit of the road with everyone' has passed into the language. He died in 1922.

19

"OCH, IT'S YE that's the play-boy. Shure this very minyet ye have it in yer mind to make the poor lonely widdy, Mrs. Mackesy, on the airliest possible occasion."

"I shouldn't be surprised meself to see her Mrs. Monaghan before long," was Terry's retort.

"That'll do ye now," cried Monaghan, lighting his pipe. "Ye may accuse me o' coortin' whin ye see me scarin' the cattle wid a red tie, an' not before. But go on wid ye there an' if ye don't persuade her before evenin' I'll say ye have no pluck. An' if I wor you to-day, I'd lave the carpentherin' alone an' stick to the joinin'; ye'd find it more profitable."

Monaghan disappeared round Dolan's corner with a laugh, and Terence Mackesy continued his journey down the street. When he arrived at his destination, he paused at the door, and looked up at the signboard. The artist who had inflicted this atrocity on the establishment has passed away, and, as nothing but good may be said about the dead, the design will be here merely reproduced without any accompanying criticism.

dAnIELmaCk
inthErTainminT
for mAn an Baste.

NICHOLAS P MURPHY was at Clongowes Wood College and later was called to the English Bar. His only surviving work is a collection of Midland sketches set in 'Ballybeg', the name of which is taken as in the plays of Brian Friel as the typical Irish small town. He died in 1914.

Mrs. Mack had often but in vain, inveighed against the inscription during her husband's life-time, and now that he was a twelvemonth dead, and according to the laws of usage, no longer a moral entity, she thought it high time to replace the monstrosity by something less calculated to drive away respectable customers.

Nicholas P Murphy *A Corner in Ballybeg* (London, 1902).

Main Street Gorey Co Wexford
(Lawrence Collection, National Library).

20

Earl Street, Mullingar (Lawrence Collection, National Library).

21

Glenmacnass, Co Wicklow (Lawrence Collection, National Library).

THE GLEN OF THE HORSE

"YONDER'S the cleft in the Mountain, their 'Glen of the Horse,'
Lonely, with bulwarks of granite to left and to right
Lifted above its great boulders, its bracken and gorse
Hiding the rillet that gurgles in giddy delight
Hurrying down to the valley of grey Glenmalure.
What is the legend that haunts it, of wizard or sprite,
Mortal devil or angel or dragon impure?"

"This. I have reason to know it, none living so well.
I am a part of the story that blackens the Glen.
Ever the name of it rings in mine ear like a knell;
Ever its memory darkens my path among men . . .

"It was an evening of summer in red "Ninety-Eight'
When, as we climbed from the Valley, my troopers and I,
Up by the mule-path, and drew in the breezes, elate,
Reaching the Pass of Imahl and the moorlands on high,
Suddenly rose from a gully the torrents had torn
Wide in the heather a Horseman in Rebel's array,
Leapt with his steed from the cover he lay in forlorn,
Sprang like a hare when it starts at a loud 'hark-away!',
Turned for a moment to scan us, then, striking his spurs
Deep in the sides of his chestnut, away to the height.
Out toward the brown Lugnaquillia through bracken and furze
Rode for his life o'er the moors in the face of the night.

George F S Armstrong *Stories of Wicklow* (London, 1886).

GEORGE FRANCIS ARMSTRONG was born in Co Dublin in 1846 and after graduation from TCD in 1892 he was appointed professor of history and English literature at the then Queen's College, Cork. He was much impressed by his mother's family, the Savages of Ards, published their history in 1888 and added Savage to his name in 1890. He had a high reputation in Ireland towards the end of the century, to the extent that several Irish papers suggested he be appointed Poet Laureate on Tennyson's death in 1892. He died in Co Down in 1906.

The Abbey, Killeigh King's
County 1885 (Mathews
Collection). *The Abbey* is a house,
part of which, as the name
suggests was once monastic
property, situated in the village of
Killeigh, five miles south of
Tullamore, King's County. The
property was confiscated during
the reformation and it passed to
the Tarleton family in th late
sixteenth century. The
photograph shows John William
Tarleton (1833-1896) with his
eldest son John. The property was
sold to its present owners, the
Mathews, in 1917.

Killeagh Abbey, Tullamore.

24

Once upon a time and a very good time it was there was a moocow coming down along the road and this moocow that was coming down along the road met a nicens little boy named baby tuckoo . . .

His father told him that story: his father looked at him through a glass: he had a hairy face.

He was baby tuckoo. The moocow came down the road where Betty Byrne lived: she sold lemon platt.

> *O, the wild rose blossoms*
> *On the little green place.*

He sang that song. That was his song.

> *O, the green wothe botheth.*

When you wet the bed first it is warm and then it gets cold. His mother put on the oilsheet. That had the queer smell.

His mother had a nicer smell than his father. She played on the piano the sailor's hornpipe for him to dance. He danced:

> *Tralala lala,*
> *Tralala tralaladdy,*
> *Tralala lala,*
> *Tralala lala.*

Uncle Charles and Dante clapped. They were older than his father and mother but uncle Charles was older than Dante.

Dante had two brushes in her press. The brush with the maroon velvet back was for Michael Davitt and the brush with the green velvet back was for Parnell. Dante gave him a cachou every time he brought her a piece of tissue paper.

James Joyce *A Portrait of the Artist as a Young Man* (New York, 1916).

JAMES JOYCE (1882-1941) is probably Ireland's greatest modern writer and certainly her most written about. An intense classical and Thomistic training fitted him to be his own best philosophical and aesthetic interpreter and his purpose 'to forge in the smithy of my soul the uncreated conscience of my race' was to his own mind at least, achieved, though whether the triple imposition of silence, exile and cunning was necessary or not has not been proved. *Ulysses* (1922) remains his finest achievement but *A Portrait of the Artist as a Young Man* (1916) is the most revealing. The style of *Dubliners* (1914) a collection of stories about his city, places it as a 19th century work, *Exiles* (1918) his play (rejected by Bernard Shaw for obscenity) is interesting but not great, his poetry is interesting but not great, his poetry is embarrassing and no one has yet been able to prove that *Finnegan's Wake* (1939) was not a joke - Olympian perhaps but a joke all the same.

MORIARTY unwisped the reins from the saddle of the harness and placed them in the small hands of his mistress, who, as an afterthought, had unlatched the Tara brooch and slipped off the cloak.

"Arrah, what have yiz been afther?" said Moriarty, looking back at the strewn garments as though he had only just discovered what the child had been doing. "Glory be to God, if you haven't left the half of yourself behint you on the road - sure what way is that to be behavin'. Now look here, and I'll tell you for onct and for good, if you let another stitch off you, back yiz'll go, dunkey and all, and it's Mrs Driscoll will give you the dhressin' - musha! but you're more thrubble than all me money - *let up wid thim reins and don't be jibbin' the dunkey's mouth!*"

The last sentence was given in a shout as he ran to the donkey's head just in time to avert disaster.

26

Moriarty sometimes spoke to Miss French as though she were a dog, sometimes as though she were a horse, sometimes as though she were his young mistress. Never disrespectfully. It is only an Irish servant that can talk to a superior like this and in so many ways.

"I'm not jibbing his mouth," replied Miss French. "Think I can't drive! You can hold on to the reins if you like, though, and, see here, you can smoke if you want to."

"It's not you I'd be axin' if I wanted to," replied Moriarty, halting the donkey on a part of the path that was fairly level, so as to get a light for his pipe before they emerged into the sea breeze on the cliff top.

H de Vere Stacpoole *Garryowen* (London, 1910).

HENRY DE VERE STACPOOLE was born in Kingstown in 1863, the son of Rev William Church Stacpoole. He was educated at Malvern College at St Mary's Hospital and practised medicine. His most famous book *The Blue Lagoon* (1915) - a romance of a shipwrecked boy and girl growing up on a South Sea Island - made his reputation. Earlier novels about Ireland were *Patsy* (1908), *Father O'Flynn* (1914). *Garryowen* (1910) is the story of a racehorse.

Ass and Trap, The Mall, Newtown barry, Co Wexford. [Lawrence Collection, National Library] c. 1905.

27

THOMAS KING MOYLAN was born in 1885 and became chief clerk of Grangegorman Hospital. He was the author of many stage comedies which became very popular with amateur companies. *The Curse of the Country* deals with the perennial economic problems of emigration and protectionism v. free trade and is notable for the character of the Irish merchant, Darcy Killigan who 'has a shop, a series of them in fact, all under one roof, than which Harrod's Stores never stocked a wider variety of wares. It was his boast that no man, or woman for that matter, needed anything from cradle to coffin that he could not supply.' He died in 1958.

GREG. Is there no chance of raising it locally; there ought to be plenty of money round here.

JOHN. The money is in the banks earning one-and-a-half to two-and-a-half per cent., but it won't come my way. They look on me as mad because I said the engine might be taken up for aircraft work. The fastened on that and made a laugh of me. Aircraft was only one outlet; it means a cheap traction for them here, cheap power for their threshing and ploughing and mowing; the industry would mean more employment for Kilglennon and sweep away the dull, hopeless look of it. Those lads down at the Brothers' Schools—lads who will afterwards be building up the wealth of the States, or Canada, or England, if the prospect of being made Clerk to the Union does not keep them stuck here—these lads would have something to look forward to if their fathers would only back me up now. Think of it, Gregory; think of all those brainy fellows being lost, generation after generation, lost to us for the want of an outlet at home!

GREG. Aye, 'twas only the other day I was trying to track down in my mind where all my school-chums had gone. Only yourself and myself were on the Old Sod.

JOHN. There was Tom Geary, full of divilment. Can you fancy him in a fashionable London practice. And Harry Brown, who used to run that little paper with all the local skits in it, he's managing a big paper in New York. Paddy King is an engineer in India; Callaghan is boss of a contracting firm of builders in South Africa; Lacey is running a huge farm in Canada; Stenson is in the Chinese Customs, top-dog over a crowd of Celestials. What a nation we'd be, Gregory, if all those chaps were back here again, working and prospering as they have done abroad. Lord! Ireland wouldn't be big enough to hold us—nor a nation on the earth strong enough to keep us down.

GREG. John Silent, I'll have to re-christen you. I thought I had some "gift of the gab," but you've developed the most surprising flow of language since I saw you last.

JOHN [*smiling*]. I don't know when I said as much. I suppose it is getting on my favourite topic, and having you to talk to. Round here they judge you by the paper you read, and a fellow like me, who doesn't read any, is looked on with suspicion. I get sick of the alternate praise and denunciation of Redmond and Carson, Sinn Feiners and Covenanters, William O'Brien and John Dillon. It concerns me more where my socks are made than what was said last night in the Orange Lodge, the Masonic Hall, or the A.O.H.

GREG. "Them's my sentiments," John, and if everyone took the same interest in the origin of their clothes we'd be able to afford much better ones. Look at all the money we spend on the importation of that item alone. Look at all a woman spends; look at all she spends on even one small section—her underwear. Many a man makes a point of getting "home-grown" collars, ties, and shirts; but ask the average Irishwoman where her underwear is made, and what will she say? [*MOLLIE passes the window and comes to the door.*]

JOHN [*smiling*]. I can guess what she'd say, and I know for certain what the neighbours would say. Catch me asking the average Irishwoman anything about her clothes, or where they came from.

MOLL. [*entering*]. I'm an average Irishwoman, John, but you needn't be afraid to ask anything about my clothes, though from Adam I couldn't tell you where anything I have came from; I'm quite satisfied to get them.

[*JOHN and GREGORY look embarrassed. Then JOHN introduces GREGORY and MOLLIE*].

JOHN. Miss Regan this is Gregory O'Neale, a very old friend of mine. Gregory, Miss Regan. [*They shake hands heartily.*]

MOLL. [*to GREG.*] What wild deeds were you inciting John to do just now?

MALACHY SCALLY came from Kilbeggan, the distillery village where the famous Tullamore Dew was first manufactured. The design of the shop was based on one sen in Liege and it was erected by direct labour with the assistance of the architect T F MacNamara. Scally's business declined afterwards because the shop proved to be too grand for the clients. It is now owned by Glessons.

Scally's Shop, Williams Street, Tullamore, 1912 (Lawrence Collection, National Library).

29

THE DEAD AT CLONMACNOIS.

In a quiet watered land, a land of roses,
    Stands Saint Kieran's city fair:
And the warriors of Erin in their famous generations
    Slumber there.

There beneath the dewy hillside sleep the noblest
    Of the clan of Conn,
Each below his stone with name in branching Ogham
    And the sacred knot thereon.

There they laid to rest the seven Kings of Tara,
    There the sons of Cairbré sleep—
Battle-banners of the gael, that in Kieran's plain of crosses
    Now their final hosting keep.

And in Clonmacnois they laid the men of Teffia,
    And right many a lord of Breagh;
Deep the sod above Clan Creidé and Clan Conaill,
    Kind in hall and fierce in fray.

Many and many a son of Conn, the Hundred-Fighter,
    In the red earth lies at rest;
Many a blue eye of Clan Colman the turf covers,
    Many a swan-white breast.

T W Rolleston
'The Dead at Clonmacnoise' Sea Spray (Dublin, 1906).

The Shannon is a glorious river, broad and deep, and brimming over, extending from source to sea a distance of two hundred miles, and 'making its waves a blessing as they flow' to ten Irish counties . . . Six miles from Athlone we pass the Seven Churches of Clonmacnoise (once, as its name signifies, the Eton of Ireland, 'the school of the sons of the nobles') by whom despoiled and desecrated we English need not pause to enquire; and close to these a brace of those famous Round Towers which have so perplexed the archaeological world, and which according to Frank were 'most probably lighthouses which had come ashore at night for a spree and had forgotten the way back again.'

S Reynolds Hole *A Little Tour in Ireland* (London, 1896).

THOMAS WILLIAM HAZEN ROLLESTON was born in Shinrone, King's County in 1857. He was one of John O'Leary's circle of young men though older than Yeats or Hyde. He became an active champion of the Gaelic League in 1896 when Hyde and MacNeill accepted his challenge and were able to prove that Irish could be used as a precise language for philosophy and science. He helped found the Irish Literary Society in England in 1893 and his book *Imagination and Art in Gaelic Literature* (1900) had much influence. He wrote much verse but his lasting claim to literary fame (apart from the lyric printed here) was his editing with Stepford Brook of *The Treasury of Irish Verse* (1900). He died in 1920.

THE ROADS OF IRELAND

There are many fine roads in Ireland,
  Travelling from the city to the town;
There are straight level roads in Ireland
  And roads for ever going up and down.

There are beautiful fair roads in Ireland,
  Meandering by the woodland and the stream,
Running silver white across the valley
  Out to where the far blue mountains dream.

There are many fine sea roads in Ireland,
  Dashed by the bright salty spray,
Where the warm smell of whin and white clover
  Travel with the traveller all the way.

There are many many roads in Ireland,
Crossing the land from sea to sea.
But of all the highways and the by-ways
  There is only one road for me:

It's the way of high adventure when the morning dew is there,
  It's childhood and the river running free,
It's Youth's delicious rapture and the promises of Life
  When the golden moon has risen from the sea.

There are many many roads in Ireland,
  Long roads, old roads, and new.
Oh! tell me when you're dreaming and romancing,
  Is there only one road for you?

'Hal D'Arcy *Poems* (Dublin,
1930).

Little is discoverable about HAL
D'ARCY except that in spite of her
name she was a lady. She wrote one
novel *A Handful of Days* (1914) and
several books of verse including *The
O'Donoghue* (1907) and *Poems*
(1930).

Market days, Dundalk, c. 1905

Afloat

The City of Dublin Steam Packet Company carried the mail between Kingstown and Holyhead from 1851 to 1920. At first they used paddle-steamships and then from 1896 they used four turbine steamships called after the four provinces of Ireland. They were capable of 24 knots and had a deserved reputation for efficency. In 1920 they were replaced by Railway steamers run by the LNWR.

Mail Boat, Kingstown c. 1905 [Lawrence Coll., National Library].

Th' anám an Dhia but there it is -
  The dawn on the hills of Ireland!
God's angels lifing the night's black veil
  From the fair, sweet   face of my sireland!
O Ireland isn't it grand you look -
  Like a bride in her rich adornin'?
And with all the pent-up love of my heart
  I bid you the top o' the mornin'!

This one short hour pays lavishly back
  For many a year of mourning;
I'd almost venture another flight,
  There's so much joy in returning -
Watching out for the hallowed shore,
  All other attractions scornin':
O Ireland! don't you hear me shout?
  I bid you the top of the mornin'.

For thirty summers, *asthore machree*,
  Those hills I now feast my eyes on
Ne'er met my vision save when they rose
  Over memory's dim horizon.
E'en so, 't was grand and fair they seemed
  In the landscape spread before me;
But dreams are dreams, and my eyes would ope
  To see Texas' sky still o'er me.

Oh! often upon the Texan plains,
  When the day and the chase were over,
My thoughts would fly o'er the weary wave,
  And around this coast-line hover;
And the prayer would rise that some future day -
  All danger and doubting scornin' -
I'd help to win for my native land
  The light of Young Liberty's mornin'!

John Locke 'The Exile's Return or Morning on the Irish Coast' in
Irish Literature V [*Philadelphia, 1904*].

JOHN LOCKE was born in Callan, Co Kilkenny in 1847. He joined the IRB in
1863 and contributed to James Stephens' Fenian journal *The Irish People*.
He had the characteristic career of journalism, prison and exile in America.
His poem, 'The Exile's Return' was almost the anthem of the home-looking
Irish-American. He died in New York in 1889.

WINIFRED LETTS was born in Dublin 1882. She contributed several plays to the early Abbey repertoire, notably *The Challenge* (1909) but her lasting claim to fame is her well-known poem 'A Soft Day' which was printed in the first of two collections of poetry, *Songs of Leinster*.

New Ross Harbour, Co Wexford, c. 1908 (Lawrence Collection, National Library).

THE HARBOUR

I think if I lay dying in some land
   Where Ireland is no more than just a name,
My soul would travel back to find that strand
   From whence it came.

I'd see the harbour in the evening light,
   The old men staring at some distant ship,
The fishing-boats they fasten left and right
   Beside the slip.

The sea-wrack lying on the wind-swept shore,
   The grey thorn bushes growing in the sand
Our Wexford coast from Arklow to Cahore -
   My native land.

The little houses climbing up the hill,
   Sea daisies growing in the sandy grass,
The tethered goats that wait large-eyed and still
   To watch you pass.

The women at the well with dripping pails,
   Their men colloguing by the harbour wall,
The coils of rope, the nets, the old brown sails,
   I'd know them all.

And then the Angelus - I'd surely see
   The swaying bell against a golden sky,
So God, Who kept the love of home in me,
   Would let me die.

Winifred Letts Songs from Leinster [*London, 1914*].

Ballyhack Co Wexford [Lawrence Collection, National Library].

JAMES MURPHY was born in Dublin in 1839 and after some period as a teacher in Bray was appointed Professor of Mathematics to the Catholic University under Newman's successor, Woodlock. He wrote many romantic historical novels about Ireland, most notably *The shan Van Vocht* (1883). He died in Kingstown in 1913.

IT WAS with a heart beating with conflicting emotions that Eugene found himself in the officers' quarters of the Thunderer, wherein at a large table sat the captain and a number of gentlemen resplendent with all the gorgeousness of naval uniform. If he had had the time to analyze these emotions he would have found the principal one to be a vague sense of disappointment and loss and disaster. Not every man in warfare on sea or land must run the risk of these - they are the incidents of his profession; but for others. Simple as was the little barque in appearance that was even then making her rapid way through the deep waters to the bottom, she bore important fortunes. The future of a gallant and brave nation struggling into the light of freedom was in her keeping, and mayhap the safety of a powerful and friendly fleet. He was convinced, from all that he had heard the night before, that the only chance for success attending the great venture France was about to make in Ireland's cause, was in making the Eastern coast their point of debarkation; and that unless the present intention of the Republican leaders were altered, sorrow would come to the cause now engaging the attention of the high-hearted men whom he had left last night - and misfortune to a French army and fleet.

James Murphy The Shan Van Vocht [*Extract from* Irish Literature [*Philadelphia, 1904*]].

Regatta at Boat Club, Wexford. [*Séamas de Vál Collection, Oulart, Co Wexford*].

'Ireland has, practically speaking, no mercantile marine. A few coasting and cross-channel steamers running to continental ports is all that is left of the once great commercial fleet of Ireland ... Why have we not this marine? We have the material in abundance of which sailors are made. We have £50,000 of money lying idle in our banks. It is because we have not the spirit of a free people—because we are taught to be dependent and look to and trust in a foreign parliament when the people of other nations are taught to look and trust in themselves'

IT CHANCED that this Sabbath morning a brigantine was lying alongside the quay, her captain standing near the whell, and a couple of "hands" forward. I had invited them to Trinity Church, and had given some of my little books to them, when, as I was returning to ascend the shore-plank, I saw an old man seated on the windlass forwards. He was dressed unlike an ordinary seaman, wore a tall black hat, black frock-coat, and had the air of a past respectability strongly marked upon his face, which bore the marks of deep care and sorrow. He sat in the hot sunlight, kicking his feet against the deck, and scarcely looked up when I drew near and saluted him.

"I tell you what it is," at last exclaimed he passionately, as I spoke a few words to him, "I have seen sorrow enough to drive any man out of his right senses. I was not always thus," he said, and he looked up with his sunken eyes into my face, "only two years ago I was happy, and look at me now; then I was master of my own ship, now I am before the mast; then I had my dear wife, now I am alone in this earth."

"It comes before me now again," he said dreamily, and his face grew ashen pale, - the snow-crowned hills around - the frozen Neva, - the craft lying frozen up alongside one of those great buildings to which she was secured by iron rings and hawsers. "My men had all left save two, for we were regularly shut up for the winter at St. Petersburg, and these two men after a time got tired of the snow, and ice, and cold, and went home; but the wife, she still stuck to me, and we made the best of it; it was cold and dreary enough, but we loved each other, and were company to one another, though it was so far from home. Well, one of those great men, to whom I had applied, had sent me two Russians as care-takers of the ship, of whom he gave me a good character, and though I never liked their looks much, still I did not like to encourage myself in doubting them; they had little to do with us, nor we with them; they lived forward in the forecastle to themselves, and smoked away, or slept away their time - one man watching by day, another by night. Well, sir, one day," and his voice trembled, "I had to send a particular letter home to the owners, and I did

not like to send it by the men, so as I knew the way to the post-office I went myself, and as I returned" - here he grasped the windlass, and trembled violently - "I caught sight of the ship, and there was a dense smoke rising forward and another aft. I rushed down like a madman - you must know it was a very lonely part of the river, and no other ship lay near her - down the companion I ran, calling out, 'Wife, wife! where are you - where?' - oh! that awful moment! I saw her lying dead before me, - her very head cleft in twain with a hatchet blow, and her very ear-rings torn from her ears, and her poor dead face turned downwards. The two Russians had done it, and then set fire to the ship. I don't remember much more then; she was buried; and my heart gave way. I followed her to the grave alone; I heard that the English Consul brought the murderers before the Government, but they did nothing; and now look at me," - and his burning eyes wearily fastened themselves on mine, - "I am broken-hearted, going down from bad to worse, with that awful scene ever rising before my mind. I see it as I sit here; I see it as I take the wheel; I see it as I lay out aloft; I see it in my berth; I see it in my dreams; and he wearily drooped his head upon his chest, and relapsed into silence. "I trust," I said, "that you will see her again, not as when you saw her last, still and pale in death, but radiant in joy, and clothed with the robe of the Redeemer's righteousness."

[*Rev*] *J Duncan Craig*, Real Pictures of Clerical Life in Ireland [*London, 1875*].

THE REV J DUNCAN CRAIG was born in 1831 and after graduation from Trinity took orders. He ministered in Kinsale and Dublin where he was the vicar of Trinity Church in Lr. Gardiner Street. He became an authority on Provencal literature but was in no other sense liberal. His two books, *Bruce Reynall MA* (1898) and *Real Pictures of Clerical Life in Ireland* (1875) are noted for their pro-Orange, anti-Catholic bias. Phrases like '—when Rome Rule or Home Rule arrives in Ireland—for the terms are synonymous' appear in his writing but his books give a racy if heavily slanted view of Irish life.

'Every dog has his day.'
　　Well, dear, do you remember,
How you and I found a golden day
　　In the midst of a bleak December?

You smiled at the chance of our meeting,
　　I blushed as I turned away,
While our little world stood by in amaze,
With hands upheld in dismay.

We loosened the chain of our little boat,
　　And each took an oar in hand.
You spoke no word, but you looked at me,
　　And we rowed for love's sweet land.

You said, 'All earth's beauties I see in your face.'
　　I said, 'All earth's music you're speaking.'
And the keel of our little craft grated the while
　　On the silvery shore of our seeking.

You looked at me and I smiled on you -
　　(O sweet! it was golden weather) -
Then we laughed as the boat glided back from the
　　　　　　　　　　　　　　　　　shore
　　And we pulled from the land together.

For you thought, perhaps, of another face,
　　And I - let pass, you remember,
Not half we said on that summer's day
　　We found in a bleak December.

Dora Sigerson *Verses* (London, 1893).

DORA SIGERSON SHORTER was born in Dublin in 1866, the eldest daughter of George Sigerson, the Gaelic scholar and scientist. A minor versifier of the Renaissance she was sponsored by George Meredith but came in for rather a lot of criticism for her lack of formal technique. Her most famous poem, 'Sixteen Dead Men' was about the 1916 leaders. 'One Day in December' was written for her husband, Clement Shorter, editor of *The Illustrated London News*. She died in 1917.

Below: Trinity College Regatta, Chapelizod c. 1900 (Lawrence Collection, National Library).

WE are going to talk, if you please, in the ensuing chapters, of what was going on in Chapelizod about a hundred years ago. A hundred years, to be sure, is a good while; but though fashions have changed, some old phrases dropped out, and new ones come in; and snuff and hair-powder, and sacques and solitaires quite passed away - yet men and women were men and women all the same - as elderly fellows, like your humble servant, who have seen and talked with rearward stragglers of that generation - now all and long marched off - can testify, if they will.

In those days Chapelizod was about the gayest and prettiest of the outpost villages in which old Dublin took a complacent pride. The poplars which stood, in military rows, here and there, just showed a glimpse of formality among the orchards and old timber that lined the banks of the river and the valley of the Liffey, with a lively sort of richness. The broad old street looked hospitable and merry, with steep roofs and many coloured hall-doors. The jolly old inn, just beyond the turnpike at the sweep of the road, leading over the buttressed bridge by the mill, was first to welcome the excursionist from Dublin, under the sign of the Phoenix. There, in the grand wainscoted back-parlour, with 'the great and good King William,' in his robe, garter, periwig, and sceptre presiding in the panel over the chimneypiece, and confronting the large projecting window, through which the river, and the daffodils, and the summer foliage looked so bright and quiet, the Aldermen of Skinner's Alley - a club of the 'true blue' dye, as old as the Jacobite wars of the previous century - the corporation of shoemakers, or of tailors, or the freemasons, or the musical clubs, loved to dine at the stately hour of five, and deliver their jokes, sentiments, songs, and wisdom, on a pleasant summer's evening. Alas! the inn is as clean gone as the guests - a dream of the shadow of smoke.

Lately, too, came down the old 'Salmon House' - so called from the blazonry of that noble fish upon its painted sign-board - at the other end of the town, that, with a couple more, wheeled out at right angels from the line of the broad street, and directly confronting the passenger from Dublin, gave to it

something of the character of a square, and just left room for the high road and Martin's Row to slip between its flank and the orchard that overtopped the river wall. Well! it is gone. I blame nobody. I suppose it was quite rotten, and that the rats would soon have thrown up their lease of it; and that it was taken down, in short, chiefly, as one of the players said of 'Old Drury,' to prevent the inconvenience of its comind down of itself. Still a peevish but harmless old fellow - who hates change, and would wish things to stay as they were just a little, till his own great change comes; who haunts the places where his childhood is passed, and reverences the homeliest relics of by-gone generations - may be allowed to grumble a little at the impertinences of improving proprietors with a taste for accurate parallelograms and pale new brick.

Then there was the village church, with its tower dark and rustling from base to summit, with thick piled, bowering ivy. The royal arms cut in bold relief in the broad stone over the porch - where, pray, is that stone now, the memento of its old viceregal dignity? Where is the elevated pew, where many a lord lieutenant, in point, and gold lace, and thunder-cloud periwig, sate in awful isolation, and listened to orthodox and loyal sermons, and took French rappee; whence too, he stepped forth between the files of the guard of honour of the Royal Irish Artillery from the barrack over the way, in their courtly uniform, white, scarlet, and blue, cocked hats, and cues, and rufles, presenting arms - into his embalzoned coach and six, with hanging footmen, as wonderful as Cinderella's and out-riders outblazing the liveries of the troops, and rolling grandly away in sunshine and dust.

Sheridan Le Fanu The House by the Churchyard [*Dublin, 1904*].

SHERIDAN LE FANU was born in Dublin in 1814 the son of a dean of the Church of Ireland and grand-nephew of the dramatist, Richard Brinsley Sheridan. He wrote one historical novel, *Torlogh O'Brien* (1847) but already while still a young man had won a special fame as the author of 'Phadrig Crohore' - an Irish Lochinvar. He is best remembered as the author of such novels as *The House by the Churchyard* (1863) and *Uncle Silas* (1864). His shorter pieces of macabre writing collected in *In a Glass Darkly* (1872) are among the finest and most skilfully wrought examples of the *genre* and in *Carmilla*, easily the finest vampire story ever written, he anticipated his more famous fellow Trinity man, Bram Stoker, who did not produce *Dracula* till 1897. In his time he was editor of *The Dublin University Magazine* and *The Evening Mail*. He died in 1873.

On the River Liffey at Chapelizod, c. 1904 [Lawrence Collection, National Library].

CROSSING the bridge we enter Chapelizod once a favourite residence for Dublin citizens, and still possessing some traces of the old world respectability which characterised it at the period of which Le Fanu wrote in his famous novel. Between the two approaches from the main street to the Protestant Parish Church, is an old-fashioned house, which is evidently the actual "House by the Churchyard" that plays so prominent a part in the story.

Weston St J Joyce *The Neighbourhood of Dublin* (Dublin, 1912).

"YOU SEE," were Davie's reassuring words, "there's plenty of room to *sit* upright" (which was strictly true; but I am not very tall, and he is short). "Some people make a point of head-room, but I never mind much about it. That's the centre-board case," he explained, as in stretching my legs out, my knee come into contact with a sharp edge.

I had not seen this devilish obstruction, as it was hidden beneath the table, which indeed rested on it at one end. It appeared to be a long low triangle, running lengthways with the boat and dividing the naturally limited space into two.

"You see she's a flat-bottomed boat, drawing very little water without the plate; that's why there's so little headroom. For deep water you lowere the plate; so, in one way or another, you can go practically anywhere."

I was not nautical enough to draw any very definite conclusions from this, but what I did draw were not promising. The latter sentences were spoken from the forecastle, whither Davies had crept through a low sliding door, like that of a rabbit-hutch, and was already busy with a kettle over a stove which I made out to be a battered and disreputable twin brother of the No. 3 Rippingill.

"It'll be boiling soon," he remarked, " and we'll have some grog."

My eyes were used to the light now, and I took in the rest of my surroundings, which may be very simply described. Two long cushion-covered seats flanked the cabin, bounded at the after end by cupboards, one of which was cut low to form a sort of miniature sideboard, with glasses hung in a rack above it. The deck overhead was very low at each side, but rose shoulder high for a space in the middle, where a "coach-house roof" with a skylight gave additional cabin space. Just outside the door was a fold-up washing-stand. On either wall were long netracks holding a medley of flags, charts, caps, cigar-boxes, hanks of yarn, and such-like. Across the forward bulkhead was a bookshelf crammed to overflowing with volumes of all sizes, many upside down and some coverless. Below this were a pipe-rack, an aneroid, and a clock with a hearty tick. All the woodwork was painted white, and to a less

ROBERT ERSKINE CHILDERS was born in Glendalough Co Wicklow the son of an Irish mother and an English father but was as he often insisted '. . .by birth, domicile and deliberate choice, an Irishman.' He was educated at Haileybury and Trinity College, Cambridge, but lived in Ireland from 1919. He wrote the famous and prophetic adventure yarn, *The Riddle of the Sands* in 1903 and took a leading part in the Howth Gun-running of 1914. He took the Republican side in the Civil War and was arrested while carrying a gun given to him as a present by Michael Collins. He was court-martialled and shot in Beggars Bush Barracks on 24 November 1922.

jaundiced eye than mine the interior might have had an enticing look of snugness. Some Kodak prints were nailed roughly on the after bulkhead, and just over the doorway was the photograph of a young girl.

"That's my sister," said Davies, who had emerged and saw me looing at it. "Now, let's get the stuff down." He ran up the ladder, and soon my portmanteau blackened the hatchway, and a great straining and squeezing began. "I was afraid it was too big," came down; "I'm sorry, but you'll have to unpack on deck - we may be able to squash it down when it's empty."

Erskine Childers The Riddle of the Sands [*London, 1903*].

Kingstown Harbour 1900 [*Lawrence Collection, National Library*].

The Great Eastern docked at Dublin: designed by Brunel and used for laying cables in the Atlantic, this was the first iron-clad vessel of its kind.

Canal Quay, Bagenalstown, Co Carlow
(Lawrence Collection, National Library).

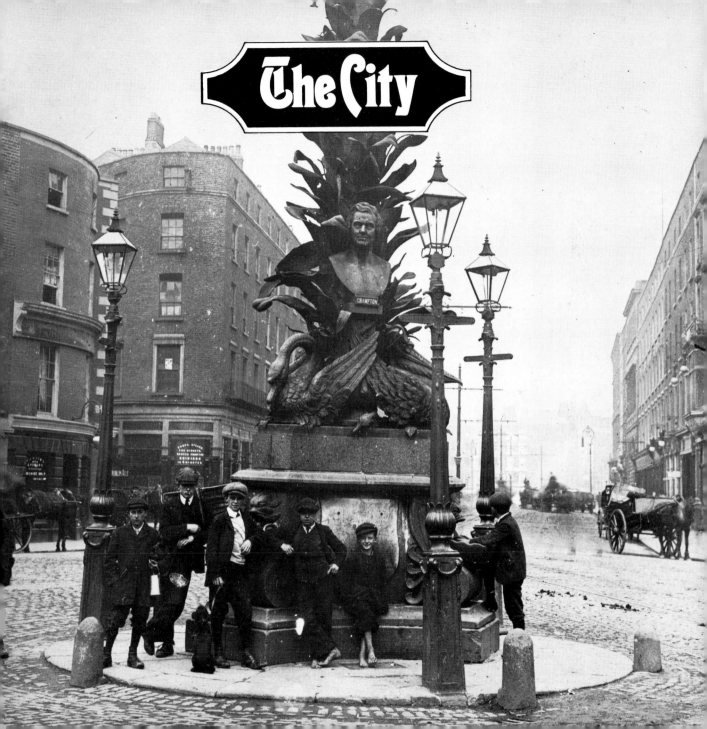

The City

Michael's Lane Dublin c. 1900
(Lawrence Collection, National Library).

There's a gray fog over Dublin of the curses,
It blinds my eyes, mavrone; and stops my breath,
And I travel slow that once could run the swiftest,
And I fear ere I meet Mauryeen I'll meet Death.

There's a gray fog over Dublin of the curses,
And a gray fog dogs my footsteps as they go,
And it's long and sore to tread, the road of Connaught.
Is it fault of brogues or feet I fare so slow?

There's a gray fog over Dublin of the curses,
But the Connaught wind will blow it from my way,
And a Connaught girl will kiss it from my memory
If the Death that walks beside me will delay.

(There's a gray fog over Dublin of the curses,
And no wind comes to break its stillness deep:
And a Connaughtman lies on the road to Connaught
And Mauryeen will not kiss him from his sleep - Ululu!)

Nora Hopper, 'The Grey Fog' in *Irish Literature* (Philadelphia, 1904).

FROM 1850 onwards Dublin had increasingly attracted immigrants from the provinces but had never been able to provide enough work for them. So it was that by 1900, 87,000 out of a total population of 300,000 lived in slum tenements and of the 5,000 tenements, 1,500 had been condemned as totally unfit for human habitation. Dublin's infant mortality rate was 168 per 1,000 births while that of the country as a whole was only 101. Tuberculosis and other diseases were rife as was alcoholism.

NORA HOPPER was born in Exeter in 1871, the daughter of an Irish officer in the British Army. Her poetry and prose are very delicate and filled with a rather romantic view of Irish life, as this poem shows. Yeats in his misty period announced that her *Ballads in Prose* (1894) 'haunted me as few books have ever haunted me'. She died in 1906.

"What would it be about, Mick?"

"Well, I'll tell you, Geraghty, what it would be about. It would be an Act for finding out first, by a jury iv reg'lar cliver fellows, in what diraction a lad's taste lay, so that the boy might be taught the right thrade, and not cram him with a thrade that he had no likin' for. Bekase it's the most murdherin' foolishness for a father or mother to say, 'I'll make Tom a carpenther; Jack a sweep; Larry a tinker; and Mat a smith.' The lads is not consulted at all, and they have no likin' or taste for the thrades they are put to, and then what's the consequuince? Why, first it

Glencree Reformatory c. 1899
(Lawrence Collection, National Library).

takes twiced as much money and time to make them larn anythin'. Secondly, their lugs is well warmed for them, and they're backs well scarified bor not gein' quick enough at what they'll never be anythin' at. Thirdly, when they're out iv their time and work at their thrades they'll get the blessin' backwards iv everybody that has dailin's with them. Fourthly, they'll get a revinge against everybody from the abuse they get, and get into no ind iv quarrels and ructions, and to keep up their sperrets they take to dhrink. Fifthly, when people come to see the botches they are, they won't imply them, and then the lads commence to starve and rob to make out a livin', and that's the road to the gallows. Now, Terry, as I tould you, my Act would remidy that state iv affairs as far as it could be remidied, bedase the choice ive the thrade wouldn't be left to the fancy iv parents and guardians, but would be found out by the jury, who would study the child's wishes, and find out what he would be most inclined for. And a thrade or business a boy has a care for, he will larn it aisy, and if he could do anythin at any thrade he will sartinly do most at the wan he took a fancy to."

"Well, Mick, I have known boys that if you had a grand jury sittin' on them, you couldn't find out what was their taste, and you see there you'd be bet."

"No, Terry, my 'Cure for Starvation Act' provides for them sort iv lads, bekase in all the industhrial schools, reformathories, and wherever else thrades was taught, I'd have such boys insthructed in at laist three different thrades, so that if they failed at wan they could turn to another, and if they failed in all, they could do a little in aich; the same as the big shops does at present, for formerly what is in wan big shop now, was spread over a dozen or more."

"There is somethin' in that, Mick, sartinly, I admit."

"To be sure there is, Terry. You never hear foolishness out iv my mouth at all, bekase, as Lanty often says, 'them that buys him for a fool loses their money,' so I, for a great dale more raison, say the same ive myself. Sure I'll give an instance in point which comes complate to hand intirely, and that is in conniction with wan iv my speculations. I'm talkin' now ive the failure iv the Irish Church Missioners to show converts in Connaught. You see, Terry, the fathers and mothers iv Missioners didn't know what thrade was shuited to them, and they made them Irish Church Missioners instead iv makin' them tinkers and sweeps, that they would have taken on to betther, bekase they couldn't be worse as Missioners than they are. But talkin' o' them reminds me that I'd betther now tip the head Missioner a letther, afeerd the former wan went asthray, or the Missioners think it is impossible I could do what I said."

"Yes, Mick, that's a good idea, and you will have plenty iv time, for, afther Lanty comes in with the thripe, it will take some time to do, before we can have our dinner."

Mick McQuaid on *Education* in *The Shamrock* Saturday, March 4, 1893,

COL WILLIAM FRANCIS LYNAM though born in Galway in 1845 spent most of his life in Dundrum and Clontarf. After retiring from the 5th Royal Lancashire Militia he lived in almost hermetic solitude. The adventures of his character, Mick McQuaid ran in *The Shamrock* from January 19, 1867 till beyond the author's death in 1894. Mick is the archetypal philosophical witty demotic Irishman whose comical adventures are laced with acute observations upon 19th-century Ireland.

On the beach in front of this dainty mansion a young lady was sitting on a ridge of shingle, bleached by sun and sea-water to perfect cleanliness, which afforded a comfortable resting-place. The young lady seemed much at her ease. Her skirt of blue serge was turned up over a second skirt of white and blue and caught up at the back in what used to be called "fishwife" fashion - the bodice fitting her slight supple figure easily, perfectly; a little foot in a dark-blue stocking, and an incomparable shoe peeped forth as she supported an open book on one knee, and a wide-brimmed sailor hat almost hid her face as she bent over the page.

A big brown boat drawn up beside her made a shelter from the level rays of the sinking sun. Altogether she presented a pretty picture of quiet enjoyment.

As the last strains of the band died away a gentleman in boating attire strolled slowly across the grass, paused, looked round as if searching for somethng, and then came straight over the shingle towards her.

She heard his step and looked at her book with renewed attention, nor did she move till he stood beside her. Then she raised her face, an interesting, rather than a pretty face, somewhat brunette in complexion, and pale, with a warm paleness - a small, oval face, with a delicate chin and a very slight downward curve at the corners of the soft red mouth, that gave a pathetic expression to her countenance when in repose. Her eyes, too, which were her best feature - large eyes, with long, dark lashes, had a wistful, far-away look, more suited to a saint than to their piquante owner.

The man who paused beside her was tall and slender, with a grace of movement not usual in an Englishman. He was darker, too, than ordinary Anglo-Saxons, who rarely possess such blue-black hair and flashing dark eyes as his. His well-cut, refined, but determined mouth was unshaded by moustaches, though a strong growth of black beard showed through his clear olive-brown skin. He smiled a soft, caressing smile as he threw himself on the sand at her feet, saying: "I thought you had gone on the pier with Callander?"

"No; he has gone to the station to meet Mr. Standish, and Mabel has had the honour of a command from the Grand Duchess to drive with her."

The saintly-pathetic expression entirely disappeared, as she spoke with a swift, arch smile, and a

Esplanade Bray 1903 (Lawrence Collection, National Library).

56

flash of scorn from her "holy eyes."

"Ah," he returned, in an amused tone, "why did *you* not go to meet your beloved guardian?"

"I never meant to go. I came out of the way to listen to the band *here*. Music is so charming as it comes fitfully on the breeze, and I enjoy it most alone."

"Well, it is over now, so I may venture to stay?"

"Oh, yes, if you like! But I am tired of sitting here. I want to match some silks. Do you mind, Mr. Egerton?"

"Not at all. As Madame de Stael says, '*être avec ceux qu'on aime -*'"

"It sounds just as well in English," she interrupted, laughing. "'To be with those we love is all-sufficient, etc., etc., etc.'—yes, it is a pretty sentiment."

"You are not in an amiable mood to-day, Miss Wynn. What book is this? Let me carry it for you. Ah! 'The Great Lone Land.'"

"Yes, it is charming—thank you," giving it to him.

"Don't you think it would be cruel to waste this lovely evening matching silks in a stuffy shop? Let us go along the common towards the pier. We may meet some of your party returning."

"Yes, let us go along by the sea." She turned as she spoke, and directed her steps to a low grassy embankment which protected the common on the shore side.

Annie F Alexander *Blind Fate* (London, 1891).

ANNIE FRENCH ALEXANDER was born in Dublin in 1825, the daughter of Robert French, a Dublin solicitor. She published in all forty novels which ranged from high romance to gothic mysteries. Her best known work was *The Wooing O't* (1875). *Blind Fate* (1891) is a mystery story which led a publisher's hack to contrive the following less than deathless quatrain:

In Mrs Alexander's tale
  Much Art she clearly shows
In keeping dark the mystery
  Until the story's close.

She died in 1902.

Marine Hotel Bray 1903

(Lawrence Collection, National Library).

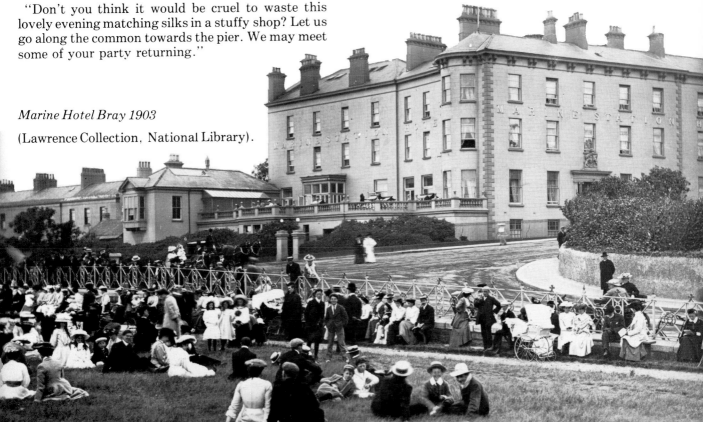

Her mother knew it was time to get out of bed when she heard a heavy step coming from the next room and going downstairs. A labouring man lived there with his wife and six children. When the door banged she jumped up, dressed quickly, and flew from the room in a panic of haste. Usually then, as there was noting to do, Mary went back to bed for another couple of hours. After this she rose, made the bed and tidied the room, and went out to walk in the streets, or to sit in the St Stephen's Green Park. She knew every bird in the Park, those that had chickens, and those that had had chickens, and those that never had any chickens at all - these latter were usually drakes, and had reason on their side for an abstention which might otherwise have appeared remarkable, but they did not deserve the pity which Mary lavished on their childlessness, nor the extra pieces of bread with which she sought to recompense them. She loved to watch the ducklings swimming after their mothers: they were quite fearless, and would dash to the water's edge where one was standing and pick up nothing with the greatest eagerness and swallow it with delight. The mother duck swam placidly close to her brood, and clucked in a low voice all kinds of warnings and advice and reproof to the little ones. Mary Makebelieve thought it was very clever of the little ducklings to be able to swim so well. She loved them, and when nobody was looking she used to cluck at them like their mother; but she did not often do this, because she did not know duck language really well, and feared that her cluck might mean the wrong things, and that she might be giving these innocents bad advice, and telling them to do something contrary to what their mother had just directed.

The bridge across the lake was a fascinating place. On the sunny side lots of ducks were always standing on thir heads searching for something in the water, so that they looked like only half ducks. On the shady side hundreds of eels were swimming about - they were most wonderful things: some of them were thin like ribbons, and others were round and plump like thick ropes. They never seemed to fight at all, and although the ducklings were so tiny the big eels never touched any of them. Even when they dived right down amongst them. Some of the eels swam along very slowly, looking on this side and on that as if they were out of work or up from the country, and others whizzed by with incredible swiftness. Mary Makebelieve thought that the latter kind had just heard their babies crying; she wondered, when a little fish cried, could its mother see the tears where there was already so much water about, and then she thought that maybe they cried hard lumps of something that was easily visible.

After this she would go around the flowerbeds and look at each; some of them were shaped like stars, and some were quite round, and others again were square. She liked the star-shaped flowerbeds best, and next she liked the round ones, and last of all the square. But she loved all the flowers, and used to make up stories about them.

James Stephens *The Hill of Vision* (London, 1922).

JAMES STEPHENS was born in Dublin in 1880 (not, as he often used to claim, on the same day as James Joyce). He was sent to an industrial school in 1886 for begging and afterwards served as a clerk in several firms. He soon became accepted into Dublin's literary circles as much for his talk as for his writing. He wrote poems and wildly imaginative, quirky prose including *The Crock of Gold* (1912) and *Here Are Ladies* (1913). He was Registrar of the National Gallery from 1915 to 1924 and in later life won fame as a very idiosyncratic broadcaster. He died in 1940.

Winter in St Stephen's Green c. 1904 (Lawrence
Collection, National Library).

Of priests we can offer a charmin' variety,
Far renowned for larnin' and piety;
Still, I'd advance you, widout impropriety,
 Father O'Flynn as the flower of them all.

   Here's a health to you, Father O'Flynn,
   Slainté, and slainté, and slainté agin;
     Powerfullest preacher, and
     Tinderest teacher, and
   Kindliest creature in ould Donegal.

Don't talk of your Provost and Fellows of Trinity,
Famous for ever at Greek and Latinity,
Dad and the divels and all at Divinity,
 Father O'Flynn'd make hares of them all.
  Come, I venture to give you my word,
  Never the likes of his logic was heard,
    Down from Mythology
    Into Thayology,
Troth! and Conchology, if he'd the call.

Och! Father O'Flynn, you've the wonderful way wid you,
All the ould sinners are wishful to pray wid you,
All the young childer are wild for to pray wid you,
 You've such a way wid you, Father avick!
  Still, for all you're so gentle a soul,
  Gad, you've your flock in the grandest conthroul;
    Checkin' the crazy ones,
    Coaxin' onaisy ones,
Liftin' the lazy ones on wid the stick.

And though quite avoidin' all foolish frivolity,
Still at all seasons of innocent jollity,
Where was the play-boy could claim an equality
 At comicality, Father, wid you?
  Once the Bishop looked grave at your jest,
  Till this remark set him off wid the rest:
    "Is it lave gaiety
    All to the laity?
Cannot the clargy be Irishmen too?"

   Here's a health to you, Father O'Flynn,
   Slainté, and slainté, and slainté agin;
     Powerfullest preacher, and
     Tinderest teacher, and
   Kindliest creature in ould Donegal.
   Alfred P Graves *Father O'Flynn and other Irish Lyrics* (London, 1899).

ALFRED PERCIVAL GRAVES was born in Dublin in 1846, the son of Charles Graves who afterwards became Bishop of Limerick. He graduated from Trinity in 1871 and became in turn assistant editor of *Punch*, Home Office Clerk and Inspector of Schools. He was the father by his second wife of Robert Graves the romantic poet and gadfly critic, whose book of World War I, *Goodbye to All That* (1929) spurred him to write a most entertaining book of reminiscences called *To Return to All That* (1932). Famous as the author of the song 'Father O'Flynn' and as a translator from Irish his greatest contribution to the Gaelic Revival was in the sphere of Irish music. He died in 1940.

As part of the Tercentenary celebrations on Thursday, 7 July 1892 a procession was held from the Examination Hall to the Leinster Hall where delegates from other universities presented addresses. Later in the day there was a garden party at The Royal Hospital, Kilmainham and in the evening a performance of Sheridan's *The Rivals* (an appropriate choice for an assembly of Irish dons) was given at the Gaiety Theatre. The celebrations were presided over by Provost George Salmon, then a distinguished septuagenarian. At the Tercentenary banquet, the evening before, Lecky the distinguished historian had prayed ' . . . that the spirit that animated this university in the past may still continue. Whatever fate may be in store for us, whatever new powers may arise, may this university at least, be true to itself . . . '

Trinity College, Dublin Tercentenary 1892
(Larry O'Connor Collection, Dublin).

Fisherwomen in front of old Tholsel, Wexford, 1895

HERSELF AND MYSELF
An Old Man's Song.

'T was beyond at Macreddin, at Owen Doyle's weddin',
  The boys got the pair of us out for a reel.
Says I: "Boys, excuse us." Says they: "Don't refuse us."
  "I'll play nice and aisy," says Larry O'Neil.
So off we went trippin' it, up an' down steppin' it -
  Herself and Myself on the back of the doore;
Till Molly - God bless her! - fell into the dresser,
  An' I tumbled over a child on the floore.

Says Herself to Myself: "We're as good as the best of them."
  Says Myself to Herself: "Sure, we're betther than gold."
Says Herself to Myself: "We're as young as the rest o' them."
  Says Myself to Herself: "Troth, we'll never grow old."

As down the lane goin', I felt my heart growin'
  As young as it was forty-five years ago.
'T was here in this *bóreen* I first kissed by *stóireen* -
  A sweet little colleen with skin like the snow.
I looked at my woman - a song she was hummin'
  As old as the hills, so I gave her a *pogue*;
'T was like our old courtin', half sarious, half sportin',
  When Molly was young, an' when hoops were in vogue.

When she'd say to Myself; "You can court with the best o' them."
  When I'd say to Herself: "Sure, I'm betther than gold."
When she'd say to Myself: "You're as wild as the rest o' them."
  And I'd say to Herself: "Troth, I'm time enough old.'

Patrick Joseph McCall, 'Herself and Myself' in Irish Literature VI
(Philadelphia, 1904),

PATRICK JOSEPH MCCALL was
born in Dublin in 1861. His *Fenian
Nights Entertainments* was serialised
in *The Shamrock*. These were tales
of the Fianna told in 'seanchaí' style
and very popular in their day. He is
chiefly remembered as the author of
many fireside songs including
'Follow Me Up To Carlow', 'Kelly of
Killaine' and 'Boolavogue'. He died
in 1919.

TALL, and gaunt, and stately, was "Master Ben;" with a thin sprinkling of white, mingled with the slightly-curling brown hair, that shaded a forehead, high, and somewhat narrow. With all my partiality for this very respectable personage, I must confess that his physiognomy was neither handsome nor interesting: yet there was a calm and gentle expression in his pale grey eyes, that told of much kind-heartedness - even to the meanest of God's creatures. His steps were strides; his voice shrill, like a boatswain's whistle; and his learning - prodigious! - the unrivalled dominie of the country, for five miles round was Master Ben.

Although the cabin of Master Ben was built of the blue shingle, so common along the eastern coast of Ireland, and was perched, like the nest of a pewit, on one of the highest crags in the neighbourhood of Bannow; although the aforesaid Master Ben, or (as he was called by the gentry) "Mister Benjamin," had worn a long black coat for a period of fourteen years - in summer, as an open surtout, which flapped heavily in the gay sea-breeze - and in winter, firmly secured, by a large wooden pin, round his throat - the dominie

was a person of much consideration, and more loved than feared, even by the little urchins who often felt the effects of his "system of education." Do not, therefore, for a moment, imagine that his was one of the paltry hedge-schools, where all the brats contribute their "sod o' turf," or "their small trifle o' prates," to the schoolmaster's fire or board. No such thing; - though I confess that "Mister Benjamin" would, occasionally, accept "a hand of pork," a kreel, or even a kish of turf, or three or four hundred of "white eyes," or "London ladies," if they were presented, in a proper manner, by the parents of his favourite pupils.

In summer, indeed, he would, occasionally, lead his pupils into the open air, permitting the biggest of them to bring his chair of state; and while the fresh ocean breeze played around them, he would teach them all he knew - and that was not a little; but, usually, he considered his lessons more effectual, when they were learned under his roof; and it was, in truth, a pleasing sight to view his cottage assemblage, on a fresh summer morning; - such rosy, laughing, romping things! "The juniors," with their

Artane Schools (Lawrence Collection, National Library).

rich curly heads, red cheeks, and bright, dancing eyes, seated in tolerably straight lines - many on narrow strips of blackened deal - the remnants, probably, of some shipwrecked vessel - supported at either end by fragments of grey rock; others on portions of the rock itself, that "Master Ben" used to say, "though not very asy to sit upon for the gossoons, were clane, and not much trouble." "The Seniors," fine, clever-looking fellows, intent on their sums or copies - either standing at, or leaning on, the blotted "desks," that extended along two sides of the school-room, kitchen, or whatever you may please to call so purely Irish an apartment: the chimney admitted a large portion of storm or sunshine, as might chance; but the low wooden partition, which divided this useful room from the sleeping part of the cabin, at once told that Master Ben's dwelling was of a superior order.

Mrs S C Hall *Sketches of Irish Life and Character* (London, 1909).

MRS C HALL (nee Anna Maria Fleming) was born in Dublin in 1800 but spent much of her long life in England. She had a prodigious output of verse, novels, burlettas and opera. Her most appealing books are those which deal with Ireland and which are based upon girlhood memories of life in Wexford and upon frequent visits. Her observations as a visitor to Ireland are a rich source for the detail of Irish life in the 19th-century. She seems to have remained professionally Irish in spite of her exile. She died in 1887.

Founded by Edmund Rice of Callan, Co Kilkenny at the beginning of the 19th-century, the Christian Brothers established schools in most towns of any size. The schools gave a religiously committed education to the children of lower and lower-middle class Catholics. The Christian Brothers remained apart from the national school system with its mild attempt at religiously integrated education. Later in the century the Christian Brothers were noted for their skill in preparing pupils for the new state examinations. In the early 20th century, for one reason or another, a large proportion of the revolutionaries passed through the Christian Brothers schools. To the Brothers the revolution was the proof of their contention that they had taught the children of the Irish poor and had taught them well.

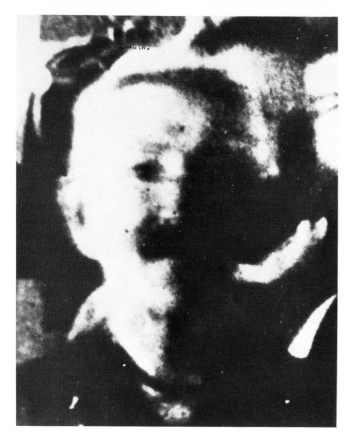

Matt Talbot [Taken from a group Phot. of workers of the firm of T. & C. Martin] c. 1915 (Paddy Laird Collection).

MATT TALBOT was born in 1856 in the poor area of Dublin's north side. He lived for most of his long life in Rutland Street where he looked after his mother until she died. He was employed as a storeman in T & C Martin's timberyard on the North Wall. In the lockout of 1913, in spite of O'Casey's accusation, he supported the workers' stand but refused to have anything to do with violent picketing. In his young days he was a heavy drinker and a close friend of the original of O'Casey's character, 'Fluther' Good, in *The Plough and the Stars* (1926). Later on he led a life of asceticism and prayer. He died at the age of 69 in Granby Lane, on his way to the Dominican Church in Dominick Street.

[*The silhouette of the tall figure again moves into the frame of the window speaking to the people.*]

PETER [*unaware, in his enthusiasm, of the speaker's appearance, to FLUTHER*]. I was burnin' to dhraw me sword, an' wave it over me -

FLUTHER [*overwhelming PETER*]. Will you stop your blatherin' for a minute, man, an' let us hear what he's sayin'!

VOICE OF THE MAN. Comrade soldiers of the Irish Volunteers and of the Citizen Army, we rejoice in this terrible war. The old heart of the earth needed to be warmed with the red wine of the battlefields . . Such august homage was never offered to God as this: the homage of millions of lives given gladly for love of country. And we must be ready to pour out the same red wine in the same glorious sacrifice, for without shedding of blood there is no redemption!

[*The figure moves out of sight and hearing.*]

FLUTHER [*gulping down the drink that remains in his glass, and rushing out*]. Come on, man; this is too grand to be missed!

[*PETER finishes his drink less rapidly, and as he is going out wiping his mouth with the back of his hand he runs into the COVEY coming in. He immediately erects his body like a young cock, and with his chin thrust forward, and a look of venomous dignity on his face, he marches out.*]

THE COVEY [*at counter*]. Give us a glass o' malt, for God's sake, till I stimulate meself from th' shock o' seein' th' sight that's afther goin' out!

ROSIE [*all business, coming over to the counter, and standing near the COVEY*]. Another one for me, Tommy; [*to the BARMAN*] th' young gentleman's ordherin' it in th' corner of his eye.

[*The BARMAN brings the drink for the COVEY, and leaves it on the counter. ROSIE whips it up.*]

BARMAN. Ay, houl' on there, houl' on there, Rosie!

ROSIE [*to the BARMAN*]. What are you houldin' on out o' you for? Didn't you hear th' young gentleman say that he couldn't refuse anything to a nice little bird. [*to the COVEY*] Isn't that right, Jiggs? [*The COVEY says nothing.*] Didn't I know,

Tommy, it would be all right? It takes Rosie to size a young man up, an' tell th' thoughts that are thremblin' in his mind. Isn't that right, Jiggs?

[*The COVEY stirs uneasily, moves a little farther away, and pulls his cap over his eyes.*]

ROSIE [*moving after him*]. Great meetin' that's gettin' held outside. Well, it's up to us all, anyway, to fight for our freedom.

THE COVEY [*to BARMAN*]. Two more, please. [*To ROSIE*] Freedom! What's th' use o' freedom, if it's not economic freedom?

Sean O'Casey, *The Plough and the Stars* (1926).

St Patrick's Close Dublin 1902, showing the typical street market. The cathedral has been bled out of the picture out of a vanished sense of decorum. (Lawrence Collection, National Library.)

Rathmines Road, Dublin, c. 1900.

Royal visit 1903, Grafton Street, Dublin

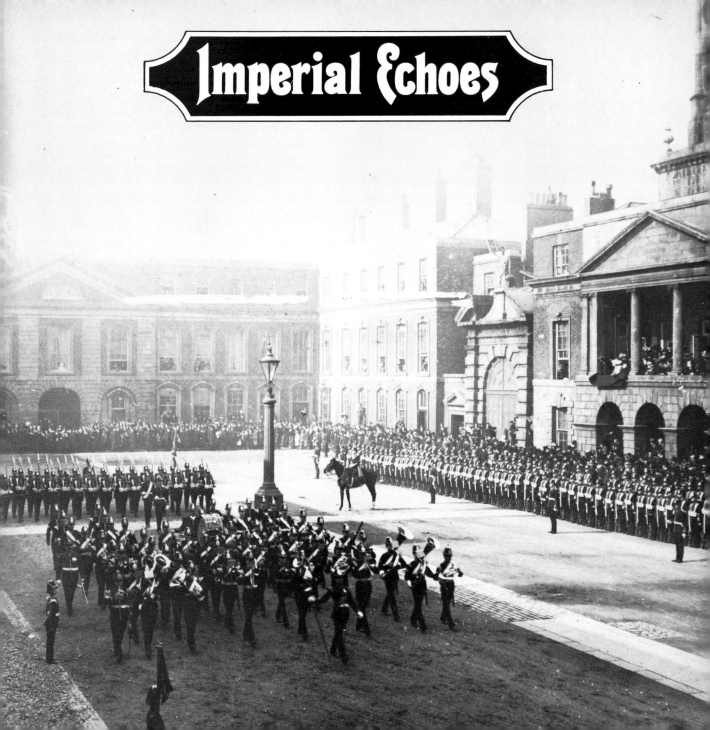

Imperial Echoes

THE annual occasion had come round once more, and, duty over for the day, the afternoon of March 17th saw Sergeant O'Callaghan, in all the glory of best tunic, with buttons highly polished, boots properly shone, trousers nicely stretched, sallying from the barracks, "every inch a soldier," to find the house of Mr. Kelly, whither he had been invited to spend the afternoon and evening in the company of a few friends.

Kelly was a retired sergeant of the 200th, who had left the Service on the expiration of his time, and now lived on his "pinsion," supplemented by "a bit av civilian wurrk." He was a lone widower, whose house was kept by his daughter, and had been O'Callaghan's faithful friend for many years.

There are traits about a smart soldier's walk which seem magnetic to one's vision. The upright carriage, the easy, regular stride, the free and graceful head-poise, the steady, fearless glance. And such was Pat O'Callaghan's on this glorious afternoon, well exemplifying the admonition of an old drill instructor to a squad of recruits, "Never mind if yer pockets contain only the price of a pint, walk as if you owned the side of the street you are on, and were shortly coming in for the other side."

"Ah, Pat, me bhoy, sure an' I've bin afther thinkin' av ye the whole blissid day! How are ye, at all, at all? Permit me to introjuce ye to

Curragh Camp Co Kildare (Lawrence Collection, National Library).

72

ex-Sergeant Maloney, late av the Cowldstrame Guarrds, an' two or three av me civilian friends.''

Such was the reception accorded to O'Callaghan on his arrival at Kelly's house.

The introduction over, a bottle of whisky appeared, the cards were produced, and the first part of the visit was spent in quiet enjoyment. Later on came supper, more whisky, anecdotes, music and songs, and by midnight the revellers were in a somewhat hilarious condition.

"Come, Maloney, ye great hulkin' blaygard, jist tell the comp'ny in yer best shtoile yer wan an' only shtory, how ye visited Her Majesty the Queen (God bless her!) an' how she thrated ye to a dhrop av the crathur."

At this Maloney, a big, raw-boned, grizzled Irishman, with a humorous twinkle in his blue eyes, awakes from semi-repose, and, pulling himself together, favours the company with the following yarn.

Frank Byrne *An Irish Stew* (London, 1916).

FRANK BYRNE is known to literary history as the author of a series of sketches of Irish life called *An Irish Stew*. His phonetic rendering of the brogue becomes at times extreme but the picture of Ireland he gives in his six stories is realistic and not unsympathetic.

Her inches were hardly proportionate to her years, and these measured three. She balanced the deficiency by breadth, and toddled about on the fattest of short legs. She was not pretty after the angelic pattern, and was all the more engaging.

It would be difficult for her biographer to say which were the more adorable; her smile, that raced like a pink radiance from the soft little chin to the crystal blue eyes, or the two perpendicular lines of thought and fearful anxiety that sometimes sprang between the mobile brows, and generally furnished the occasion for stamping her foot at some refractory subject, or were brought into play by an earnest insistence on having the unanswerable answered without delay.

As most of her hours were spent out-of-doors, and hats were antipathetic to her, it followed that few of her subjects enjoyed sight of the carefully combed and curled little poll that left her mother's hands every morning. Instead, they had the more disturbing, if less elegant, picture of fine brown silk rolling and shaking, like the floss of a King Charles, in the dearest confusion imaginable round and about the bright little face. The invasion of curls just permitted the pretty upward play of brown eyelashes against the protruding arch of brow, so that the big blue eyes looked out from a forest of winter shade. She had the divinest of mouths, an arched rosy bud, formed as a child's mouth rarely is, sweet and perfectly shaped, with an imperious claim upon kisses. Not to wish to kiss her, was to prove yourself inhuman. She was never dirty, though not exactly a precisian in the matter of raiment. It would not be safe to trust her with an orange, if it were intended she should sit upon the chairs of civilization, an emblem of spotless childhood; but she could be relied upon any day to pass a neighbourhood where mud-pies were being manufactured and not succumb to the burning temptation to bemire herself.

Such was Norry, the uncrowned queen of a remote little town on the edge of a glorious Irish lake. Like the Oriental philanthropist, she loved her fellow-men. Her existence was based on the first law of Christianity, with such a surprising result that her fellows of all classes, creeds, sexes, and ages worshipped her.

74

She was not of the order of female infant that is content to stay indoors and play with dolls. Nor were outdoor games the chief delight of her life. What she liked was the making and sustaining of universal acquaintances.

She woke with the dawn preoccupied with the fortunes of Tommy This and Molly That, and chattered about them while she graciously submitted to the encroachments of soap, water, bath-towel, and brush; and she was still discoursing of them in passionate interludes while Marcella fed her upon bread and milk and porridge in the kitchen.

She it was who welcomed all new-comers into the town—tramps, travellers, and visitors. Her formula was as rigid and unchanging as royal etiquette. She drew no line between beggars and noblemen, but simply said to the trousered male: "Man, what's your name?" If there were any geniality in the reply (and there usually was), she as invariably added: "The

blessings of Dod on you. Kiss me!" Upon her lips, however, the command took the form of *tish*. The person in petticoats she addressed as "'oman," and if the 'oman happened to be accompanied by a baby, it was an exciting moment for Norry.

Hannah Lynch *Autobiography of a Child* (London, 1899).

HANNAH LYNCH was born in Dublin in 1862 and was the most literary of the young ladies who joined Anna Parnell's *Ladies Land League* in 1880. When Parnell's paper, *United Ireland*, was suppressed and its editor, William O'Brien, was sent to jail she removed the type to Paris and edited it there. Her most famous book of fiction, *Autobiography of a Child* (1899) caused something of a stir because of the unabashed detail of the reminiscence and the excellence of the writing. Much travelled and the author of many books describing her journeys she died in 1904.

The system of police however in Ireland presents some defects. It is too military in its organisation, and not sufficiently civil or domestic. The barrack mode of life makes the men indolent. It does not appear customary for them to parade the towns and country in beats, as in England. On fair and market days the constables are seen here and there among the people, and on the occasion of a party or faction fight, or in the case of an arrest or a search for arms, they muster in force, but otherwise they are very idle.'

An Englishman *A Walking Tour Round Ireland in 1865* (London, 1867).

Girl on Horse Tricycle/RIC Depot/Phoenix Park c. 1899 (Lawrence Collection, National Library).

The Gallant Irish yeoman
   Home from the war has come,
Each victory gained o'er foeman,
   Why should our bards be dumb?

How shall we sing their praises
   Or glory in their deeds,
Renowned their worth amazes,
   Empire their prowess needs.

So to Old Ireland's hearts and homes
   We welcome now our own brave boys
In cot and hall; 'neath lordly domes
   Love's heroes share once more our joys.

Love is the Lord of all just now,
   Be he the husband, lover, son,
Each dauntless soul recalls the vow
   By which not fame, but love was won.

United now in fond embrace
   Salute with joy each well-loved face.
Yeoman, in women's hearts you hold the place.

   Oliver St J Gogarty *Ode of Welcome* (Dublin, 1902).

OLIVER ST JOHN GOGARTY, born 1878, was the great Corinthian of his period. Renowned for his poetry, drama, athleticism, wit and style he was a skilful surgeon, an aviator, the man who owned Ireland's first Rolls-Royce (a butter coloured one) and a senator of the Irish Free State. Joyce's description of him as 'stately plump Buck Mulligan' is somewhat inaccurate as far as the 'plump' is concerned but stately he was and Buck he became to the great pleasure of Dublin. His poetry and novels are in eclipse but his wit and Graecian temper is disclosed in *As I Was Going Down Sackville Street* (1937) and *It Isn't This Time Of Year At All* (1954) which are still celebrated. The piece published here was an *Ode of*

Welcome printed in *Irish Society* in June 1902 to celebrate the return of the Irish regiments after their victorious campaigns in the Boer War. It should be read acrostically for Gogarty's alternative message. He died in 1957.

Marlborough Barracks c. 1900 (Lawrence Collection, National Library).

"Read out the names!" and Burke sat back,
  And Kelly drooped his head.
While Shea - they call him Scholar Jack -
  Went down the list of the dead.
Officers, seamen, gunners, marines,
  The crews of the gig and yawl,
The bearded man and the lad in his teens,
  Carpenters, coal passers - all.
Then, knocking the ashes from out of his pipe,
  Said Burke in an offhand way:
"We're all in that dead man's list, by Cripe!
  Kelly and Burke and Shea."
"Well, here's to the Maine, and I'm sorry for Spain,"
  Said Kelly and Burke and Shea.

"Oh, the fighting races don't die out,
  If they seldom die in bed,
For love is first in their hearts, no doubt,"
  Said Burke; then Kelly said:
"When Michael, the Irish Archangel, stands,
  The angel with the sword,
And the battle-dead from a hundred lands
  Are ranged in one big horde,
OUr line, that for Gabriel's trumpet waits,
  Will stretch three deep that day,
From Jehoshaphat to the Golden Gates -
  Kelly and Burke and Shea."
"Well, here's thank God for the race and the sod!"
  Said Kelly and Burke and Shea.

Joseph Clarke, 'The Fighting Race' in *Irish Literature II* (Philadelphia, 1904).

JOSEPH IGNATIUS CONSTANTINE CLARKE was born in Kingstown in 1846. He joined the Board of Trade in 1863 and remained there till 1868 when he resigned 'for patriotic motives'. Afterwards he had a distinguished career as journalist and editor in America. He wrote one of the many 19th-century plays about Robert Emmet in 1888 and a 'metrical romance', *Malmorda* in 1893, beginning
  To me by early morn
  Came memories of old Ireland by the sea.
'The Fighting Race' about the Spanish-American War of 1898 is the only one of his poems to have lasted. He died in 1925.

78

MULLINGAR BARRACKS was built in 1814-1815 and hardly
surprisingly named after the Irish-born hero of Waterloo. Wellington
Barracks it remained until 1922 when Irish troops under Brig McGuire
took over on January 10. For the rest of the year it was the
demobilisation centre for the stood-down RIC. The barracks was closed
in 1928 and not reopened till 1939 at the beginning of the Emergency.
Both photographs are taken from the main gate, the squad facing the
camera from the Manchester Regiment and the others from the
Connaught Rangers who garrisoned the place in 1904.

Military Barracks, Mullingar 1904 (Lawrence Collection, National
Library).

Somer's Fort c. 1897 (Lawrence Collection, National Library).

"All but one, remember that—all but one!" said the priest.

"Thank ye kindly, Father, I shan't forget. Thank ye, Andy, an' you, too, young sir; I'm much beholden to ye. I hope some day I may have it to do a good turn for ye in return. Thank ye kindly again, and good-night." He shook my hand warmly, and was going to the door, when old Dan said:

"An' as for that black-jawed ruffian, Murdock—" He paused, for the door suddenly opened, and a harsh voice said:

"Murtagh Murdock is here to answer for himself!" It was my man at the window.

There was a sort of paralyzed silence in the room, through which came the whisper of one of the old women:

"Musha! talk iv the divil!"

Joyce's face grew very white; one hand instinctively grasped his riding-switch, the other hung uselessly by his side. Murdock spoke:

"I kem here expectin' to meet Phelim Joyce. I thought I'd save him the throuble of comin' wid the money."

Joyce said in a husky voice:

"What do ye mane? I have the money right enough here. I'm sorry I'm a bit late, but I had a bad accident - bruk me arrum, an' was nigh dhrownded in the Curragh Lake. But I was goin' up to ye at once, bad as I am, to pay ye yer money, Murdock." The Gombeen Man interrupted him:

"But it isn't to me ye'd have to come, me good man. Sure, it's the sheriff himself that was waitin' for ye', an' whin ye didn't come" - here Joyce winced; the speaker smiled - "he done his work."

"What wurrk, acushla?" asked one of the women. Murdock answered, slowly:

"He sould the lease iv the farrum known as the Shleenanaher in open sale, in accordance wid the terrums of his notice, duly posted, and wid warnin' given to the houldher iv the lease."

There was a long pause. Joyce was the first to speak:

"Ye're jokin', Murdock. For God's sake, say ye're jokin'! Ye tould me yerself that I might have time to git the money. An' ye tould me that the puttin' me farrum up for sale was only a matther iv

forrum to let me pay ye back in me own way. Nay, more, ye asked me not to tell any iv the neighbors, for fear some iv them might want to buy some iv me land. An' it's niver so, that whin ye got me aff to Galway to rise the money, ye went on wid the sale, behind me back - wid not a soul by to spake for me or mine - an' sould up all I have! No, Murtagh Murdock, ye're a hard man, I know, but ye wouldn't do that! Ye wouldn't do that!"

Murdock made no direct reply to him but said, seemingly to the company generally:

"I ixpected to see Phelim Joyce at the sale to-day, but as I had some business in which he was consarned, I Kem here where I knew there'd be neighbors - an', sure, so there is."

He took out his pocket-book and wrote names: "Father Pether Ryan, Daniel Moriarty, Bartholomey Moynahan, Andhrew McGlown, Mrs. Katty Kelligan - that's enough! I want ye all to see what I done. There's nothin' undherhand about me! Phelim Joyce, I give ye formil notice that yer land was sould an' bought be me, for ye broke yer word to repay me the money lint ye before the time fixed. Here's the sheriff's assignment, an' I tell ye before all these witnesses that I'll proceed with ejectment on title at wanst."

Bram Stoker, *The Snake's Pass* (London, 1891).

BRAM STOKER in Dublin in 1847 was called afer his father, Abraham Stoker, a Dublin Castle clerk. Though bookish and solitary as a child he became a successful athlete at Trinity and there developed the interest in theatre that drew him from the safety of the Civil Service and led him to the more colourful and certainly more dramatic office of manager to Henry Irving. His first published work was *The Duties of Clerks of Petty Sessions in Ireland* but the fame of this was eclipsed by a gothic romance called *Dracula* (1897). Few of many books written during a lifetime of prodigious labour are still of interest the only one to come near the success of *Dracula* being *The Lair of the White Worm*. His only work set in Ireland was *The Snakes Pass* (1891) from which this excerpt so reminiscent of his friendly rival, Le Fanu, was taken. He died of exhaustion in 1913.

Soldiers and families on Killiney Strand c. 1904
(Lawrence Collection, National Library).

This is the Children's War, because
  The victory's to the young and clean.
Up to the Dragon's ravening jaws
  Run dear Eighteen and Seventeen.

Fresh from the Chrisom waters pure,
  Dear boys, so eager to attain
To the bright visions that allure,
  The fierce ordeal, the red pain.

The light is yet upon their curls:
  The dream is still within their eyes;
Their cheeks are silken as a girl's,
  The little Knights of Paradise.

O men with many scars and stains,
  Stand back, abase yourselves and pray!
For now to Nineteen are the gains
  And golden Twenty wins the day.

Brown heads with curls all rippled over,
  Young bodies slender as a flame,
They leap to darkness like a lover;
  To Twenty-One is fall'n the game.

It is the Boy's War. Praise be given
  To Percivale and Galahad
Who have won earth and taken Heaven.
  By violence! *Weep not, but be glad.*

Katherine Tynan 'The Children's War' from *Late
Songs* (London, 1917).

KATHERINE TYNAN was born in
Clondalkin in 1861. An active
Parnellite she left after the O'Shea
affair. She became a member of the
O'Leary salon where she met Hyde
and formed a passionate but demure
friendship with the young Yeats. She
wrote many books of poems and
light novels. Her poetry has a
freshness and an innocence that is
characteristic of a woman who for all
her fame and company retained the
simple catholicism of her girlhood.
One of her last appearances in print
was in a letter to the *Irish Times* of
April 21, 1928. She died in 1931.

A DMP group, Vice-regal Gardens, Dublin Castle with Commissioner Sir John Ross of Bladenbury seated Centre (Garda Siochana Museum, Phoenix Park).

THE MERRY POLICEMAN

I was appointed guardian by
The Power that frowns along the sky,
To watch the tree and see that none
Plucked of the fruit that grew thereon.

There was a robber in the tree,
Who climbed as high as ever he
Was able, at the top he knew
The apple of all apples grew.

The night was dark the branch was thin,
In every wind he heard the din
Of angels calling - "Guardian, see
That no one climbs upon the tree."

And when he saw me standing there
He shook with terror and despair,
But I said to him - "Be at rest,
The best to him who wants the best."

So I was sacked, but I have got
A job in hell to keep me hot.

The Dublin Metropolitan Police were (like the City of London Police in the metropolitan area) a force distinct from the general constabulary, the RIC. The force dates from 1836. By 1901 their district included 36 square miles manned by six divisions of uniformed men and seventh division (G Division) of detectives, known as 'G-men' long before Hoover, and the main non-military adversaries of Michael Collins. Their height regulations (at least six feet) made them in general a taller force than the RIC and they took great pride in their dignified appearance which was added to by their tall silver-faced helmets. They were unarmed and bitterly opposed a suggestion made in 1917 that they be amalgamated with the RIC. They pointed out with pride that they were a city and civil force unlike the RIC which was rural and semi-military. The time of their greatest unpopularity was during the lock-out of 1913. Their best known member is the folk-hero constable with the polysyllabic name, 'Mor-i-ar-i-tee.'

86   *Dublin Castle Guard* (Lawrence Collection, National Library)

CLAVERING sat on the side of an extremely narrow bed and looked at the horn lantern which hung from a bracket in the wall. There was so little room that by stretching out his arms he could span the cell from side to side; but, as this fact had the one merit of ensuring him privacy - since the guard and the prisoner and the prisoner's bed could not all fit in together - he minded it the less.

Straight opposite him, sunk deep in the old masonry of the Bermingham Tower, was an unglazed slit about a foot square.

In the three days since his arrest he had not been able to glean much of the fate of his fellow-conspirators, beyond the negative fact that he was so far the only one in government hands - the sole harvest of Rathlin's carefully-prepared reaping.

They had extracted nothing from him by question or cross-question, by cajolery or threat; but neither had they told him anything. He felt like a live man snatched suddenly into a tomb, with the knowledge that he had left those he valued most in the world in imminent peril.

Miriam Alexander *The Port of Dreams* (New York, 1913).

MIRIAM ALEXANDER was born in Birkenhead but was educated in and later lived in Dublin. A strong supporter of the Gaelic League she left it about the same time as Hyde for much the same reasons. Her best novel, *The Port of Dreams* (1912) is set in Ireland and Scotland at the time of the *'45* and contains a dramatic account of Prince Charlie's escape. The novel has the 'modern' theme of cowardice.

'At the Vice-regal lodge, the Chief Secretary meets the officials and the 'crows'. Next day he goes to the Castle, curious perhaps to see that notorious institution of which he has heard so much. As he approaches the place he beholds or may behold a conspicuous building hard by, from which a green flag flies defiantly. 'What the devil is that?' he may ask; for in his general ignorance he may take the building to be part of the castle. However he soon finds himself close to the castle gates and is perhaps consoled by seeing the Union Jack fluttering in the breeze.

'But,' he asks, 'what is this building which flies the emblem of Irish nationality at the very gates of the citadel?' He is told that it is the City Hall. If he is a typical Chief Secretary he says, 'Damned rebels' and takes shelter in the fortress.

R Barry O'Brien *Dublin Castle and the Irish People* (London, 1912).

Within the great hall of the Castle of Kilkenny had assembled, in two days after the arrest of Beatrice, the court of the county Palatine, at which she should be tried for the murder of her husband. This spacious apartment was crowded by the feudal lords of the territory governed by de la Spenser, and its passages and approaches were guarded by their retainers. In the principal seat, which was placed upon the dais, sat the Lord Eustace le Poer, according to his seignorial dignity as Seneschal of the district. The chair of state in which he reclined was canopied with richly embroidered tapestry, on which was emblazoned the royal arms of England and the achievements of the houses of le Spenser and le Poer. The Seneschal was attired in the costume of a civilian, his long and flowing robes giving increased dignity to his somewhat mournful aspect; his eye intelligent and was guarded in front and at the closely fashioned sleeves and cuffs with rich fur, and girded by an embroidered girdle buckled about the waist. Over this tunic he wore a mantle of gorgeous velvet, arranged with considerable elegance, and drawn over his right shoulder and across the left arm. The countenance of the feudal lord had assumed an expression of deep sorrow, which none doubted that he truly felt; but, as befitted his office and high jurisdiction, it was calm and dignified. Beneath the Seneschal sat Walter Cotterill, of Kells, sergeant-at-law, who was to speak to the accusation. This functionary was of a grave and somewheat mournful aspect; his eye intelligent and contemplative, his lip inquisitorial, and his hair of an iron grey. No one would hope favour from him, or fear injustice. He was habited in his long full-slieved gown. From his girdle depended his official badge of distinction, the ink horn, with its accompanying pen-case. His head was uncovered, but on his left shoulder rested, attached to the neck of his gown, a circular cap composed of a roll of velvet of rich material. From this hung a long broad band or scarf which was gathered into his girdle; to the other side of this cap a loose hood was attached which fell negligently about his head and shoulders. At his girdle he wore the gypciere or large purse common at the period. Around the hall and seated within canopied niches, or stalls, formed of dark oak, and which had, above each, the banner of arms belonging to the feudal baron to whom it appertained, were assembled the lords of the county Palatine all arrayed in their massive mail suits, the iron sternness of their array being somewhat softened by the graceful draperies of their richly embroidered surcoats. Beneath those leaders upon a bench reserved for them sat the sovereign of the corporation and some of the most wealthy burgesses of Kilkenny. Before the superior judge was placed the prisoner, and at her right hand sat Thomas Derkyn, the lieutenant of de Cantaville, beside whom stood a young and elegant-looking knight, who was known to be Robert Cantaville, the nephew and successor of the murdered chieftain. The unfortunate lady, Beatrice de Cantaville, reclined in the chair placed for her, evidently very much exhausted.

Paris Anderson *The Warden of the Marshes* (Kilkenny, 1884).

PARIS ANDERSON was a lieutenant in the Kilkenny Militia and is known to have lived in Dublin in 1837. His only novel, *The Warden of the Marshes* was published in 1884. It is set in fourteenth-century Kilkenny and has as one of its characters the famous witch, Dame Alice, 'the love-lorn Lady Kyteler' of Yeats's poem 'The Tower'. The book's main interest is in the historical accuracy of the description of the dress etc. of the period.

Visit of the duke and duchess of York to the marquis and marchioness of Ormond, 1899.
Front L—R: *Lady Eva Dugdale, Viscountess de Vesci, Marchioness of Ormonde, Duchess of York, Lady Beatrice Butler, Lady Constance Butler, Hon. Hugh Downey.*
Back L—R: *Viscount de Vesci, W T Seigne, Sir Charles Cust, Duke of York, Marquis of Ormonde, Lord F Fitzgerarld, Mr Monerliffe, Earl of Eva.*

EDWARD VII AND ALEXANDRA arrived in Dublin on 21 July 1903, their visit previously arranged for March 1902 having been cancelled owing to poor relations between Dublin and London at that time. The visit coincided with the safe passage through the Lords of the Irish Land Purchase Bill and this was regarded, perhaps a little desperately as a good omen. The Dublin Corporation refused by 40 votes to 37 to offer an address of welcome and William M Murphy had the wit to refuse a knighthood. The visit was the usual sequence of visits to schools, hospitals and the like accompanied by appropriate overeating. Mannix, the president of Maynooth at the time avoided an awkward situation by flying the King's racing colours instead of the Union Jack. The Royal party left from Cork on August 1, full of the 'warmest regard' for the Irish people.

Kilkenny High Street, decorated for the visit of Edward VII and Queen Alexandra, (Lawrence Collection, National Library).

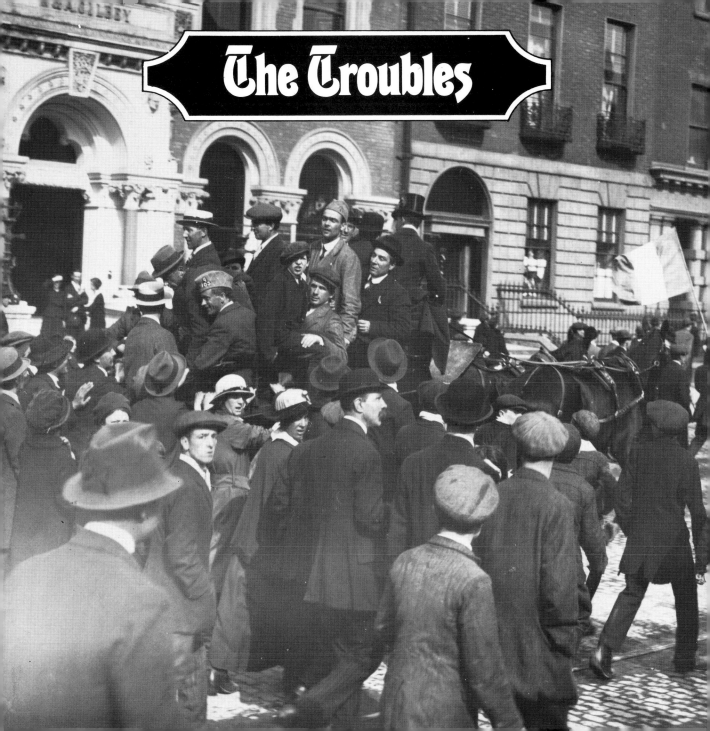

The Troubles

THE IRISH WORKER was founded by Jim Larkin in 1910 as the organ of his Irish Transport and General Workers Union. It became the workers' main newsheet during the labour troubles of 1913. These began with the dismissal of members of the tramway workers who were Transport Union members and was followed by a general lock-out of 24,000 Dublin men and women. Larkin and Connolly had joined forces and in face of extreme police and army brutality the Irish Citizen Army was formed on 23 November 1913. (Sean O'Casey's first published book was a history of the Army of which he was a member. It was published in 1914 by Maunsel at 1d.) The workers' headquarters were at Liberty Hall, the offices of the ITGWU in Beresford Place. The lock-out ended in apparent failure in January 1914 but its effects were widespread both socially and politically. The head lines in the photgraph refer to the failure of a government commission to bring the two sides together in December 1913. The Daily Herald was for many years the leading English Labour paper.

Of the events in SEAN O'CASEY's early life few made such an impression upon him as the labour agitation of 1912-1913 which led to the formation of the Citizen Army. Jim Larkin became his hero and his strident play *The Star Turns Red* (1940) was dedicated 'to the men and women who fought through the Great Lockout of 1913'. In *Juno and the Paycock* (1924) his most popular play it was characteristic that the role of women in labour agitation should be appreciated and emphasised.

Mary [*tying a ribbon fillet-wise around her head*]. I don't like this ribbon, ma; I think I'll wear the green - it looks betther than the blue.

Mrs. Boyle. Ah, wear whatever ribbon you like, girl, only don't be botherin' me. I don't know what a girl on strike wants to be wearin' a ribbon round her head for, or silk stockins on her legs either; it's wearin' them things that make the employers think they're givin' yous too much money.

Mary. The hour is past now when we'll ask the employers' permission to wear what we like.

Mrs. Boyle. I don't know why you wanted to walk out for Jennie Claffey; up to this you never had a good word to say for her.

Mary. What's the use of belongin' to a Trades Union if you won't stand up for your principles? Why did they sack her? It was a clear case of victimization. We couldn't let her walk the streets, could we?

Mrs. Boyle. No, of course yous couldn't - yous wanted to keep her company. Wan victim wasn't enough. When the employers sacrifice wan victim, the Trades Unions go wan betther be sacrificin' a hundred.

Mary. It doesn't matther what you say, ma - a principle's a principle.

Mrs. Boyle. Yis; an' when I go into oul' Murphy's tomorrow, an' he gets to know that, instead o' payin' all, I'm goin' to borry more, what'll he say when I tell him a principle's a principle? What'll we do if he refuses to give us any more on tick?

Mary. He daren't refuse—if he does, can't you tell him he's paid?

Mrs. Boyle. It's lookin' as if he was paid, whether he refuses or no.

Sean O'Casey, *Juno and the Paycock* (London, 1925)

92

Workers on the steps of Liberty Hall, 1913 (Keogh Collection, National Library).

THE PRICE OF FREEDOM

MAN of Ireland, heir of sorrow,
  Wronged, insulted, scorned, oppressed,
Wilt thou never see that morrow
  When thy weary heart may rest?
Lift thine eyes, thou outraged creature;
  Nay look up, for man thou art,
Man in form, and frame, and feature,
  Why not act man's god-like part?

Think, reflect, inquire, examine,
  Is it for this God gave you birth -
With the spectre look of famine,
  Thus to creep along the earth?
Does this world contain no treasures
  Fit for thee, as man, to wear? -
Does this life abound in pleasures,
  And thou askest not to share?

Look! the nations are awaking,
  Every chain that bound them burst!
At the crystal fountains slaking
  With parched lips their fever thirst!
Ignorance the demon, fleeing,
  Leaves unlocked the fount they sip;
Wilt thou not, thou wretched being,
  Stoop and cool thy burning lip?

History's lessons, if thou'lt read 'em,
  All proclaim this truth to thee:
Knowledge is the price of freedom,
  Know thyself, and thou art free!
Know, O man! thy proud vocation,
  Stand erect, with calm, clear brow -
Happy! happy were our nation,
  If thou hadst that knowledge now!

Denis F McCarthy, *Poems* (Dublin, 1884).

Colonel Maurice Moore, the younger brother of the writer, George Moore, was born at Moore Hall, the family home in Co Mayo. He became a colonel in the Connaught Rangers and as a military expert and a close personal friend of Redmond was an obvious choice to become Inspector-General of the Irish Volunteers when that force was founded by Eoin MacNeill on 25 november 1913.

Eleven months before the Ulster Volunteers had been formed to defend the position of Ulster within the Union. MacNeill had analysed this and other moves in the North in an article published in *An Claidheamh Soluis*, the Gaelic League newspaper. This was later issued as a pamphlet, 'The North Began' and the conclusions reached by MacNeill encouraged the IRB, the radical wing of nationalism, to form a similar body themselves. When the meeting at the Rotunda, Dublin, established the force, it was in fact under the control of the IRB, although many Redmondites were members. The movement spread rapidly over the country, as had MacNeill's earlier movement, The Gaelic League. In the case of Athlone, the subject of our picture, it incorporated an earlier Midland Volunteer Force which had been established two months before.

DENIS FLORENCE MCCARTHY was born in Dublin in 1817 and followed a not untypical 19th-century career as a better-off Irish Catholic. He studied law was called to the bar but did not practise, dabbled in journalism, wrote verse, translated Calderon and became Newman Professor of English Literature. In an unsigned review in the *Catholic University Gazette* 1854, the writer, almost certainly Newman, himself, said of his poetry that, 'beautiful as they are and undoubtedly popular, promise ever more than they display.' His earliest poems were written for the newly-founded *Nation* and his main publications are *The Bell Founder* (1857), *Book of Irish Ballads* (1869) and *Poems* (1884). He died in 1882.

Volunteer parade being reviewed by Colonel Maurice Moore, December 1914 in Athlone (Phot. Simmons, Old Athlone Society).

The Kilkenny by-election of August 1917 was the last of a series of four that year in which the Sinn Fein member ousted the sitting Redmondite. The others were at North Roscommon, South Longford and East Clare (where de Valera had his momentous victory in July). As a result of the aftermath of 1916 majority opinion had gone over to the more radical nationalism. This change was confirmed when the older nationalist party was routed in the general election of 1918.

Markiewicz addressing Sinn Fein supporters at Co Kilkenny election 1917 (Keogh Collection, National Library).

MARTIN: I know who it was
Hung the blue flowers over the decent cross,
Who put the white flowers into the earth itself,
Who bought the cross maybe, and who, I'll swear,
Made the perpetual masses go up
From the slow priests like a thin incense drifting
Before the throne of God.
MICHAEL.   Though it's all finished
I'll tell you Martin, I would give big money
Put into your fist now, God help me so,
To have that knowledge, so I would.
MARTIN.   I'll tell you.
Have you ever searched out in your sleeping
By a slow hand comes from the hills?
MICHAEL.   I have not;
Not lately; when I was a boy.
MARTIN.   Ah, surely,
Are not those the shining hours men do be having?
I was one time waked that way: something came
And drifted about me, falling from the sky,
Or rising from the earth. Then I went up
Through the grey darkness creeping from the room,
And looked out to a world that the big years
Cannot destroy. Over the Seven Churches
The wood was scarfed in a white drifting mist
In the world's greyness; and, just like a spirit

Thinking and thinking in a kind of coat
That the wind blew about, it sat there dreaming,
While from the middle of itself a song
Came bursting out. It was all quiet that time;
There was nothing about so early as that;
But just that kind of spirit there whose heart
Went bursting up and breaking into a song
Where all songs mixed, that filled up all the world,
And went up in a tumult to the sky.
And I, Michael, I could have been burned up
With the gladness came on me; I could not move,
I trembled so that time.

Darrell Figgis, *Teigue* (Dublin, 1918).

O'Connell Street, April 1916 (Keogh Collection, National Library).

DARRELL FIGGIS (alias Michael Ireland) was born in Rathmines in 1882. He was taken to India as a child but returned to Ireland in 1913. His was the main influence (according to himself) in the Howth gun-running of 1915. Prominent as a Free State back-room boy, he drew up the constitution for the new state. He committed suicide after an unhappy love-affair in 1925. He published a book of poetry, *A Hill of Vision*, in 1909 and a novel, *Children of the Earth* (1918). *Teigue*, an unactable, sub-Yeatsian verse-play was written in 1918.

The destruction of Sackville Street was partly brought about by looters but most of the damage was done by the ruthless use which the British made of artillery. Connolly was mistaken in his belief that a capitalist power would not destroy property. The efficient use of field guns was one of the reasons the insurgents were so quickly defeated. By the Friday of Easter Week the flames engulfing the street had reached the GPO and Pearse and garrison had to leave by Henry Street. They surrendered next day. Perhaps £2m. worth of damage had been done to the street.

Immediately after the insurrection of 1916 about 3,500 people were arrested. Of these nearly 2,000 were sent to England for internment but after further enquiries 1,300 were released and most of the others were held only until Christmas. Of the leaders fifteen were executed and 75 given penal servitude for various terms. It was these who were released in the summer of 1917, their zeal for independence hardened by their stay in enemy prisons.

PADRAIC PEARSE was born in Dublin in 1879 the son of an Irish mother and an English father. He was educated at the Christian Brothers School in Westland Row and graduated from the Royal University, became a barrister but rarely practised. His keen interest in the Irish language led to reasonable attempts at writing in that language and effective work for its restoration as editor of its journal, *An Claidheamh Soluis*. His ideal of a free and Gaelic Ireland led to the founding of St Enda's, a school for boys at Rathfarnham. He joined the IRB in America and became first President of the Provisional Irish Republic which was promulgated on the steps of the GPO on Easter Monday, 1916. He and his brother Willie were executed in Kilmainham on May 3rd, 1916.

FORNOCHT DO CHONAC

Fornocht do chonac thú,
A áille na háille,
'S do dhallas mo shúil,
Ar eagla go stánfainn.

Do chualas do cheol,
A bhinne na binne,
'S do dhúnas mo chluas,
Ar eagla go gcloisfinn.

Do bhlaiseas do bhéal,
A mhilse na milse,
Is do chruas mo chroí,
Ar eagla mo mhillte.

Do dhallas mo shúil,
Is mo chulas do dhúnas,
Do chruas mo chroí,
Is mo mhian do mhúchas.

Do thugas mo chúl
Ar an aisling do chumas,
'S ar an ród do romham
M'aghaidh do thugas.

The burial of Arthur Griffiths, 1920 (Lawrence Collection, National Library).

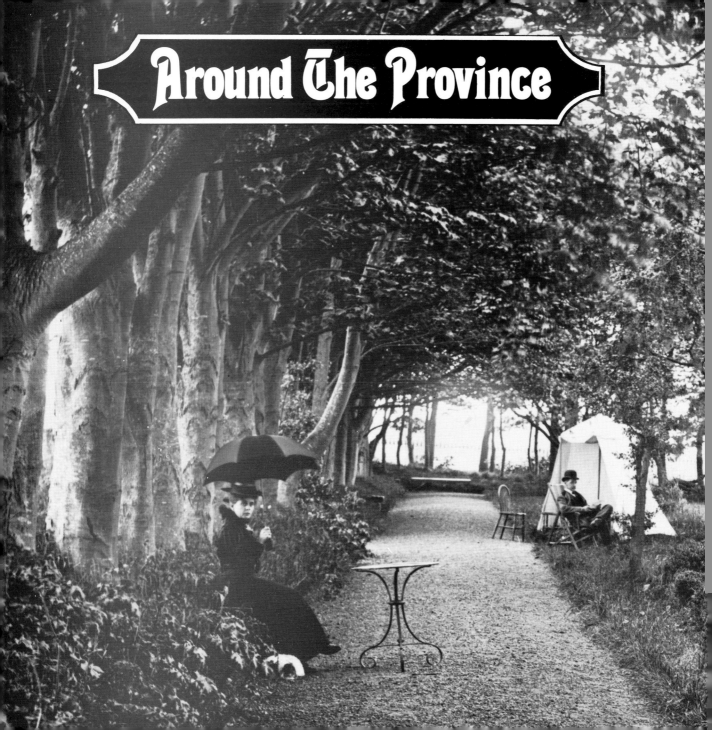

Around The Province

THE DEATH OF DIOGENES,
THE DOCTOR'S DOG.

VETERINARY SURGEON
                        Take muzzle from mouth,
And the can from his tail;
He's as dead from the drought
    As the deadly doornail.
I fear he has found hydrophobia - not even Pasteur
    may avail.

DOCTOR
When I rambled around
    In the ground that was Greece,
I was given the hound
    By the King's little niece;
And rather were finded ere I found him to gaze on his
    saddest surcease.

CHORUS [*Scholars of the House*]
He was given the hound
    By the seed of a King,
For the wisdom profound
    Of his wide wandering.
But was it the donor, or owner, or dog that was led by
    a string?

The poem was written for the Dublin University
Magazine [14 February 1903] and should be spoken
with a 'w' for 'r' lisp.

John Pentland Mahaffy (Keogh Collection, National Library) *1917.*

SIR JOHN PENTLAND MAHAFFEY was born in 1839 in Vevey, Switzerland, the son of a Donegal clergyman who was Chaplain to the British Embassy in Geneva. He entered Trinity in 1855 and took orders and was elected Fellow in 1864. He was given the chair of Ancient History in 1871 and became Provost after much delay and despair in 1915, a post he held until his death in 1919. He was a polymath noted for the breadth rather than the precision of scholarship. Famous for his rather bullying wit he was responsible for such epigrams as 'Irish bulls are always pregnant'. He is also remembered as the man who refused to join the platform party at the Thomas Davis Centenary celebrations (20 November 1914) because of the presence of 'that man Pearse'. He apoted Gogarty in much the same way as earlier he had befriended Wilde and had considerable influence upon his writings.

WADEBRIDGE [*putting down the book*]. It is not for me to stand between her crime and its punishment.

THE BISHOP [*gratified*]. Ah!

WADEBRIDGE: Nor for me to stand between her and you.

THE BISHOP [*mystified*]. And me?

WADEBRIDGE. The woman condemned to death in your name, as you say, was Mabel Debenham.

THE BISHOP [*in a strangled voice*]. Mabel Debenham! . . . killed her child . . . What child?

WADEBRIDGE. As I believe, your child.

THE BISHOP [*almost screaming*]. My child!

WADEBRIDGE [*producing an envelope*]. Judge for yourself. There is the photograph of mother and child taken a month ago.

THE BISHOP [*glaring at it*]. Mabel and . . . taken a month ago . . . my child, and she had the heart to kill it!

WADEBRIDGE. As you had the heart to kill her.

THE BISHOP. To . . . No, no. [*Mastering himself.*] I spoke in good faith, Wadey. I spoke in good faith . . . and I am not afraid. [*Going towards him pitifully.*] Take me to her, Wadey; take me to her. . . .I will be with her at the end.

WADEBRIDGE. At the end she was alone. She is dead.

Conal O'Riordan, *Rope Enough* (Dublin, 1914).

CONAL HOLMES O'CONNELL O'RIORDAN was born in Dublin in 1874. He became a director of the Abbey in 1909 and revived *The Playboy* in spite of great opposition. His earlier work appeared under the pseudonym Norreys Connell. His first play *The Piper* was put on in the Abbey to a hostile reception. Later plays were *Rope Enough* (1913) *His Majesty's Pleasure* (1925) and *The King's Wooing* (1929). Though a career as a soldier was frustrated by a spine injury he managed to serve in both World Wars, as YMCA welfare officer and Air Raid Warden. Many of his novels are about the Service. He died in 1948.

The Zoological Gardens in Phoenix Park was founded in the early 1830's only a few years after the Jardin des Plantes in Paris and Regent's Park Zoo in London. It remains famous for its successful breeding of lions, records of which go back to 1857. The Royal Zoological Society of Ireland is its governing body, the President and Council meeting for breakfast every Saturday morning. This civilised practice has been going on for more than a hundred years.

In the Zoo 1904 (Lawrence Collection, National Library).

To the intelligentsia of Dublin, this play might not appear a very striking drama. "Melodramatic propaganda" would probably be their description of it, but here in Ballycullen it was as one of the great Greek tragedies of old in Athens. For all his soul might have dwindled sadly in very truth, what man was there amongst them at all who had not spoken out of his dream sometime of dying for Ireland? Of how, maybe, as he went down some grass-grown boreen, where the hawthorn blossoms in Maytime fell and were blown on a light wind like fragrant, tinted snow, and for all its rich colour of the fields at sunset, the shadow over all had seemed to him the deadly shadow of England. And then he had spoken to the girl walking by his side, of "fighting the bloody British Government," of "Dying from a bullet in some rebellion or another," of being "murdered mebbe in jail, the way they murdered Wolfe Tone." "And waht whoud you do then?" Then there had come, probably, a little strained, beseeching look into the eyes of the girl as she put her soft arm about his neck, her brown, troubled head upon his shoulder, and sobbed her request that he would not go. And he had not gone, only marrying the girl a little later, and wondering ever since at the "wildness" of himself, and he a young fellow. No Irish dramatist had seen this material, and yet it was the complete expression in tragi-comedy of Ireland - the Ireland of all the dreams, and all the songs, and all the dying. Many a young man would be behaving just like this after to-night's performance, and both the young women and the old would be weeping little, silent tears as they tried to remember or to picture themselves in the disquieting, in fact desperate, position of Sara Curran. But over all the audience, over its face as one man, would be clouding a curious mixture of expression, combative, satirical, critical, comical, tragical really in its full significance.

Already Michael Dempsey had taken the Ballycullen Dramatic Class on to the stage, and they were all stiffly awaiting the rise of the curtain. One of the girls, she who was to play the part of Ann Devlin, complained of a little faintness, and someone rushed to get her a mineral. The man who was to play Michael Dwyer brought out a bottle of whiskey from his pocket, and took a good, long drink. Then the little drop-curtain which had been so badly painted by Ambrose Donohoe, the handy man, screeched upward, and the play began.

One might have seen immediately that, although possessing the curious, intimate connection with Irish life already suggested, it was made distant from Irish life by several focuses of unreality. It possessed no verisimilitude as a picture of the period, and, in the second place, was no transcript of life, inasmuch as the method of presentation was as far removed from realism as it is possible for anything to be. And yet it did not appear as any kind of spontaneous romance; one could not call it a folk-play. The lines were spoken haltingly, with a poor accent, which did not fully express their meaning. The entrances and exits and the situations were most crudely effected. Yet were the people gripped, for no other reason than because it was a play about Robert Emmet. Indeed, Michael Dempsey need not have gone to such pains to give a great performance. Merely to have stood there on the very middle of the stage in his top boots with gold tassels, white trousers and black cut-away coat, his arms folded, and a lock of hair brushed down upon his forehead, would have been quite sufficient. In fact, from one aspect of Ballycullen's point of view, the whole thing was quite unnecessary. The drunken ballad-singers had told them all they wanted to know about Robert Emmet, and this was exactly how they had always seen Robert Emmet dressed up in a picture. Into their dull minds was crowded a sudden warfare of conflicting thoughts.

Brinsley MacNamara, *The Clanking of Chains* (Dublin, 1920).

BRINSLEY MACNAMARA was born John Weldon in the village of Delvin, Co Westmeath in 1890. He was actor, playwright, essayist and novelist, famous for two widely differing Irish 'classics', the novel *The Valley of the Squinting Windows* (1918) and the play, *Look at the Heffernans* (1926). The first caused a minor riot in his home village on the night of 28 May 1918 when a copy was publicly burnt. The second is a typical Abbey comedy still performed by many amateur companies throughout Ireland. The great achievement of MacNamara as stated fifty years ago by A E Malone was 'in assisting Ireland to see itself as something less than a nation of demi-gods'. Two novels, *The Clanking of Chains* (1920) and *The Mirror in the Dusk* (1928) in different ways contribute to the removal of this romantic myopia, the first in its account of the disillusionment of the Nationalist dream and the second in its truth about Irish rural life. He died in 1963.

Cast of play in Father Mathew Hall, 1917 (Old Athlone Society).

Skating at Johnstown Castle, Co Wexford c. 1885
(Séamas de Vál Collection, Oulart).

BRIGHT sunshine, pure invigorating air, and ice in perfect condition had combined to make Miss Fetherstone's skating party an emphatic success. The young people from the Rectory were there, and a few more - considering the depleted condition of the neighbourhood, it was quite a considerable gathering; but no one ever refused an invitation to the Priory, however short the notice. All day the picturesque banks of the pond had echoed merry laughter and ceaseless chaff, and the ice-imprisoned Undine in the depths had hummed a welcome to the steel-shod feet which had never ceased to plough its frozen surface. Even now, when the afternoon was fast giving place to night, and stars began to twinkle here and there in the darkening blue above, enthusiastic skaters were still pursuing each other in games, or taking station for quadrilles on the smooth, grey ice.

Kate and Gerald were slowly climbing the steep path that led up to the house. She looked very handsome, a tall graceful figure in her furs, and recent exercise had given to her cheeks the touch of colour which they sometimes lacked.

Gerald walked beside her, swinging a pair of skates in either hand. Earlier in the day he had found opportunity to acquaint her with the recent occurrences at Liscarrick, but their conversation had been interrupted and fragmentary, as occasion served. Now he had given her the whole tale, beginning with the Squireen's proposal to Mrs. Delaney, and going on to Molly's adventure on the Bog road, and her understanding, as yet unannounced, with Jack Whalen.

Miss Fetherstone was deeply concerned. She was genuinely delighted at the news of Molly's engagement to her cousin, and was already considering in her warm heart what she could do to make smoother their path for the young lovers, but Mrs. Delaney's position and the attitude she assumed moved her at once to pity and anger.

"It's incredible!" she cried hotly. "That a woman in your sister-in-law's position could stoop to even *think* of such a creature as O'Hara. Why, the man drinks, if there were nothing else."

"I don't think Emmie knows that," said Gerald.

"But she's bound to find it out, sooner or later."

"Yes," he assented, "she's bound to find it out, and if I can manage it, it will be sooner, not later."

George H Jessop, *The Shamrock Grows* (1911).

GEORGE H JESSOP was born in Dublin in 1850 and went to America after graduating from TCD. He was editor of *Judge* and contributed to other humorous papers. His collection of sketches, *Gerald French's Friend* (1889) deals with the adventures of a prodigal Irishman in the US and of the characteristic immigrant Irish types he meets on his travels. The piece printed from *The Shamrock Grows* (1911) is about the Ireland of the latter-day squireens when the horse still had a higher place in society than most humans and all endings were happy. He died in 1915 in Hampstead having become a Catholic shortly before his death.

At last the waltz died languorously away, and he led her into the hall. "Shall we go out to the terrace, or would it be too cold outside?" he asked, with an unconscious note of pleading in his voice.

"No, it's not cold now; besides, I have a wrap here," Zoe answered, picking up a light cloak from one of the hall chairs, and throwing it round her shoulders.

"Good," said Barry, and they went out.

Miss Delaney's house was delightfully situated - high up on Killiney Hill, among tall trees, and commanding a full view of the bay from Bray Head on the south side right round to the Hill of Howth on the north-east. When the two reached the terrace, they stood for a moment lookng out over the sea, enjoying the fresh night air after the heat inside. A yellow moon was shining, and the low murmur of the sea came to them, borne on the faint breeze that gently stirred the trees. The night was beautifully fine, and quite warm now, and yet there was a vague, elusive something of sadness in the air, the regretful brooding of autumn.

"What a night!" Barry murmured, by way of marking time, for he was rather in a whirl.

"Delicious - beautiful!" Zoe answered, and she really meant it and felt it - but still she was fingering her trinkets and patting her hair.

"Let us go round to the side - it's quieter there - will you?" said Barry after a moment, again with the unconscious pleading note. He had the rare gift of a deep musical voice, and sincere emotion gives to that sort of voice most compelling inflections. Zoe felt its charm and its appeal; she gave him a little quick nod of the head and a smile. "If you like," she agreed. He led her round to the south side of the house, and then along to the end of that part of the terrace.

"We don't want to sit down, do we?" she said, going to the edge and leaning on the low stone balustrade.

"Whatever you like," said Barry, coming near to her. "I'd sooner have this - as the only seat is in the shadow there."

Then there fell a silence as they stood in the moonlight, the man, as he watched her hungrily, too oppressed with feeling to be able to find a word, and the girl, staring at the distant misty hills of Wicklow, seemingly quite unconscious of her companion's eager glances, but only seemingly.

W F Casey, *Zoë* (London, 1911).

W F CASEY is chiefly famous for two plays *The Man Who Missed the Tide* and *The Suburban Groove* which were presented in the Abbey in 1908. These dealt, unusually for the time and place with upper middle class characters in Dublin. *Zoë* (1911) deals with the same social class and is an account of the heartless flirtations of the eponymous heroine in a city mainly dedicated to golf, bridge and theatre. Casey afterwards became editor of the London *Times*.

*Couple outside the Royal Irish Yacht Club Kingstown
c. 1901* (Lawrence Collection, National Library).

IRISH ASTRONOMY

A Veritable Myth, Touching the Constellation of O'Ryan,
Ignorantly and Falsely Spelled Orion.

O'Ryan was a man of might
  Whin Ireland was a nation,
But poachin' was his heart's delight
  And constant occupation.
He had an ould militia gun,
  And sartin sure his aim was;
He gave the keepers many a run,
  And wouldn't mind the game laws.

St. Pathrick wanst was passin' by
  O'Ryan's little houldin',
And, as the saint felt wake and dhry,
  He thought he'd enther bould in.
"O'Ryan," says the saint, "avick!
  To praich at Thurles I'm goin',
So let me have a rasher quick,
  And a dhrop of Innishowen."

"No rasher will I cook for you
  While betther is to spare, sir,
But here's a jug of mountain dew,
  And there's a rattlin' hare, sir."
St. Pathrick he looked mighty sweet,
  And says he, "Good luck attind you,
And, when you're in your winding-sheet,
  It's up to heaven I'll sind you."

O'Ryan gave his pipe a whiff -
  "Them tidin's is transportin',
But may I ax your saintship if
  There's any kind of sportin'?"
St. Pathrick said, "A Lion's there,
  Two Bears, a Bull, and Cancer" -
"Bedad," says Mick, "the huntin's rare;
  St. Pathrick, I'm your man, sir."

So, to conclude my song aright,
  For fear I'd tire your patience,
You'll see O'Ryan any night
  Amid the constellations.
And Venus follows in his track
  Till Mars grows jealous raally.
But faith, he fears the Irish knack
  Of handling the shillaly.

Charles Graham Halpine, 'Irish Astronomy' in *Irish Literature IV*
(Philadelphia, 1904).

CHARLES GRAHAM HALPINE alias 'Pte Myles O'Reilly' was born in Oldcastle, Co Meath in 1829, the son of the rector, the Rev N J Halpin (the 'e' he added later). A student at TCD he did not graduate but followed a career in journalism which took him to America. At the outbreak of Lincoln's war he joined the famous 'FIghting 69th' and rose to the rank of general. He enrolled the first negro regiment in the Federal Army and was placed high on the Southern States' blacklist. His songs, including 'Not a star from the flag shall fade' were very popular throughout the army and the north United States. He died in 1868 after an accidental overdose of chloral, taken to cure insomnia.

The 'Leviathan of Parsonstown' as it was christened remained the largest telescope in the world until 1917. Its six-foot diameter enabled the local clergyman to walk right through it, a distance of fifty-eight feet when it was opened in 1845. The builder of the telescope, the third earl of Rosse, discovered that the *nebulae* was a star system separate from our galaxy and many millions of miles further away than had been thought.

Telescope at Birr Castle 1889 (Lawrence Collection, National Library).

"Rock candy is sweet, but it isn't soft!" flashed Sadie.

"Yes," retorted Katie, " and you're soft, but you aren't sweet!"

"You must say what's in the script!"

"I'm only an amateur!" cried Katie shrilly; "I won't be 'musted'!"

"It's plain to be seen that you are only an amateur," was the crushing retort.

"And I," Shaun announced, wearily passing his fingers through his dark hair, "happen to be stage manager. Go on with the play."

"Why doesn't my husband write to me?" lamented Mrs. O'Grady, her voice rising and falling like the *keen* of a Banshee.

"Good heavens!" exclaimed Brian, quite astounded; "is that a new bit in the play?"

"Of course it isn't," snapped his sister; "Hold your tongue, Belinda, and prompt!"

"My name is Brigid," wailed the prompter, "and if I hold my tongue, how can I prompt?"

"Proceed, 'Viola,'" said Shaun, in dull tones.

"'How softly the sun sinks to rest! The -'"

"But you know," interrupted Denis, "that's a foolish expression! How else could the sun sink?"

"I know of a place where it sets with an unearthly bang." Patsy informed them.

"Where's that?" was the breathless inquiry.

"Kingstown, Dublin."

"After these two exhibitions of crass ignorance," remarked Shaun dryly, "we will proceed with the play."

Katie began again, accordingly: "'How softly the sun sinks to rest! The golden glory in the west -'" here she stopped, and appealed to Shaun.

"Is it supposed to be poetry?" she asked.

"*No!*"

"'Shines,'" continued Katie, "'like - like -'"

"You're all wrong, " interposed Mrs. O'Grady; "begin all over again."

"Why didn't you prompt?"

"You wouldn't take the last prompt!"

Katie's retort was interrupted by the entrance of Barney, cheery, debonair, and inclined to be a little dictatorial.

"Sorry to be so late," said he, "but I met Thady O'Reilly, and he kept me. I mean, I kept him."

"What's he doing?" asked Brian, "getting drunk, I suppose!"

"Certainly not," returned Barney, "Thady is always sober as a judge, and as foolish too."

"I was rehearsing the first scene, Mr. O'Hagan," Katie told him, with great dignity.

"Then go ahead," said Barney, beginning, as usual, to stage-manage the whole thing.

"'How softly'" began Katie, for the third time, "'the sun sinks to -'"

"Oh, speak up, Viola!" advised Barney; "why you wouldn't be heard without ear trumpets!"

"People don't usually shout their sentimental sentiments."

"Neither do they mumble them."

Mary B Pearse, *The Murphys of Ballystack* (Dublin, 1917).

MARY BRIDGET (afterwards Brigid) PEARSE was born in Dublin in 1893, the youngest sister of Padraig. She was an eager recipient of his youthful romanticism, deprecated his later militarism and was estranged from the family after 1916. She compiled a family history in 1919 but this led to further dispute with her sister Margaret. She wrote, acted in and produced many plays but her main publication was a sub-Somerville and Ross account of small town Irish life, *The Murphys of Ballystack* (1917). It was the country viewed from the town in a sentimentalised and condescending way and the writing notably lacks the Irish cousin's experience, talent and bite. She died in 1947 after a history of recurring neurosis.

The Corsican Brothers (1856) was one of the most famous of the romantic melodramas specially devised for the aristocratic theatregoers of mid-century London and New York. The London impresario most closely associated with the play was Charles Kean, the son of the great Irish Regency actor, Edmund Kean. This story of twin brothers who feel each other's pain became vastly popular. In the major London theatres of thetime stage machinery had reached its peak of ingenuity and a remarkable device made specially for the play and known since as the Corsican trap allowed a ghost to seem to rise and drift across the stage. Boucicault brought the play to Ireland and its popularity with amateur groups became as great as that of Boucicault's own successes, *The Colleen Bawn* and *The Shaughraun*.

Cast of *The Corsican Brothers*, Carlow Lay College 1886 (St Patrick's College, Carlow).

The station consists of a small shed built of stone, with a slated roof, somewhat out of repair, and containing a single wooden bench for the benefit of waiting passengers. The inner walls of this edifice are chipped and grimy, and their decoration is furnished by railway time-tables (generally a month or two out of date - a trifling drawback, since nobody ever dreams of consulting them), interspersed with large posters announcing weekly and monthly fairs, and auction bills regarding sales of hay and oats and other farm produce. In another small box-like erection at one end of the platform, and close beside the solitary gate which gives ingress and egress to the station, is the ticket-office. Within it the station-master sits with the utmost official pomp, and from it he directs the activities of his sole subordinate, a youth of some sixteen summers, who might, from his chief's manner, be a complete staff at a large terminus rather than one forlorn-looking lad. The arrival of a train brings forth the station-master to the platform with an air of great grandeur. There is quite a touch of magnificence in the manner in which, when "she is signalled from the Junction," he emerges from the ticket-office, locking the door behind him. Descending passengers are treated strictly according to their class. First-class (rare birds these) with high distinction, third-class with contumely, and second-class (to which most of us adhere) with moderate respect, pleasingly informed with cordiality according to the place we occupy in Mooney's affections.

Railway Station, Athboy Co Meath 1904

For Bartholomey Mooney, station-master of Aghole, is a respecter of persons undisguisedly and deliberately, and his high esteem of the qualities fitted for his own office does not include impartiality. Indeed, a less impartial person it would be difficult to discover - even in Ireland. This is the more remarkable since, according to his own account, his favourite axiom is: "Be civil to all, but familiar with few." So far as his practice goes, the reverse would be more correct, for he is familiar with almost everybody and civil to none.

Ella MacMahon *Irish Vignettes* (London, 1928).

The station was exceedingly clean; and when we left it, and an erect, intelligent, well-dressed station-man, who at about half a mile from it, in a well appointed uniform, appeared standing on the green bank, motionless as a statue, I could not help feeling that his outstretched arm not only showed us the way we were to go, but, morally speaking, demonstrated most indisputably the facility with which a railway, wherever it runs, establishes habits of order, discipline and cleanliness, which would have been declared impossible to inculcate.

Sir Franci B Head *A Fortnight in Ireland* (London, 1952).

ELLA MAC MAHON was daughter of the Rev J H MacMahon who was chaplain to the Lord Lieutenant of Ireland in the '90's'. Her best of about twenty novels deals with working-class seduction and betrayal, the critical event, taking place on an Easter Monday excursion to Bray. The piece printed, a pen-picture of a station-master, is typical of her style and comes from *Irish Vignettes* (1928).

Railway Station, Dundalk 1910 (Lawrence Collection, National Library).

Fitzwilliam Square, Wicklow (Lawrence Collection, National Library).

King Edward at Maynooth
(Lawrence Collection, National Library).

Select Bibliography

HISTORICAL BACKGROUND
J. C. Beckett. *A Short History of Ireland* (London, 1952. 5th edition, 1973).
J. C. Beckett. *The Making of Modern Ireland, 1603-1923* (London, 1966).
F. S. L. Lyons. *Ireland Since the Famine* (London, 1971).
T. W. Moody. *The Ulster Question 1603-1973* (Cork, 1974).
T. W. Moody and J. C. Beckett (ed.), *Ulster Since 1800.* 2 series: (1) *A political and economic survey;* (2) *A social survey* (London, 1955, 1957).
Patrick Flanagan. *Transport in Ireland* (Dublin, 1969).
L. M. Cullen. *Six Generations* (Cork, 1970).
A. T. Q. Stewart. *The Ulster Crisis* (London, 1967).
Belfast Telegraph. 1 Sept. 1970. This centenary edition of the paper has many excellent articles on Ulster life at the turn of the century.

FOLKLIFE
E. E. Evans. *Irish Folk Ways* (London, 1957).
E. E. Evans. *Mourne Country: landscape and life in south Down* (Dundalk, 1951).
Alan Gailey. *Irish Folk Drama* (Cork, 1969).
G. B. Adams (ed.) *Ulster Dialects* (Holywood, Co. Down, 1964).
Ulster Folklife (Holywood, Co. Down, 1955).

WRITERS
R. J. Hayes (ed.) *Sources for the History of Irish Civilization. Articles in Irish periodicals.* 10 vols (Boston, Mass. 1970). This provides a guide to magazine articles on and by Irish authors.
D. J. O'Donoghue. *The Poets of Ireland* (Dublin, 1912. Reprint, New York, 1970).
S. J. Brown. *Ireland in Fiction,* with an introduction by D. J. Clark (London, 2nd edition, 1919. Reprint, Shannon, 1968).

B. T. Cleeve. *Dictionary of Irish Writers.* 3 series: (1) *Fiction* (Cork, 1967); (2) *Non-fiction* (Cork, 1969); (3) *Irish* (Cork, 1971).
Rann. No. 20 (Belfast, June 1953).
This magazine has several valuable articles on writing in Ulster as well as a useful bio-bibliographical list of Ulster authors, 1900-53.
S. H. Bell, N. A. Robb and John Hewitt (ed.). *The Arts in Ulster, a symposium* (London, 1951).
S. H. Bell. *The Theatre in Ulster* (Dublin, 1972), *Irish Booklore* (Belfast, 1971).
Lennox Robinson. *Ireland's Abbey Theatre* (London, 1951).
Malcolm Brown. *The Politics of Irish Literature* (London, 1971).
Ulick O'Connor. *Oliver St John Gogarty* (London, 1964).

OLD PHOTOGRAPHS
Maurice Gorham. *Ireland from old photographs.* (London, 1971).
Theodora Fitzgibbon. *Taste of Ireland: Irish Traditional Food* (London, 1968).
Noel Nesbit. *The Changing Face of Belfast* (Belfast, 1968).
Kieran Hickey. *The Light of Other Days: Irish life at the turn of the century in the photographs of Robert French* (London, 1973).

Acknowledgements

For kind permission to reprint copyright material the following acknowledgements are made:

For James Berry to the Dolmen Press; for George Birmingham to Irish University Press; for M. McDonnell Bodkin to Gill and Macmillan Ltd; for Joseph Campbell to Simon Campbell; for Padraic Colum to the Dolmen Press Ltd; for William Cronin to Gill and Macmillan Ltd; for M. E. Dobbs to Brigadier N. C. Dobbs; for St J. Ervine to his literary executors; for George Fitzmaurice to the Dolmen Press Ltd; for the poem from "Amhráin Chlainne Gaedheal" to Conradh na Gaeilge; for Lady Gregory to the Lady Gregory Estate and Colin Smythe Ltd, Publishers; for Joseph Guinan to Gill & Macmillan Ltd; for Stephen Gwynn to Blackie & Son Ltd; for Douglas Hyde to the Dr Douglas Hyde Trust; for James Joyce to Jonathan Cape; for Sir Shane Leslie to Desmond Leslie; for Robert Lynd to Mills and Boon Ltd; for Patrick MacGill to T. C. Johnston; for Brinsley MacNamara to Mr O. Weldon; for Rutherford Mayne to Miss Ginette Waddell; for Alice Milligan to Gill and Macmillan Ltd; for F. F. Moore to the Hutchinson Publishing Group Ltd; for George Moore to J. C. Medley and R. G. Medley, and to Colin Smythe Ltd, Publishers; for T. K. Moylan to James Duffy & Co, Ltd; for Sean O'Casey to Macmillan Ltd; for Padraic Ó Conaire to Sáirséal agus Dill; for Liam O'Flaherty to the author and Jonathan Cape Ltd; for Enrí O'Muirgheasa to Miss Maeve O'Muirgheasa; for Moira O'Neill to Mrs Susan Skrine; for M. B. Pearse to Gill and Macmillan Ltd; for Forest Reid to Stephen Gilbert; for Grace Rhys to the author and J. M. Dent & Sons Ltd; for A. McK. Ros to her literary executors and Chatto and Windus Ltd; for G. W. Russell to his literary executors; for Somerville and Ross to Sir Patrick Coghill and Chatto and Windus, and to John Farquharson Ltd; for James Stephens to Macmillan & Co. Ltd; for E. L. Voynich to William Heinemann; for L. J. Walsh to his literary executors; for William Butler Yeats to M. B. Yeats, Miss Anne Yeats and The Macmillan Company of London and Basingstoke.

For kind permission to reproduce photographs the following acknowledgements are made:

To H. D. H. Cooper for photographs from the Cooper Collection; to the Cork Examiner; to the Crawford Municipal School of Art, Cork; to the Gárda Síochána Museum; to the Garrick Society; to the trustees of the Ulster Folk and Transport Museum for photographs from the Green Collection; to the governors of the Linenhall Library; to the director of the National Library of Ireland for photographs from the Lawrence Collection; to the Offaly Research Library; to the Old Kilkenny Society; to the deputy-keeper for photographs from the Northern Ireland Public Records Office; to the officers of the Royal Irish Academy; to Peter Verschoyle for photographs from the Rose Shaw Collection; to the headmaster of Portadown College for photographs from the Sprott Collection; to the director of the State Paper Office, Dublin; to Mrs L. Stephens and Trinity College Library, Dublin; and to the trustees of the Ulster Museum, Belfast, for photographs from the Welch and Hogg Collections; also to J. K. C. Armour; S. H. Bell; Arnold Crawford; Séamus de Vál SP; Revd Mother M. Enda of Foxford; Edmond Flaherty; Miss Gavin of Roscommon; Stephen Gilbert; M. J. Glynn; Fred Heatley; Liam Jordan of Ballinasloe; Sean MacGinnea; Harry McKnight; Don MacMonagle; Mr Matthews of Killeigh, Co. Offaly; Larry O'Connor; Mr Desmond Wynne of Castlebar.

Every effort has been made to trace the owners of copyright material used in this book. In the event of omission the publisher would be glad of notification.

Index of Authors

*Numbers in brackets refer to
Ulster (1), Connacht (2),
Munster (3) and Leinster (4)*